Name All the Animals

Praise for NAME ALL THE ANIMALS

'This is Smith's first book, but if her quite beautiful consciousness of the world, of love, loss, and the unfathomable bond between human beings dead and alive is anything to go by, she's one to watch' TIME OUT

'Smith's clear-eyed, tender portraits of her family and teachers are filled with gentle comedy and lyrical sadness. She reaches through her own pain and the warp and weft of teenage life to some universal understandings about how we deal with death' TIMES EDUCATIONAL SUPPLEMENT

'Clear-eyed and free from self-pity, Smith's memoir is a powerful and heartbreaking coming-of-age story' INK

'An eloquent, taut and unsentimental expression of the intensity of a strong sibling relationship . . . It is a story about the passion of first love, and a plea for acceptance because that love was taboo' THE TIMES

'Smith's prose quietly gleams with understated poetic images, and her dialogue is crisp and exact. She conveys with admirable poise and restraint the quiet tragedy of ordinary people expected to cope with the unthinkable. A thoughtful and beautifully written reminder that, among all the gory, shock-value memoirs currently popular, sometimes the truth can be as rich as fiction' Stephanie Merritt, ZEMBLA

About the Author

Alison Smith's writing has appeared in *McSweeney's* and various anthologies. She lives in Brooklyn, New York. This is her first book.

NAME
ALL THE
ANIMALS

Alison Smith

Scribner

First published in Great Britain by Scribner, 2004
This edition published by Scribner, 2005
An imprint of Simon & Schuster UK Ltd
A Viacom Company

1 3 5 7 9 10 8 6 4 2

Simon & Schuster UK Ltd
Africa House
64–78 Kingsway
London WC2B 6AH

www.simonsays.co.uk

Simon & Schuster Australia
Sydney

A CIP catalogue record for this book is available from the British Library

ISBN 0-7432-5234-9
EAN 9780743252348

Printed and bound in Great Britain by
Bookmarque Ltd, Croydon, Surrey

for Roy

This is a true story.

Some names and details have been changed.

Out of the ground God formed every beast of the field and every bird of the air, and brought them to the man to see what he would call them, and whatever the man called every living creature, that was its name.

GENESIS 2:19

Not everything has a name.

ALEKSANDR SOLZHENITSYN

Prologue

THE SPRING MY brother, Roy, turned twelve we discovered an abandoned house in the gully by the old railroad tracks. Roy saw it first.

"Look at that." He pointed and his skinny arm trembled.

The funny thing about this house was that its entire front half had been ripped away, as if a large claw had reached out of the sky and torn it clean off. The remaining rooms of the house were still furnished. Wallpaper, water-stained and peeling, hung on the decaying walls. Snow clung to the seat cushions. Rusted pots and pans languished in the kitchen cupboards. It was as if the house's owners had stepped out for a moment and while they were gone someone had torn their home in half.

"What happened to it?" I asked.

Roy lay down under a crabapple tree, placed his chin on his hand, and stared at the house. I lay down next to him. "I don't know," he said. He scratched the back of his head, took a deep breath, and suggested we take a closer look.

"Are you crazy?" I asked.

"No," he said. He got to his feet.

"What if it's dangerous? What if it's haunted?"

"Come on, Al." He walked toward the house.

Over the next few months, Roy was drawn back to the abandoned house again and again. Each time he crossed its threshold, stepping over the splintered floorboards, he removed his baseball cap as if he were entering a church. All spring we lay in the field outside the ruined house. The ground warmed under us, the snow melted into runnels.

One day he asked me, "What do you think happened to them?"

"Who?"

"The people who used to live there."

I glanced at him. He was squinting up into the trees. "Maybe they found a better house," I said.

"No." He rolled away from me. "That's not it."

"Then what do you think happened?"

"I think they just left one day. They got in their car and drove away and never came back."

"Where'd they go?"

He turned toward me, pulled up a sliver of new grass, and said, "Maybe they're still on the road."

Part I

The Storm

1

I STARTED SKATING at nearly the same time I took my first steps. Mother taught me how on the outdoor rink at the local park. Every weekend she took me there and we skated in circles the wobbly gait of the swamp-skater, pushing off with the serrated tip. The spring after I turned fifteen, the ice melted as it did every April, and still I showed up, like clockwork, my skates slung over my shoulder. I watched the ice dissolve back into Allen's Creek. Mother drove down and met me, popped open the passenger-side door of the family camper-van, and said, "Hop in. I've got a surprise for you." That day I skated on an indoor rink for the first time. There was something in the long mile of that white room, in the coolness of the air and the smell of the ice—like the inside of a tin cup—and all the while outside I knew the sun was tapping on the roof, warming the tiles, begging to be let in. I was hooked. I joined the rink's figure skating academy.

The girls at the Rochester Skating Academy in 1984 were a hardy bunch—great jumpers, who raced around the rink backwards at high speeds. I was the one in the corner by the sidewall pushing my wire-rim glasses up my nose, my stockings bunched at the knees. I did not jump. My spins were slow and careful. But I did have one thing going for me. I was good at Patch.

Patch was named for the sectioning of the ice into six-by-eight-foot strips or patches. The first thing to do when you get to your assigned patch is carve two adjacent circles, using an instrument called a scribe (which looks like an overgrown compass). On that huge number eight you try to skate the perfect figure. It's harder than it looks—keeping the cut line of the blade arced, the skate moving at a good clip, never straying from the two circles. It was my favorite part of the day: the collective silence of concentration, drilling over and over a single blade turn, the subtle weight shifts, from front to back, right to left. This measured intricacy, the repetitive devotion it required—it was the closest you could get to praying on ice.

In late July, three months after I started my indoor skating career, I had an accident during morning Patch Hour. While practicing the 180-degree turn in the center of the eight, I slipped and fell. Sixteen pairs of eyes looked up from their patches and stared at me. I tried to stand up. My leg warmers slid down over my heels. I moved to adjust them, and then I saw it. In the center of the eight, at the fulcrum of the north and south circles, lay a spot of blood. A darkening stain ran across the crotch of my skating dress. I crossed my legs.

Moments later, in the bathroom at the Rochester Skating Rink, dark flowers of blood spread across the toilet water. I called Mother from a pay phone in the hall.

"It's your first," she whispered into the phone. She was at the architecture firm where she worked as a secretary.

"I've got blood all over me!"

"All right. I'll meet you in the bathroom, the one by the soda machine."

"Bring a bucket."

"Oh stop," she said. "It's not that bad."

I waited for Mother in the stall farthest from the door. When she entered, her low heels clip-clopped across the floor. She went straight for the last stall and opened the door. My skates were still on, the laces loosened. I had crammed half a roll of toilet paper between my legs. She slouched, one hand on her hip. "Alroy," she whispered as she shook her head. It's not my name. It's ours, my brother's and mine. A pet name she made up, combining Roy's name and mine into a single shorthand. "That bad, Alroy?" she asked.

I nodded and gazed up at her.

My mother stood in her homemade wraparound skirt with the blue flowers. She had tucked a white summer blouse into its ribboned waist. She wore her hair short, in a Dorothy Hamill cut, and in the humidity it curled out around her ears like wings. She slid her purse off her shoulder, pulled out a pack of extrathick sanitary pads, a bottle of pills, and a collapsible camping cup. She crossed over to the sink, filled the cup with water, and thrust both her hands under my nose. One held the cup, the other two pink pills.

"Take these."

I swallowed the pills. She ran her hand over my forehead. I pushed her away. She handed me a pad and backed up. Through the metal door I heard her sigh. She tapped her foot. I leaned back. The flusher jabbed me in the kidneys. I peeled the white adhesive strip off the back of the pad and slid my skating dress down.

Mother drove me home. After she set me up in bed with a bottle of Midol and a copy of the Psalms, she made no proud speech about my initiation into womanhood, offered no advice on the prevention of menstrual cramps or the application of sanitary pads. She cleared her throat, ran her fingers through her hair, and said, "I'll tell Daddy. You tell Roy."

And with that she left me and returned to work.

When Roy showed up outside my bedroom door later that afternoon, he was holding a portable radio. He had just come from his morning job as a groundskeeper at a local country club and was already dressed for his second summer job as a cashier at Tops Supermarket. The stiff red uniform vest, boxy and oversized, hung on his narrow frame. Wrapping a leg around the door, he leaned into the room. "Hey, little sister, who's your superman? Hey, little sister, who's the one you want?" he crooned along with Billy Idol. Then he pulled back, hit his head against the doorframe, and tumbled to the ground, moaning in mock pain.

"Roy-dee," I hollered, from under the covers.

"Little Sister," he hollered back, pulling himself up.

Billy Idol was not his music of choice. He was more a fan of the Police and the Who, but he knew this song drove me crazy. Whenever the local station played it, he rushed toward me, his arms out, singing at the top of his lungs.

I yelled over the sound of the radio. "I'm sick!"

"What?" he yelled back.

I pointed at the radio. He turned it down.

"I'm sick."

He walked into the room. "How do I look?" Under the uniform vest he wore an orange Hawaiian shirt and maroon running pants.

"Terrible. Everything clashes."

"Good!" His head bobbed up and down. "It's your turn to do the dishes."

"Will you do them?"

He glanced over at me. "What's wrong with you?"

"Nothing."

His hands thrummed out a beat against the door. "I thought you said you were sick."

I could feel the blood rushing to my head. My face grew hot. "I have my period."

"Your what?"

"My *period!*"

The thrumming stopped. I could hear him breathing; his lungs were congested. "Oh," he said.

He became engrossed in the pattern of his Hawaiian shirt. His hair was long; he had let it grow now that he was not in school. It ran over his ears and scrolled out around the base of his skull. The sun was shining in the window over the porch, and the evergreens' bright needles shimmered in the windless afternoon. He stepped into the room, picked up my skates, and started swinging them by the laces.

"Don't touch those," I said. I reached across the bed, grabbed them from him, and shoved them under the blankets.

He cleared his throat. "It's supposed to rain tonight," he said.

"What do you want, Alroy?"

"It's your turn to do the dishes."

"You do them."

"No, you."

"No, you."

"No, you."

"Loser," I said.

"Dweeb."

"Mutant."

"Moron!" And then he lost it. He broke into a grin. Paper white teeth, three dimples—one on either side and a little dent in his chin.

"Alroy," I said.

He disappeared behind the door again. He coughed once. The breath rattled in and out of him. He had just recovered from a nasty bout of bronchitis. One hand on the door, the other on the doorframe, he leaned back into the room and smiled. From my position on the bed I saw only half of him. A slice of brown hair, tan skin, and the hideous orange and red.

Outside a mourning dove cooed. The sun beat down on us through the back window, no trace of the coming storm. It was four in the afternoon. I looked away. I felt a slip in the air, a nearly imperceptible change in temperature. I turned to catch him, but he had already left.

I fell asleep, my hands wrapped around my skates. I slept straight through without eating supper, without going to my evening job at the Sisters of Mercy Convent. And as I slept a storm gathered over Lake Ontario, ten miles to the north. At one o'clock the sky broke open. Rain pelted the ground, rivered into the gullies along Penfield Road. It rained all night, and it was raining the next morning when Roy left for work. Friday, July 27, 1984. Father stopped him at the front door.

"What are you going to do," Father asked, "in the rain?"

Roy tossed the keys to the van from his right hand to his left and hitched up his shorts. "We'll wash the golf carts," he said.

At 5:51 A.M. Father opened the front door for him. Roy ducked into the driving storm. He was gone. It was not for another two hours, when it was too late, that I would walk into the kitchen and see. He had done the dishes after all.

2

WHEN THE OFFICERS came by the house at seven that morning, the only sound was the rain on the roof, the water rushing out of the gutters. They stepped in out of the storm, stood in the front hall, their hats in their hands, the soft gray of their coats blending into the gray outside. There were two of them. The one on the left held out a badge, nestled in a brown leather case. But this—the official nature of the visit—wasn't what worried me. It was the tilt of their heads, the shuffle of their feet. You could almost smell the pity. Mother held a hand to her throat and trembled. She begged them not to say it.

Mrs. Smith, there's been an accident.

I ran when the officers told us—slammed out the front door, tore down the street. The rain soaked through my slippers. One of the officers came after me. He caught up with me in front of the Wilsons' house, grabbed my shoulder, and pulled me to him. His mustache bristled in the damp air. His large hands lay heavy on my thin arms. "They need you," he said.

"Who?"

"Your parents. They need you now. To be strong."

After the officers left, our neighbor Mr. Henderson drove us in his acid green Dodge Dart over to the factory where Father worked. When we drove up to the plant, Father was standing on the curb waving his arm as if he were hailing a taxi. His tie was tucked in between two buttons on his shirtfront to keep it from dangling in the factory's machinery. I moved to the front seat so that they could sit together in the back. The rain slowed.

"Where is he?" Father asked as he climbed in and sat down.

When Mother told him, Father tried to stand up in the back of the car. Mr. Henderson fiddled with his left turn signal and pulled back into the traffic. The rain poured down outside, and the old Dart's defroster sputtered and coughed against the fogged windshield. Just as we got back to the house, the storm subsided. Sunlight washed over the leaves on the sugar maple in our front yard, and the tree glowed. I had never seen it light up like that—as green as a traffic light. That's when we found them, the neighbors, scattered across the lawn.

They did not come with casseroles and frozen pies. They just got in their cars and drove to us, or opened their front doors, forgetting to close them, walked into our yard, and stood there. On the lawn, the doorstep, they all held some part of themselves: an arm pressed to a chest, a hand up across a forehead. Mrs. Henderson wore only one earring. Mrs. Wilson clutched a telephone to her chest, the wall cord trailing behind her as she ran across the street. By mid-morning there were twenty-five of them draped across the living room and the dining nook, sniffling into their hands, passing boxes of Kleenex.

The phone was already ringing. There were still more people to tell. Mother picked up her blue address book. She opened to the As and reached for the phone. Halfway there she froze. "I can't do this," she said. "I can't tell people."

I took the book. I told her that I'd do it. There was a phone in the basement, away from the crowd. Sitting on the floor in the half-dark, the address book balanced on my knee, the door to the toy cupboard at my back, I placed the black rotary-style phone on the floor next to me and I started dialing.

Almost everyone had already heard. Some knew more than I did. The boys who worked at the golf course knew. Some had gone home. Some had called their parents from the pro shop. Mrs. Whitman screamed the moment she heard my voice. "One of the boys told me, but I could not believe it," she said. "When I heard your voice I knew it was true."

Some people wanted details: what road, at what angle, when, how much damage. I could not answer their questions. I did not know what happened.

I called the girl up the street. Roy was to have had a date with her that night. A shy, studious boy, he had gone on very few dates. This would have been his third. She listened to me tell her that there had been an accident, that Roy was gone, and then she said, "Thank you for calling." She hung up.

Upstairs, Mother's tennis friends arrived. Fresh off the wet court, Mrs. Volkmouth led the pack of them. I sat on the stairs and watched as they congregated in the front hall—lost, stricken, useless—their freshly laundered tennis whites fluttering. Whenever anyone opened the front door, a breeze rattled the silver-plate crucifix and the pleated skirts flew up. Our foyer became a sea of floating white poplin.

The clergy descended—Father Haskins with the Sisters of Saint Joseph in tow. They organized things a bit, got a prayer circle going in the living room, and pulled Mother in. It wasn't so bad. It gave her something to do. They wanted Father to join as well, but he just wandered from room to room clutching a dustrag in his hand.

I would have sat on the third step of the stairs by the front hall for the duration of that long, dark day if it weren't for Mrs. Volkmouth. At some point she patted Mrs. McGill on the shoulder, stepped away from the tennis whites, walked into the living room, and planted herself on a brocade-covered footstool. Her Spalding tennis racket clasped in her right hand, she pressed the back of her left against her damp cheek. She needed something, I could tell. She caught sight of me and waved me over.

"Coffee." Her voice was an octave lower than usual. "I must have coffee." I poured her a cup of Father's leftover morning brew. She took one sip, pursed her lips, and again she touched the back of her hand to her cheek. "It's stale." Her voice quavered when she spoke. She leaned forward, the mug cradled in her upturned palm, and said, "We need a fresh pot."

I found the directions under Mr. Coffee's lid and the filters in the low cupboard next to the canned goods. I made my first pot of coffee. The adults guzzled it down and came back asking for more. Once I started, I could not stop. I set up camp in the kitchen and served coffee all that morning and well into the afternoon. The house overflowed with strangers. I listened to Mother call out my brother's name, and Father weep in the hall. I loved Mr. Coffee's domed middle, his beige and fake chrome façade, the odd-sized serving pot, the beginning hiss as the first drops hit the hot glass.

As each new wave of mourners burst in the front door—wild-eyed, dropping their purses and umbrellas—they called Mother's name. They pushed through the tennis ladies and the Sisters of Saint Joseph, found Mother at the center of the prayer circle. They gasped, they cried. That got everybody else in the circle crying. I followed behind the newcomers, picking up umbrellas and purses. I waited as they wept on Mother's shoulder. When they finished, I asked if they took cream or sugar.

Morning passed into afternoon. I handed around more mugs of coffee. Father's life insurance company called. Mother chose an undertaker. Then at three in the afternoon, Father started to climb the stairs, got halfway up, and froze. He looked down at his legs, scratched the back of his head, lowered himself onto a middle step, and remained there for the rest of the afternoon.

As I tapped the old grounds into the garbage under the sink and pulled out the box of filters, Mrs. Henderson joined me. Her youngest child, Mary Elizabeth, was my best friend.

"He's gone," she said. She touched my arm. "You know that, don't you?"

I pointed at her mug of coffee. "Do you want cream in that?"

Mrs. Henderson grabbed my finger. "Alison," she said. Then she paused and shifted her weight to her other hip. "A little cream would be nice." She smiled.

Later, Mrs. Henderson made us dinner. She brought a plate of steak and mashed potatoes to Father where he sat perched on the middle stair, but he would not touch it. She said he wouldn't even look up at her. After chasing the food around my plate for a half hour, I pushed back my chair, walked outside, picked up my bike, and went for a ride.

Following the wobbly circle of light from the lamp attached to my handlebars, I rode up and down the streets of our neighborhood. The Wilsons were home. It was Friday night—movie night. I was supposed to baby-sit for them. They had not found another sitter, and I watched them through the bay window. Mrs. Wilson bent over the table. The two brothers grabbed for the same roll on a dinner plate. I could see their mouths moving as they talked over each other.

When I got to the top of the street, I looked back at our small, white house with the Medina stone base. Reclaimed from the gully whose mouth opened out at the end of the road, our neighborhood had a damp, wild feel to it. The old houses, built right after World War II, had all but returned to the forest. Skunkweed and wild columbine grew along every back fence. Gullies and gorges opened up across the landscape. At the lazy end of every street there lurked a Dead End sign. If you ventured past the sign you would soon plunge into a swampy forest.

As I gazed out over the landscape, the neighborhood shrank; the enormous hill melted into a bump, the curving streets faded into narrow paths. I closed my eyes, released the brake, and kicked off. The wind cooled my face as the bike and I dropped down. I coasted all the way to the end of the street and came to an easy stop at the mouth of the gully. The dirt was mottled and pockmarked from the rain. A light fog crawled out of the blackness and made its way slowly up the street. I pushed my bike back onto the road and pedaled furiously toward home.

When I got there Roy's best friend, Tim, was standing on the front stoop.

"Where you been?" he said.

I shrugged, dropped my bike on the lawn, and joined him on the steps. A slight boy, just a few inches taller than me, he had thick, straight hair that fell across his forehead in one great auburn thatch. Roy had met him in tenth grade, and they had been close since. They shared the same quiet, mischievous nature. Together they had spent the last month sneaking into the local university library at night and looking up information on black holes.

Tim moved to hug me, then changed his mind and let his hands hover in the air before sliding them into the pockets of his jeans. He swallowed several times, and I watched his Adam's apple bob up and down under the pale skin of his throat.

As soon as we were inside, we climbed the stairs up to Roy's room. We passed Father on the way.

"Hello, Mr. Smith," Tim said as we stepped around him.

Father did not reply.

We sat on Roy's bed. The red-and-black-plaid bedspread curtained down around our ankles. The room smelled like him.

"I went to the junkyard," Tim told me. "I had to see the van. I had to see it before I could believe that it was real."

"Did you?" I asked.

"Yes." He pulled at a loose string on the pillowcase. "I mean I saw the van."

He described it to me. How he could find it only with the cautious help of the attendant. It wasn't even a car anymore, it was so mangled. The van had been customized for camping. We called it the camper-van, and every summer Mother and Father took us on long road trips in it. Inside, behind the driving compartment, lay cupboards, a Coleman stove, and a platform that held a mattress. None of this was visible when Tim saw the van. The attendant kept checking his watch and shifting from one leg to the other. So Tim went away.

"It didn't help. I still can't believe it," he said.

Tim left. The neighbors said good night. Once they were all gone, I realized I was alone in the house with my parents. I went back up to Roy's room. Mother showed up outside his door. I was reading Einstein's *Relativity*. I found it on Roy's desk, lying open at chapter eight: "The Idea of Time in Physics."

"What are you doing?" she asked.

I looked up at my mother. Her short brown hair curled around her tan face, her brow furrowed. There was a shine in her hazel eyes. She held a pile of laundry. It was Roy's.

"Come downstairs." She hovered in the doorway, her hand on the doorknob.

I looked down at the book. The words blurred. "I'm reading," I said.

"What?"

"A book. One of Roy's."

"Come downstairs."

I turned the page.

"Your father wants you."

"He's off the stairs?"

"Yes," she said, and she smoothed the front of a dark green T-shirt with the cross-country invitational logo on it.

I turned the pages for a while longer. After pacing the hall and visiting the bathroom and washing my hands several times, I took the stairs on tiptoe and found my parents at the dining room table, huddled in a circle of light from the one low table lamp. Father held his mother's rosary tightly in his left hand. Mother cradled Roy's laundry in her lap. They put their arms out to me.

"Baby," my father said. I walked into his embrace. "You're all I have left," he said. His face was wet with tears. I waited till he finished, then I went into the kitchen and poured myself a bowl of Cheerios.

That night I did not sleep. None of us did. I sat in Father's enormous green easy chair in the living room and watched the night pass. Just after sunrise I heard the bedsprings squeak in my parents' room, and Father's feet pressed gingerly against the old floorboards. He came downstairs, opened the front door, and picked up the morning paper. In my hidden spot in the wing chair, he could not see me. I watched him scan the front page until his eyes caught something of interest. He grasped the paper tighter. He was not wearing his reading glasses, so he had to hold the paper at arm's length. As he read, his hands began to shake. The shaking got so bad he could no longer hold the paper. It dropped to the floor. He tried to speak, but he could not. He tried to walk and he fell to his knees. He began to crawl. His arms and legs tangled in the hall rug. He called Roy's name several times, and then his voice dissolved into a long wail. He clawed at his T-shirt.

I heard Mother's footsteps as she ran down the stairs. She stopped three steps from the bottom and stared at Father. She whispered his name, examined the damage: the scratched arms, the torn shirt. She knelt down and placed a hand on his shoulder, a hand on his wet face. "Get up," she said.

He climbed into her arms. She waited while he cried. When he quieted down, she helped him up. He blinked. He touched his breast pocket as if he were checking for his wallet. They disappeared up the worn carpet of the staircase.

For a moment the world was silent. Then Mr. Wilson appeared, running across the grass in his stocking feet, his shadow flung out in front of him, painted long by the early sun. He arrived at the front steps heaving for breath, another newspaper in his hands.

"Too late," he said, and he gathered our paper, folding its fragile leaves of print. His socks were soaked with morning dew. "Where's your father?"

I pointed at the ceiling.

Mr. Wilson held the paper out in front of me. "Did you read this?"

I shook my head.

"Good." He folded it under his arm, tucking the front page out of sight. With his free hand he patted my shoulder.

I asked him, "Do you want some coffee?"

Shortly after that, the neighbors began to arrive. I gave over the coffee-making business to Mrs. Curtis, a nervous, pinched woman in a blue jumper. She brewed the coffee too weak, but I didn't much care.

The sun was high in the sky when Father came back downstairs. The house had filled with people again. This time the visitors brought food—dozens of casseroles, a few turkey pot pies, a fresh salad with peas and mayonnaise that one of them called "a green pig salad." The nuns returned. They led us in prayers. Sister Judith cornered me and recited the letters of St. Paul. Mother sat on the couch surrounded by her women friends. They read the Psalms together. She had a gentle reading voice. It wavered only slightly. She kept asking the priests, the nuns, even me when she called me over, "This is God's will, isn't it?"

Father wandered from room to room, straightening the pictures, clutching a level in his damp hand. His face was calm, almost blank. I stuck close to him. When he sat in the living room with a guest, I roamed the peopled rooms of our house, walking from bedroom, to porch, to kitchen.

Mr. Wilson caught up with me on the back porch. "About the newspaper," he said.

I stared up at him.

"There's an article in there about Roy, about the accident and—" He stopped and looked out through the rusted screens at the hazy view of the backyard. "Your parents don't want you to read it. They asked that you just pray, just look for the answer in prayer. You understand?"

We weren't good at much. Mother's father was a farmer who lost three farms and died penniless. Father's father, a telephone line repairman, died at thirty-six—complications from an ear infection. Nobody had made it to college. (Roy was going to be the first to do that. He had won a scholarship to Purdue University. He was going to study civil engineering.) But we had one talent: faith. With every ounce of our imagination we believed. My brother and I grew up in the shadow of this faith, in the great floodplain of belief. Christ was more real to me than the children I met at school. As I was walking to the school bus or down the path through the gully at the end of our street, Christ would appear to me, his long robes flowing, his white and bruised hands held out. He was my comforter, my most intimate friend. I knew only

Catholics in those early days. And our only differences were Catholic differences: the Sisters of Saint Joseph as opposed to the Sisters of Mercy. Pope John Paul the First or Pope John Paul the Second. In these surroundings you'd be hard-pressed not to believe in the existence of God. It would be like saying you did not believe in oatmeal, or motorcars, or the laws of gravity.

I went into the upstairs bathroom. I sat down on the hamper. The sun strained through the frosted glass, and diffused light bounced off the tile and shimmered across the porcelain. It filled the small bathroom with an underwater glow. I called to Him, and Christ came to me there in the small, white-tiled bathroom. He sat on the edge of the tub, His white robe bunched up in His lap, His bare feet pressed into the worn tile floor. "Yes?" He said, and He leaned in toward me, listening.

"Where is Roy? When are you going to let him come back?"

Christ stood up. He wavered for a moment on the tile floor. He touched the ends of His sleeves, stared at His feet, and left. Without a word, He walked out through the wall next to the bathroom mirror. I watched His robe trail behind Him.

God was gone. It felt like somebody had suddenly taken the needle off the record, and for the first time, the music I had heard my whole life, the music that was all around us, just stopped. I had never heard such silence. I rubbed my ears for a moment. I thought that perhaps I had gotten something stuck in them, some water from the shower. I hopped on one foot and shook my head back and forth. But there was nothing.

Downstairs, the house had filled with boys. Hunched over the spread of food in the kitchen, squatting on the stairs, slouched in the hallway, they were everywhere. Thin and lanky, red-cheeked and bright-eyed, they wore their Jesuit boys' school running gear. Mr. Bradley had brought over Roy's teammates.

Mrs. Henderson leaned over to Mrs. Wilson, who was holding her youngest, and whispered, "The entire track team? What was he thinking?"

But it was the only thing that held Father's attention in the last two days. "How's it going, boys?" he asked. "Did you get some food?" He could not stop staring. It was as if he were trying to memorize them.

The Hendersons arrived, all six of them at the door. They had been in and out for the past two days, but this time they were organized. They each held a steaming casserole dish. Mother handed the dishes to me, and I set the precarious stack in the kitchen on top of the other oven-ready dishes that had arrived. Mary Elizabeth and I decided to escape the adults. We climbed the stairs and slipped into my bedroom. She pulled herself up on the bed, bounced once, and then stared back at me. I closed the door and whispered to her, "I yelled at him. That's the last thing I did. The last time we talked, I yelled."

"I knew you were going to say that," Mary Elizabeth said. She told me that it didn't matter. That Roy would understand. I let her comfort me until I got up the nerve to ask her about the article. "Did you read it?" I asked.

"Yes."

"Don't tell me what it said. I'm not supposed to know."

"Okay."

"But will you keep it for me? In case I need it someday?"

"Are you sure?"

"Yes," I said.

She looked out my bedroom window at her reflection in the blackened glass.

One by one the neighbors drifted out into the front yard and returned to their homes. As they slowly disappeared into the night, I slipped back into the kitchen and stared at the fresh, untouched pot of coffee. I didn't drink coffee, but I poured myself a cup and tasted it. It made my lips pucker. Mary Elizabeth appeared at the door. "Put milk and sugar in it," she said. "That's what the grown-ups do."

I looked into her brown eyes. Her dark ringlets hung limp against her shoulders. I didn't want to put sugar in it. I wanted it hot and bitter on the tongue. I took another swallow, closed my eyes, and waited for the coffee to warm me.

Mary Elizabeth's mother called her name, and she left the kitchen. I stepped into the backyard. I walked to the very back and stared up at the tall pines our grandfather had planted eighteen years before, the summer after Roy was born. The moon was out. The rope swing hung from a branch of the maple tree. It brushed the ground.

I wandered out to our hideout behind the garage, near the back fence. Throughout our childhood, Roy and I had built four separate forts on that same secret spot. He was a perfectionist and insisted we tear down the old one each spring and start from scratch. The forts were our territory, off limits to the adults, except for early in the construction process, when Father was enlisted to take Roy to the lumberyard to pick out his new two-by-fours and plywood. We got better at building as the years advanced, starting with a lopsided frame covered with sturdy plastic sheeting and finally moving up to this last fort. With shingled sides, two windows, and real roof tiles, it was too good to tear down. Even Roy admitted it. And so it had stood for two years. As I leaned against the back of the garage and stared into the fort, I heard Mother calling me from the house. I did not answer her. She called again. She began to panic. Her voice rose to a scream. "Where's my child?" she demanded.

The house came to life as the guests began a mad search for me. The lights went on in my room, and the shadow of Mary Elizabeth crossed in front of the shade. Father called for me at the back door. "Baby," he said. "My baby girl, where are you?"

I shrank further into the shadows.

Nighttime did not scare Roy. He walked into it as if he were walking into a cool lake, his head flung back, the night on the lip of the sky, the first stars punching through the darkness; he was prepared to drown in it. The long call of an evening train met him as the wind crashed through the tall branches of the evergreens and the day's bright obviousness dissolved into the shapes of our imagination.

One night, after a late dinner, he had called me out to the back-yard. "Come on, Little Sister. Let's go check out the fort."

I did not answer. I stood in the circle of light by the back door, unable to dive into the darkness, afraid of every shape, every shadow.

He begged. "I'll give you my Twizzlers," he said.

But I would not budge.

"Jeez!" he cried, and let out an exasperated sigh. He stormed back toward the house and stood over me, his hands on his hips. Then Roy did something new. He took me by the hand and walked me out into the darkness. When we got to the center of the yard, he leaned over and whispered, "There is no night, Al. There's only the dark part of the day."

The night after he died, light from the house spilled out against the lawn, and my parents' voices rose across the neighborhood as they called my name into the evening air. Above me the trees rustled, every branch visible, their shadows thrown up against the sky. The grass grew silvery, the color of ice, of frozen lake water on sunny afternoons. Father was on the lawn walking toward me, but still he did not see me. From my hidden corner, I listened to Mother's voice calling for me. I stepped deeper into the yard. I remained in the darkness and let her think, for a few terrible minutes, that she had lost us both.

3

THREE WEEKS LATER, a young man walked down our drive-way, ducked around the lilac bush, stepped into the backyard, and stuck out his hand. "Hello, Mrs. Smith," he said. "Remember me?"

Mother wiped the wood stain off her fingers, set down her paintbrush, and shook his hand.

"I'm Paul. I sold your son the encyclopedias," he said. "I just came by with the purchase order."

Paul looked across the yard. The garage door was open. Just inside stood a workbench fashioned from two wooden horses and a length of plywood.

"Where's Roy?" Paul grinned and slapped his hands together. "Is he all packed for school?"

Mother sunk down onto the picnic bench and stared at her wet paintbrush.

"Mrs. Smith?" Paul ventured. "Are you okay?"

She turned the paintbrush over in her palm and stared deep into its bristles. Paul looked over toward me where I stood in the garden, a trowel held loosely in my hand. He raised his eyebrows as if to ask for help. He was just about to speak when Father pushed back the screen door and walked into the yard. He headed straight for Mother and put his hand on her shoulder.

"We forgot about the encyclopedias," Mother said.

Paul started to back out of the yard. "If this is a bad time I can always—"

"No," Father said, and he looked at Paul. He let his gaze rest for a beat too long on Paul's broad shoulders. Paul was larger than Roy, more the football player type. But his skin had the same warm, freckled tan. Paul crossed his arms over his white T-shirt. He tried

23

to smile, and the corners of his mouth quivered, bringing out the dimples in his cheeks.

Father offered Paul a seat at the picnic table.

"Roy died, Paul," Father said.

In June, Paul had come to the door selling mail-order encyclopedias for college students. Roy showed some interest, and Mother and Father bought him a set, on installment. They were to arrive, two each month, at his Purdue dorm for the first year of college. By the end of his freshman year, he would have a complete set. As Paul searched for something to say, Mother got up, walked back to the garage, put on a pair of safety goggles, and fired up her circular saw. Paul rubbed the back of his neck and stared down at the purchase order, now crumpled in his hand. "The thing is, sir," he said. "There's a no-refund policy on these encyclopedias."

When Paul left I followed him. I caught up with him near the Hendersons' driveway and tagged along until he turned and looked back at me. He made a small gesture with his hand, inviting me to join him. Paul held a clipboard and blue zipper bag of checks. As we walked, he bounced them against his thigh. "What's your mother building?" Paul asked.

"A camper-van," I said.

Paul stopped then, in the middle of the street, and looked down at me as if he were really taking me in for the first time. He was perfectly still for a moment, then he flicked his thumb against the zipper of his money bag and asked, "How can you build a camper-van?"

"I don't know, but she's doing it."

Paul's hair was parted in the middle, forming two tapering feathers that cascaded down his forehead. The soft breeze caught them and lifted them away from his face. They trembled in the wind and then settled back into an upside-down V right above his eyebrows. Paul started walking. I followed along. It was late in the day and the sun was just sliding down below the roofs of the tiny houses on our street. As we passed from house to house, sunlight fell on us for a moment and then disappeared behind the shingled façades. In that occasional, intermittent light, I gazed up at Paul.

The sun caught him from behind, and the white outline of his T-shirt glowed.

"Where do you go to school?" Paul asked.

"Our Lady of Mercy."

"Oh, the girls' school."

I nodded.

"The one with all the nuns. God, they're creepy. Look like a bunch of penguins with rulers."

I nodded again. I did not find nuns particularly creepy, but Paul could have said anything at that moment and I would have happily agreed. I liked him. I liked Paul for the simple fact that he didn't know Roy was gone. He was part of a near-extinct breed, those people who had somehow missed the newspaper article, the television coverage, the local radio reports, and the endless web of phone calls. The Before-People.

The Before-People had me in their thrall. And here I was walking alongside one of them: Paul, the Encyclopedia Boy. Just a few minutes ago he knew nothing about Roy's death. Just a few minutes ago Roy was still alive inside Paul's head. I imagined him there in Paul's mind, right under that perfect hair: Roy packing for college, Roy reading encyclopedias. In that innocence, that powerful ignorance, Roy lived.

I half-expected Paul to step through some hole in time and show me the path back to Roy, but he was entirely unaware of his special status. When we reached the end of the road, he paused, stared down at me, and gave me a quizzical look. "I got to be going. It was nice meeting you, okay," he said, and he started to walk away.

I grabbed his arm and stopped him. I pulled something out of my pocket, brushed it off, and handed it to him. It was half of an Oreo cookie. Crumbling, broken, covered in pocket lint. Paul took it, nodded, and without hesitation, brought the cookie to his mouth. He just popped it in there, lint and all, thanked me, and walked away.

4

I RETURNED FROM my walk with Paul in time to watch Mother line up her tools against the back wall of the garage. The front of her shirt was speckled with sawdust, her safety goggles were propped up on her forehead; she pulled her work gloves off her hands and slapped them against each other. A cloud of dust rose up, and she stepped away from it, waving her hand in front of her face. She sneezed once, tucked the gloves into the waist of her jeans, and slid her hands into her pockets. Father sat close by and stared at the lawn.

Mother looked up and saw me. "Where have you been?" Mother asked.

"Talking to Paul."

"Who?"

"The Encyclopedia Boy."

"You can't do that. You can't just wander off like that now." She ran her hand through her hair. The thick curls flattened under her fingers and then bounced back to life. She pursed her lips. "Your father was beside himself."

I looked over at Father where he sat on the lawn chair, his hands folded over his chest. "Baby," he said. "You're all I have left."

Mother widened her eyes, brushed the sawdust off her shirt-front, and marched toward the house.

Mother marched everywhere now. She had gotten Father and me through the wake and the funeral. She had organized everything. She never cried. And now she pushed on as if she were going to steer the sinking ship of our family back to shore. Our parents had scheduled the annual two-week camping trip to Cape Cod for that August. It was to be Roy's last family vacation before college. Mother held on to the idea of that vacation with a tenacious zeal.

Somewhere between the wake and the funeral, the newspaper article and the police report, the undertaker's office and the church, Mother bought a new van—the same make and model as the one destroyed in the accident. Then the tools came out of the garage, and she started making regular trips to the camping supply store. She bought a Coleman stove, lanterns, camping dishes, sleeping bags, and two twin pup tents. Everything that was lost in the accident, she replaced. She built what she could not buy: the platform in the back for the bed, the shelves that held our camping supplies, the wooden cupboard that served as a portable kitchen cabinet. She drew pictures of the lost things, estimated their measurements, and marched over to the lumberyard with her pencil drawings in her purse. She bought wood, screws, nails, and stain. Then she hauled it all back to our garage.

Mother had a policy for living that she often shared with her children. Her trim figure perched on the edge of a lawn chair, she would lean back in one of her rare moments of reflection and say, "Keep the best and forget the rest." Not once did I hear her complain about the poverty of her childhood, about her parents' broken marriage or her own early loneliness. She was a jolly and playful woman with a quick laugh and a ready smile. She simply erased the bad stuff. If Roy or I said something she did not approve of, she would turn, stare right through us, and reply, "You did not say that." If she heard a story she did not like, she would put her hand out toward the speaker like a traffic cop and stop them midsentence. The room would fall silent, and she would say sweetly, "That did not happen. Next topic." And then she would smile. She always smiled.

When I was twelve Roy showed me a page from his European history textbook. It was about the rise of the Soviet Empire. The page contained photos of a group of men in tweed suits sitting around a table. At first I thought the photos were identical, but as I looked more closely I saw that in the second photograph a man, third to the right, had been inked out. In his place sat a pile of black files.

"What's this?" I asked.

"They're doctored photos." Roy told me about an organization called the Kremlin. "If they didn't like you, they erased you. Just inked you out of the story. So then whatever you said or did didn't exist anymore."

"Like Mom does?" I asked.

He cocked his head to one side and laughed.

From that day on we had a secret code for Mother's rewriting of reality. After she made one of her pronouncements, she usually left the room as conversation came to an abrupt halt. And when she did, Roy would lean over and whisper, "She's playing Kremlin, Al."

Then Father would rustle his paper and look down at us sternly from his easy chair. "Don't make fun of your mother," he would say. But his mouth always quivered into a smile.

The night of the Encyclopedia Boy, Father and I sat on the lawn and looked up at the house. Down the center of the yard, we saw the trail where Mother had just walked, the leaves of grass pressed flat, their silvery backs shining against the dark earth. We listened as Mother rattled the pots and pans in the kitchen. I looked back at the garage, the wooden sawhorses, and the tools, and then I looked at my father. "What's she doing?"

The sun set behind us. The cicadas began their nightly song. Finally he spoke. "She's playing Kremlin, baby."

5

My mother was a convert. She grew up poor in rural New York, near Buffalo. Her first years were spent living in a one-room efficiency in the Basom Rooming House, where her parents tended bar at night in exchange for rent. She spent her nights at the Basom Pub. When her bedtime rolled around, her mother lined up three chairs and gave her a sweater for a pillow. She slept there behind the bar. It wasn't till she was eight years old that my grandparents scraped together the money to buy a small farm in West Shelby, down the road from Basom.

A couple times in her childhood she went to sleep-away camp—the free Christian kind, the kind that recruited. She had playmates, and three square meals a day. She had swim hour and games. And she gave her life to Christ every summer, walking up to the edge of the water, stepping into the arms of the preacher, letting the current rush around her as he leaned her back in the baptismal waters. Then she would return home to her drunken father and her stoic, unhappy mother and she would have to put Christ aside for another year.

She was the first person in her family to go to high school, and when she graduated, she left the farm for Rochester. She found a job as a bank teller and lived with other working girls in downtown Rochester, sometimes four girls in a two-room apartment. She moved a lot back then—my father is fond of telling people that it was easier for her to move than to pay rent. She dated some Catholic boys. Sometimes, on the weekends, she stayed out all night with them. When the bars closed at 2:00 A.M., my mother and the boys drove around till they found an all-night diner where they drank coffee and ate cinnamon buns till four. Then they would head over to church for the Policemen's Mass. Police officers who worked the Sunday beat could not attend services at any other time, so the Church offered this early-morning Mass for them. This was before Vatican II, when Masses were celebrated in Latin. Mother followed along in her missal, reading the English translation.

Something happened to her during those brief, early-morning Policemen's Masses. Perhaps she was still a little drunk on the cheap beer, perhaps the arms of Christ felt safer than a boy's arm, tucked around her waist, but something touched her. When she tells the story now, she will say that God spoke to her, that she was called by God. "Faith is His greatest gift," she says. "And His greatest mystery."

She found a priest at the Knights of Columbus, Father Flannigan, and asked him to teach her how to become Catholic. All that summer she drove her beat-up old convertible down Route 20 to the tiny lake town where Father Flannigan worked as a chaplain at a Catholic sleep-away camp. Three nights a week Father Flannigan taught her the Catechism, and by August, just after her twenty-first birthday, she was ready to commit herself to the Catholic Church.

The church where she attended those early Masses was called Saint Joseph's, and it was where my father attended Mass, where he was baptized and received his first communion and was confirmed. It was at Saint Joseph's where he served as an altar boy and where he first apprenticed to become a priest, before he got sick. But Mother did not know that then. It would be four more years before she would meet my father and he would take her to Saint Joseph's late at night, after a date. There, in front of the retable, my father got down on one knee before God and my mother, pulled out a ring, and proposed.

There is one way I like to picture my mother in her youth: in her car, the tiny box of the convertible with its top folded down, opening out to the night air, the radio blasting, a kerchief wrapped around her hair, her head flung back, driving under the stars and a moonless sky, heading toward Father Flannigan, driving to God.

6

AFTER DINNER, MOTHER and Father watched the news while I read on the back porch. At nine o'clock, my parents walked out onto the porch.

"Bedtime," Father said.

"Sweet dreams," Mother said.

We kissed each other good night, retired to our bedrooms, turned off the lights, and lay in the dark. In those days sleep did not come at night. Instead we stumbled upon it during the day. Curled up on the back porch lounge, head down at the kitchen table, sprawled along the grass in the backyard—sleep took us when we least expected it. And when it came for one of us, when it wrapped us in its sweet blanket of forgetting, the other two breathed a sigh of relief. Once Father left the breakfast table to fetch his glasses and did not return. After a few minutes, Mother went after him. She found him lying on the living room sofa, sound asleep. She unfolded a light summer blanket, spread it over him, and let him be.

We went to our beds at night out of habit. We went because it was expected of us. But despite our best efforts, despite warm milk and freshly laundered sheets, and (in Mother's case) sleeping pills, sleep eluded us. At night we skulked around the house. Within the first week we had worked out a system. To uphold the façade that we were getting a good night's sleep, we had to avoid each other in our nocturnal wanderings. So we took turns. We lay in our beds and listened to every squeaking floorboard—a creak in the hall, the refrigerator door opening, a light snapping on in the living room. And we waited until the silence fell back around the house. Then another of us pushed back the covers and took our turn traveling from room to room, peering out the front door into the dark neighborhood.

The night of the Encyclopedia Boy, I was restless. I kept seeing the sun flashing in and out between the houses on our street and landing on Paul with his broad, vacant grin. As I lay there, my heart pounding, I heard Father crying. The soft Ss and Os of my parents' speech crept through the wall like an animal scratching and digging into the chalk white plaster.

When they grew silent, it was Mother who walked the house first, her muffled sighs floating through the rooms. She lingered in the bathroom, ran the faucet, sipped water from one of the small paper cups by the sink, and sat on the toilet seat. She went to Roy's room next, pulled the folded T-shirts out of the drawers of his bureau, and dumped them into the hamper. She stripped the bed, piled the sheets on top. I listened to the hum and rattle of the washer-dryer and imagined her waiting in the basement for the cycle to finish. She'd sit there, on the bottom stair, feet set wide apart, elbows on her knees. The curl in her hair came out at night, in the heat, the damp. At those moments she looked like her son, the same wild brown hair falling around the ears.

She returned to bed. Father got up. He poured himself a bowl of cornflakes. The spoon rasped against the porcelain as he ate. Then I crept outside and lay on the back lawn, the cool grass tickling my neck. I listened to the barking of the neighborhood dogs. Their howls and whines formed a sort of Morse code in my mind as they called out across the damp, lush backyards. I imagined that they were planning an escape. When the barking reached a fever pitch, I knew that Shadow must be nearby. Moments later, I felt a cool muzzle nudging my hand.

Part shepherd, part Lab, Shadow had shown up one day years ago, hovering at the end of the drive, mud splattered and hungry, her skinny legs buckling. In seconds, Roy was out the front door and folding her in his arms. He put her in the tub, and before Mother had a chance to protest, he was rubbing the life back into her. We named her Shadow. After that, Shadow showed up every morning looking for Milk-Bones, which we readily supplied, and then slunk back down the road toward the gully. Roy and I had campaigned several times to adopt her, but Mother refused, saying Shadow was wild and it would be wrong to tame her. So we contented ourselves with feeding her on the sly and luring her down to the grassy fields at the end of the gully by the river, where we played fetch for hours.

The night air had grown cool, and the wind off the lake pitched up across our neighborhood and shook the trees. I pressed my face into Shadow's neck and breathed in the raw smell of the forest. In my right hand I held a paper bag. Shadow pounced on it, plunging her muzzle into the bag's side. I wrestled it from her and shoved the bag deep into the front pocket of my jeans. "No, Shadow," I whispered. "It's not for you."

I pulled a Milk-Bone from my other pocket, and she ate it out of my palm.

Then Mother came downstairs again and stood at the back door, her hazy outline hovering behind the bowed screen. Shadow and I hid in the bushes by the lilac trees and watched as Mother fingered the iron latch on the door. The door yawned open. She stepped out onto the cement walk by the back porch and blinked, adjusting her eyes to the darkness, and slid her arms up across her hips until she cupped her elbows in her open palms. She wore a short white nightgown with a pattern of yellow daisies tied together in bunches. It fell just below her knees. Her shoulders rose for a moment, and I could almost hear her inhale as her chest expanded, taking in the humid summer night. She headed straight for the garage, where she bent down and pulled up on the door handle with one hard yank. The rattle of the casters along the door's grooves echoed across the yard. She ducked inside.

From the back of the garden I peered through the latticed window on the sidewall of the garage. Sitting on a low stool by the workbench, the yellow percale cotton draped over her lap, she ran a hemstitch across the bottom edge of the new camper curtains. When she finished, she bit off the thread with her teeth, gathered the curtains in her arms, switched on the light in the cab of the van, and circled the interior, snapping the curtains into place.

As she draped the windows, the light, filtering through the thin fabric, brightened. As if from an old canvas tent lit from the inside by lanterns, brilliant yellow light streamed out of the van and set the whole yard ablaze. I blinked into the new brightness, my hand on the scruff of Shadow's neck. I could see everything now, as if it were daytime. The peeling paint on the garage, the nubby ends of the forsythia branches, the frayed rope swing. And Shadow's sandy blond coat. I waited for Mother to open the van and step out into the yard to find me, but the door did not open. The yard remained hushed and bright for a few long minutes. Then the silhouette of Mother's arm reached out across the panels of yellow light and turned some invisible knob. We fell into darkness.

I stared at the spot where, a moment before, the van had glowed. The grass grew warm under my bare feet. The hoot owls and the crickets cried. Shadow rubbed her muzzle against my pant leg and whimpered. I crouched down and put my arm around her neck. I whispered her name. A mourning dove stirred on a high electrical wire, rustled and cooed. I clicked my tongue against my teeth twice and started toward the fort with Shadow loping along behind me.

7

MY BROTHER CAME to my parents in the spring of 1966, during a snowstorm. It was mid-April, and a blizzard had pummeled Rochester with thirty-four inches of snow in two days. (This was on top of the twenty inches that fell the week before.) Ten-foot snowdrifts and fifty-mile-an-hour winds ground the city to a halt. Father dug a tunnel from the front door to the car and started the Chevy daily to make sure it would work when Mother grabbed her belly and said, "It's time."

Brought to my father unwashed, Royden Joseph Jr. shone slick and wet, his face obscured by the caul. This is a fact my father relays often, as it is his habit to remark on how dirty or clean we children were at every event. Roy was a happy baby, round and healthy, well-formed and quiet. He rarely cried, and when it came time to speak he showed no interest. He was silent.

Two and a half years later, when the labor pains started for a second time, it was December, and Mother and Father were grateful for the mere three feet of snow. They settled into the Impala with a prepacked overnight case and drove around the block where the hospital was located, counting the minutes between Mother's contractions. Just past midnight, they checked in.

When they brought me home from the hospital, my brother took one look at me and spoke his first word. "No," he said.

This was his only word for a year.

But after the first year, when he discovered that I was going to be able to walk and carry things, Roy grew accustomed to the idea of me. He even grew fond. Soon I became his only playmate. A solitary child, he did not like to socialize with other children. He preferred to be alone or in my company. We started school at Saint

Thomas More elementary. Father chose it out of all the area Catholic schools because he liked the janitorial staff. Some parents interview the teachers or the principal; ours interviewed the custodians. They believed that a well-cleaned school was a good school.

We were sickly children. Thin-necked and skinny, subject to rashes and allergies, infections and influenza. I had inherited, from my father and grandfather, the tendency for ear infections and suffered from the age of one to the age of five in some stage of infection. I required a yearly operation on my ear to widen the eustachian tube. Roy had allergies to pine, maple, oak, elm, dust, and everything else imaginable. Two or three times a year they'd get the better of him, settle into his chest, and fester there until they worked themselves into a nasty case of bronchitis. Mother spent nights with him, the vaporizer hissing on the floor beside them, Vicks VapoRub filling the room, her elbow on his pillow, her long hand covering his entire forehead as she waited for the fever to break. And he got nosebleeds—all the time. I'd find him after school in the kitchen, a dish towel bunched up around his nose, stained in large pockets of red, his head flung back as a broken vessel surged blood. I worried about this spontaneous bleeding. It seemed to increase his vulnerability. The idea that, untouched, he could bleed. It was as if the very act of going out into the world were too much for him.

I slept every night in a small blue room nestled between a cross at the head of my bed and a painting of the Sacred Heart of Jesus at the foot. Jesus' white skin, combined with the raw bruise of His heart, conspired to give Him an anemic pallor. He held His right palm out, two fingers folded, two fingers up. Roy once asked me, "What is Jesus doing with His hands?" We were lying on my bed. We'd just come in from a game of baseball, and our gloves still encased our right hands (we were both left-handed). He stared up at the portrait of Christ. "It looks like the Boy Scout salute," he said.

From the beginning Roy was a builder. He could eyeball the height of things within a quarter of an inch. He knew how to pour a foundation, hang a door, shingle a roof, build a sturdy A-frame, all before he turned ten. I do not know how he learned all of this. Probably he picked up some of it from our mother, but it seemed more as if he was born with the information. On long summer afternoons when I had fallen into reading and he could not tear me away from my book, he would slip off and look for carpenters. There was always someone in our neighborhood of small houses who had undertaken to add a family room, a porch, or a garage, and Roy always found the construction sites. If the carpenters seemed like kind men, Roy would crouch down close to them, in their sight, until they asked him what he wanted. He found ways to make himself helpful, then useful, and finally indispensable. On afternoons when he couldn't find any carpenters, he built model houses. Out of thin strips of balsa wood, he constructed replicas of all the houses in our neighborhood. He could build a model house in minutes, his hands running over the soft wood, cutting it, bending and shaping it. A few months after we stumbled upon the abandoned house, Roy built a model of it, too.

During the long spring when he was twelve and I was just nine, Roy chewed over the idea of the lost family and the empty house. It rattled his nerves. For a week of mornings early that summer, he pushed away his bowl of oatmeal and stared out the kitchen window at the ants crawling along the branches of the lilac bush. Then one day he woke up and ate two bowls of oatmeal. Some idea had turned his mood. I watched it play across his face all morning. Several times before lunch he leaned toward me, his face brightening as he began to tell me something. Then he would change his mind and sit back in the grass.

"What is it?" I asked.

But he would not talk.

The next day, Roy did not want to go to the gully to look at the house. After breakfast he walked out the back door, across the stone path to the garage. He opened the garage door, stepped inside, and closed it again. I sat outside the door, my nose in a book, waiting. He emerged an hour or so later, carrying two of Father's old leather belts. He had threaded string and wire through the buckle holes. From these makeshift loops he had hung a good-sized hammer on each belt, a screwdriver, and a carpenter's level. A small cardboard matchbox had been attached to the side of each belt and filled with nails. I scrambled to my feet.

He held out one of the belts. "Put this on," he said.

I looked at it and crinkled my nose. "What is it?"

"A carpenter's belt," he said. "We're going to make our own house."

I let the belt dangle from my hand and stared at it. He started walking in long strides toward the northwest corner of the backyard, tossing a tape measure up in the air as far as he could and then catching it behind his back. The hammer on the belt bounced against his thigh as he walked.

"Do you mean a fort?" I called after him.

He caught the tape measure behind his back, looked over at me briefly, and said, "No. I mean a house."

Behind the garage, deep in the recesses of our backyard, beyond the reach of Father's mower, skunk cabbage grew wild. When the wind blew too hard, or we stepped in the wrong spot, the stems broke and released a sour musk into the humid air. In those depths, untended by Father's meticulous hand, we began to build. After the first year, after our first sorry attempt, held together with chicken wire and plastic, Roy let go of the idea of building a real, complete house. He conceded. We called them forts.

In later years, Roy would spend hours designing the forts, drawing up plans with his slide rule and his mechanical pencils. He measured. He calculated. He walked the ground, counting feet, choosing the dimensions. He wrote supply lists and brought them to Father, who helped him find wood scraps from the local dump and bought two-by-fours and pressboard at the lumberyard. But that first year, we winged it. It took us a week to clear the land. We stunk up the whole yard pulling up the skunkweed. Mrs. Bindle, the neighborhood recluse, actually emerged from her house, her teacup balanced in one of her pale hands, and had a word with Mother about the smell.

Then we began to make the fort's main frame. It was a modest plan. One room—five feet by ten feet, with the bottom of an unused doghouse overturned and set in the middle of the room as our table. (We found a way to use the old doghouse in every incarnation of the fort.) By July, we had just about got the walls in place. Even though it listed to one side and half the roof was covered in plastic, I did not care. We were almost finished. I imagined that the rest of the summer would unfold in a happy monotony of days spent lounging about, reading books in our new hideout. Roy did not see it that way.

By the time I got to the fort the next morning, he had reams of large blue-edged paper spread out on the ground, the corners anchored down with small rocks. He was kneeling over them, a mechanical pencil clutched between his teeth, one elbow on the ground. With his right hand he scratched the back of his head meditatively. I squatted down next to him. He pointed to one corner of the thin tracing paper where the rock had rolled off. He took the pencil out of his mouth and said, "Hold that down."

I pressed my fingers to the spot. "What's this?" I asked.

"Plans for the next fort."

"But we finished the fort."

He glanced up at me and then down at his papers. "We're going to tear it down and build another one, a better one."

"What's wrong with this one?"

"In the next one we're going to add two front windows, here and here."

I slumped against the trunk of a pine tree.

After Mother turned off the lights in the van and the yard fell back into darkness, I visited the fort. Leaning against the door, I listened again for the rustle of Mother's footsteps on the grass, but the yard was silent. In the late-evening air, I could feel the crisp early-autumn wind coming off the lake. Father lay awake in the bed upstairs. Mother sat in the dark van. I pushed open the fort door, and Shadow and I stepped inside. She turned, sniffed, and again went straight for the paper bag. I thought of Roy in the yard and the night he taught me not to be afraid of the dark. I squatted down and pushed Shadow away from the bag. I rubbed her belly for a moment, and then I stood up and looked around.

This, our last fort, had two stories. The second story was an addition, one of my ill-conceived ideas. Shortly after its construction, the second story started to buckle and sag. It severely compromised the first-floor roof, and we had to put up a series of support beams that cut down the center of the narrow first floor. But the fort's main body, square and sturdy, flanked by two working windows with Plexiglas panes, was impeccably designed. It was Roy's doing.

In one corner stood a table fashioned from the old doghouse. In the other, we had placed an armchair with a broken leg and propped it up with phone books. The jerry-rigged table, the listing chair, the sagging roof, all of it, was part of the pleasure of escaping the ordered world of the adults.

In the darkness, when the grass grew as soft as water under my feet and the world had poured out every last drop of daylight until I could no longer see my hand in front of my face, I thought anything was possible. I thought that Roy had not left me; he'd only left my parents. Roy was all around me, in every shape, every sound. I could almost hear his feet on the driveway. Several times I thought I saw the shadow of his hand, the back of his head in the rustling movements of the lilac trees. Buried among these thoughts, the seed of a dangerous idea had planted itself in my mind. It had to do with the paper bag, the one Shadow could not leave alone. Every night I would arrive at the dinner table with the bag folded in a square and nestled in the bottom of my jeans pocket. During the meal, I would pull it out and hide it on my lap while I slipped food off my plate and into the bag.

When I passed the van again, it was still dark. For a moment, I thought I heard Mother's voice, but it was only the water spigot dripping on the ivy. I crept over to the hose and tightened the spigot.

Inside, Father was up again. I came upon him in the front hall adjusting the throw rugs that covered threadbare patches on the carpet. A blue shag dangled from his left hand.

"Hi," I said.

He jumped. "You scared me." He blushed. He looked down at my dirty jeans. "Where have you been?"

"I wanted a glass of milk."

"Oh." He did not take his eyes off the mud stains on the jeans.

"You want one?" I asked.

He turned back to the business with the rugs. "No," he said. "But thank you, baby."

"Sister Judith stopped by today," I said.

"Did she?"

"I told her that you were shopping for wood for the new camper-van."

Father dropped his rug. He stepped toward me. "You said that?"

"Yes."

He grabbed me by the shoulders. "You told her that?"

"Yes, I didn't—"

"Don't you ever," he said, shaking my shoulders, "ever tell anyone where we go or what we buy." He paused a moment, looked at his hands on my shoulders, and let go. "What will they think of us?"

He walked over to the living room window and stared out onto the dark street. I watched his hands tremble, the tips of his fingers pressed against the smooth glass.

8

HIS CHILDHOOD DREAM was to be a priest, to give his life to the service of God. At fifteen my father was chosen from his parish to receive a scholarship to Saint Mary's Redemptorist Seminary in Erie, Pennsylvania.

A month after his arrival at Saint Mary's, the pain started again. Throughout his childhood he had suffered lower abdominal pains so severe that he was often found doubled over on the sidewalk outside the family home in downtown Rochester. But the family doctor just said, "growing pains," and left it at that. When he went away to the seminary, the bouts of terrible pain continued. The German nuns who ran the infirmary had a different diagnosis. They came upon him curled up under the baptismal font outside the chapel one morning and whisked him off to the infirmary. They examined him and diagnosed appendicitis. If it weren't for those quick, sharp German Sisters, he would have died. As it was, his appendix burst on the operating table and the poison spilled into his bloodstream. He spent a month in the infirmary, recuperating and drinking milk shakes. The Sisters tried to fatten him up, to make this thin, pale boy into a hardy seminarian. But it did not work. By the time he returned to class, he had fallen so far behind that he failed his preliminary exams.

"It is the Lord's will," the monsignor told him, "that you never become a priest."

And with that they sent him back east. His sister Arlene met him at the train station. His mother thanked God for these small failures. She had not wanted him to leave home. But it was the seminary, his call to God, that saved his life.

Four years later, just as he graduated from high school, his mother died. There was no work in Rochester at the time and no money coming in to take care of his sisters and his elderly aunt. So every day for two weeks my father walked over to Gleason Works Tool & Die Company on University Avenue, only to be told that the factory was not hiring. Halfway into the third week, they decided to give him a try. They did not regret it. He was a good worker. His superiors offered to send him to college, to train him for management.

"Thanks all the same, sir," he said, "but I like the machine shop." And he stayed there until he retired, forty years later.

For the next seventeen years, he lived with his aunt Catherine, taking care of her and cooking all the meals. Then, in 1964, he married my mother and bought a house.

A slender man with fine black hair, keen blue eyes, and translucent Irish skin, Father approached all of life with the same gentle homage. He made contact by cleaning. Everything under his hands was straightened, wiped off, smoothed down. He could feel the dust settling on windowsills, could sense the slight tilt of a frame. He was thirty-five when he married my mother. He never missed a Sunday service.

Like a boater's paddle, Father's saints pushed him on. He sang the Latin Mass in the shower; every morning my brother and I awoke to the sound of water hitting his back and his voice, haunting, incantatory, floating out of the heat and the steam. After his shower he blessed his children with the two special relics given to him by his best friend, Brother Eddie, as a wedding present: the bones of Blessed Saint John Neumann and Blessed Saint Gerard encased in gilded copper with the inscription *Ex ossibus*.

I remember best the winter mornings when the temperature dipped well below freezing. Mother believed in the healing power of the cold. Every night she closed the heat vents that fed my parents' bedroom. She said one slept best in a chilly room. Ice formed in Father's flask of holy water. Resting in their unheated room, the relics froze, and Father never managed to warm them before he blessed us. He tried. He sat at the edge of my bed rubbing Saint

John Neumann between his palms, trying to heat up the glass plate front and the gilding before he pressed the relic to my forehead. But it was always cold. The sting of it, the sharp edge pressed softly against my skin is my most vivid memory of childhood.

He blessed Roy first. He brought the relic to his mouth, kissed it, and pressed it to Roy's forehead. He touched the relic to Roy's mouth, chest, and hands. I would drift in and out of sleep as I listened to the sound of his gentle voice repeating, "Bless his mind. Bless his throat. Bless his hands. Bless his voice."

Sometimes I would crawl into bed with Roy after Father left for work and touch that spot on his forehead where, I knew, Father had placed the relic, the bones of John Neumann. Roy was never a morning person. He would fall asleep again after Father left, waiting till the last possible moment to get up for school. So when I'd place my hand on his forehead, he'd groan and roll away from me. "Leave me alone," he'd sigh. I'd watch his side rise and fall under the covers as he breathed. I'd crawl in closer.

"Why does he do that?" I asked once. "Why does he have to touch the relic to us and bless all the parts of us?"

"He's naming them," Roy said through the covers.

"Why?"

"Because he's taking care of us." Roy sat up then. His hair was wild. It stood on end. He rubbed his eye with the back of his fist. "It's like Adam in the Garden of Eden." He tilted his head to one side, pointed with his chin as if he were indicating a garden right in front of us. "He's got to name us, like Adam named all the animals. To keep track of them."

9

BY MID-AUGUST 1984, Mother had hung up her circular saw and her safety goggles, hammered the lids on the paint cans, washed the brushes, and stepped back to admire her work. In three weeks she had planned a wake and a funeral, buried her son, bought a new van, built a bed, cupboards, and a camper kitchen, and completely stocked it with camping supplies. She packed us into this newly reconstructed van, climbed into the driver's seat, slammed into reverse, and gunned it out the rutted drive.

Every August we spent two weeks on the Cape, in Brewster, Massachusetts. We took the same route to the same campsite on the same day of the month. The first thing my brother and I did every summer, after Father pulled the van into the campsite, was walk the mile to the bayside beach. And as we walked we watched the ocean come slowly toward us through the forest, the glint of the waves, and the calm water lapping the shore. We crouched down in the dunes and stared out at the long stretch of sand. Roy and I loved the walk and the feeling that you could sneak up on the ocean, catch it unawares.

Mary Elizabeth came with us this year. She sat in the passenger seat and read the maps for Mother. Father and I bundled into the back. Her prescription sunglasses sliding down her nose, the AAA trip planner spread out on the dashboard, Mother took that ten-hour stretch of road between Rochester and Cape Cod like it was a short ride to the grocery store.

When we arrived, she pulled the new van into the old camping spot. Wash, the campground attendant, checked our name off the reservation list.

"Where's Roy?" he asked.

I looked up into Wash's weathered face and smiled. The Before-People, I thought, are going to be all over Cape Cod.

We arrived with familiar props: the bathing suits, the beach towels, the sunblock and sun visors, a cooler packed with sandwiches. Still, we found ourselves the next morning at the entrance to Nauset Beach in our street clothes, trailing our towels behind us. We stared, the three of us and Mary Elizabeth, out at the bright ocean. The weather was perfect. The sky glowed. The waves burst forward, relentless, beautiful, even bluer than the sky.

We stood there for a good half hour, just staring at the vacationers in their bright swimsuits sauntering up and down the boardwalk, their faces shining with sunblock. Then Mother took a breath, nipped over to the changing room, put on her bikini, and marched into the surf. Throwing her arms up, she gave her body over to the weight of the waves. No one loved the ocean as much as Mother and Roy. The rough water never scared them. They could ride the tall waves at the ocean beach for hours, the white crests of water frothing out along their narrow arms. Father and I would sit on the shore reading, watching their sleek, dark heads bob up and down.

Next Mary Elizabeth disappeared into the changing room and reemerged in a pink one-piece with a green visor set atop her black curls. Mother insisted on ordering the onion rings from the small white shack at the edge of Nauset Beach's municipal parking lot. They were Roy's favorite. She ate them with a grim resolve.

"Isn't this a perfect day?" she called.

Father and I stood on the boardwalk, unable to step off our little wooden island out into the expanse of sand. Mother called to us, "Come on!" She waved her hand back and forth above her head. "Please," she called. She held out an onion ring.

Wearing his gray work pants and a pair of loafers, Father stepped off the boardwalk and onto the beach. He looked down at the sand where it gathered in the heels of his loafers and kept walking. When the sand grew heavy and wet, and the water began to lap against his feet, he stopped. He stood there, a cooler in one hand, a lawn chair in the other, water lapping against the cuffs of his pants, and stared. Fine crystals of spray flew up around him. I think Father half-expected the ocean to be gone, to have ascended from this world to heaven along with his son.

Mary Elizabeth appeared at his side, her green visor obscuring the upper half of her face, looking up at him. Mother walked over and took his hand. The wind whipped the words out of her mouth, but I saw her point at his feet. He bent over and pulled off one of his loafers. She said something again, and Father nodded and stepped out of the other shoe and began to walk into the ocean in his pants and stocking feet.

"Mr. Smith. Mr. Smith!" Mary Elizabeth cried. "Stop."

"Royden," Mother called. "What are you doing?"

He got up to his knees before Mary Elizabeth went in after him. I cut out down the boardwalk and started struggling through the heavy sand toward the shore. By the time I got there, Mary Elizabeth had convinced Father to turn around. They stood on the shore again. Mother had him by the arm and was pointing at his soaking socks. He looked down at them. Mary Elizabeth pried his fingers off the chair and headed away from the water's edge. She unfolded it for him and secured it in a patch of dry sand.

"Have a seat, Mr. Smith," she said and stepped out of his way.

On the second day Mother walked down the beach, got about a hundred yards from us, and broke into a run. I pulled off my sneakers, left Mary Elizabeth to watch Father, turned back toward the dunes, and started searching for her. I walked for a half hour. The seagulls swooped and cawed, the miles of dune grass laid out before me. Finally, I caught sight of her about a mile down, in a low sandy patch between two dunes. I wanted to call out her name, but something stopped me. She ran into the tall dune grass.

There was a little shack a couple of miles down, hidden in the dunes. It was an elusive spot. The aged wood, weathered to an ashy hue, blended with the sand. Mother, Roy, and I loved that shack.

It was always deserted. No one else seemed to even know it existed. We loved that it was so hard to find, that some years it seemed to have disappeared for good. Once she started running in the dunes, I knew where my mother was headed. She wanted to sit on the shaded, sandy floor of the old shack, to step out of this unrelenting beauty. But she could not find it. Finally she stopped, sat down in the sand, and raked her hands through her hair.

There was a hardness in Mother. She had rebuilt her world once already. Moved from dirt-poor farm country outside of Buffalo to the city of Rochester, got a job in a bank, married a salaried man, and bought a three-bedroom house with a working fireplace. She was steely, single-minded, and fierce; what she said was law. But as I watched her now in the dunes alone, without her children, without the man she'd built her life around, she softened. She pulled her knees up to her chin, wrapped her arms around her shins, and put her head down.

This was what the work had been for, the weeks of preparation: to get here, the place where Mother and Roy were so happy together. How youthful she had looked that spring. Now I watched my mother—young and lithe, daughter of the Medina farmlands, winner of the West Shelby County beauty contest, singer of country tunes—I watched her age. For the first time I saw her taut body sag.

I called to her. "Mommy," I cried, a name I had not used in years.

She looked up. "Roy!" she called. "Roydie?"

I was right there, standing on a high dune, the sea grass pricking my ankles, and she could not see me. I was not the one she was looking for. It would always be Roy, the child she'd let slip through her hands. She would look for him around every corner, on every sand dune, in the face of every young man. For the rest of her life she'd chase this phantom. Like so many women, she was defined by her children. And she had let one of them die. I know she watched him on that last morning, through the bedroom window. She watched as the shadows of his hands crossed the steering wheel. She watched him, as she had every morning that summer, drive away to his summer job. Mother did not expect to find Roy on the beach, but she just had to check.

"Roydie!" she cried. "My boy?"

The wind whipped around her, and her hair flew into her face, but the beach remained quiet. Not even a gull cried. She stood up and started walking down the hill, away from me. I watched as she disappeared over the next hill, her orange flowered bikini descending like a lowering flag into the valley of dunes.

10

THE NEXT DAY we did not go back to the beach. Instead we drove out to Provincetown and took a ride on a boat. We saw several whales, their massive bodies emerging from the dark water and spitting into the bright afternoon air, their oily backs pushing up toward the noonday sun. When we returned to shore, Mary Elizabeth and Mother rented fishing poles and cast off into the murky waters at the end of the pier. Father bought me a headband in a dockside souvenir shop. He tied the braided strand around my head, securing the knot at the base of my neck. I held Father's hand as we strolled the length of Commercial Street. We must have passed up and down the narrow, crowded street seven times while Mary Elizabeth and Mother fished. The world cocooned around us. That afternoon, my hand nestled in the warmth of his palm, Father walked as if there were something broken inside of him, something floating loose in his veins that might be disturbed should he make any sudden movements.

After a while we rested on an outdoor patio. Father ordered a cup of tea, and I watched him drink it. He had been quiet on the walk, but now the quality of his silence shifted. I could tell he was puzzling over something.

"Baby?" he asked.

"Yes?"

"You know how we all have guardian angels, right?"

I hesitated a moment. "Okay."

"And they are assigned to us, to protect us in this world?"

"Uh-huh."

"What happened to Roy's angel? Where was he that morning? Did he fall asleep on the job?" He set down the cup and slid to the edge of his seat. I could smell sea salt and calamine lotion rising off his skin. "And what happens to the angel when the person he's supposed to be guarding dies?" Father looked at me for a long moment. And then he looked out onto the busy street. The sun was setting. The sky turned pink. We could just make out a slice of water shimmering between the buildings. He squinted and asked, "Do you get demoted? Do you get reassigned?"

As we watched the sky fall into darkness, I remembered an afternoon, years ago, when Father had attached a basketball hoop to the outer wall of the garage. I was seven. Roy was ten. I stood in the kitchen with Mother looking out at the back of Roy's brown, rumpled head, his face pointed up toward the sky as Father stood on the top of the ladder holding the hoop in one hand. Then suddenly Father slipped. He dropped the basketball hoop. He lost his balance. His white arms grabbed at the empty air as he tried to steady himself, and for a second, his narrow frame blurred out of focus. Mother and I stood at the sink, the water running. Soft folds of steam unfurled up our arms as we reached out toward Father, as if we could catch him through the window screen. And Roy reached with us, putting his arms out to break Father's fall. In that moment, an AM radio broadcast cutting through the evening air, the peonies drooping onto the gravel drive, the four of us held out our arms and slipped together. The four of us lost our grasp on the ladder and wavered in the air. At the last instant Father caught a lower rung of the ladder and steadied himself.

I had always thought if we lost one of us, if someone had to go, it would be Father. He hovered on the edges of life, his dainty bird feet testing the water at the beach every summer. He was afraid of the world, and because of this timidity he made every new place like home. On our camping trips, he made a kitchen out of the woods. He pumped up the Coleman stove outside our tent and cooked us breakfast on every one of his vacations. Black crows would land in silence, dropping around our campsite as the sun rose. When they cawed into the morning, Father talked to the birds.

"Hey guys. Quiet down," he told them. "I got people sleeping in that tent." And when they wouldn't, he'd join them, singing the Latin Mass, his voice dissolving into the air around us, pulling us out of our dreams. Mother and Roy and I would look at each other as Father's song buzzed in the air around the tent.

I watched Father's hand play across the mug of tea. He sighed and wrapped his ghost white hands around the dark mug, the Red Rose tea tab hanging over its rim, one single bright rose stamped on its waxy surface.

When he had finished his tea and the sun had completely set, he asked me once more. "Do you ever wonder about that, Ali?" he asked. "Do you wonder about the Angel?"

I stared into my father's face. He was an extraordinarily handsome man, I thought, with an epicene quality that lent him a youthful air, even as he slipped into middle age. More than I wanted God back, more than I wanted to feel the surety of faith that Father felt, I wanted to feel close to my father again. But I could not lie to him.

I shrugged. I played with his spoon. "I don't know," I said.

There exists only one photo of that vacation, and it is of Mary Elizabeth. She is posed outside the orange tent. Wearing a yellow halter top and green shorts, she kicks her right leg out in a Rockettes move. Her white teeth and her glasses shine in the sudden glare of the camera's flash.

11

WHEN MY BROTHER grew tired of my company or fell into one of his long silences, I would go to Mary Elizabeth's house. I showed up there in all weather, bundled or barefoot, shivering or sweating on the back stoop. Her house was across the road from ours and had the same layout: a two-story white colonial with four shuttered windows. Inside, though, the differences began. Mrs. Henderson was a collector. Whereas our mother rarely kept anything that gathered dust, Mrs. Henderson stocked her house with tiny figurines, special edition plates, racks of sugar spoons, bottles of buttons, and piles of fabric scraps.

The Henderson family was larger than ours, and several additions to their house crowded into the backyard. I spent whole days of my childhood in their home, where the rooms were dark and full of hidden treasures, where there was always a record on the turntable and the smell of home-ground peanut butter filled the air. The living room, decorated like an old-fashioned parlor, held the majority of Mrs. Henderson's pieces. A glass-top case, weighted down by a miniature ceramic shoe collection, stood in one corner of the room. More than once I stole away from the noise and the bustle in the family room, snuck into the front parlor, slipped my hand inside that case, and touched the cool smoothness of the figurines.

Mary Elizabeth possessed a doggedly practical streak that was tempered only by her appearance: long black ringlets, a tiny bottle-cap nose, and ears as small and delicate as a doll's. From birth Mary Elizabeth was organizing, sewing, cleaning, teaching, and bossing people around. She had an answer for every possible question. Her heart was huge, and her kindness toward me saved me more than once. When I could not for the life of me learn to ride a bike, she dedicated every afternoon after school to teaching me. When I was going to fail gym because I could not swim the length of the pool, she rearranged her schedule and spent an hour a day practicing strokes with me. We took the bus to school together. She got on first and saved me a seat. Every day she inspected my appearance.

"You have chapped lips. Did you know? You should use lip balm every morning," she said and showed me her Bonne Bell grape lip gloss. "I would lend you mine but that would be unsanitary." She spoke the Bible truth.

Wise and fiercely mature, Mary Elizabeth suffered as the youngest of four. She wanted to be a big sister. I was a dreamy, sloppy child eleven months her junior, prone to scabbed knees and shirt stains, forgetful of dates and unable to hold my own in conversation with adults. I was pliant, perpetually ill informed, and stubbornly naïve. I made the perfect little sister. Her older brothers and sister lived in the late-seventies era of the Bee Gees, toe socks, and feathered haircuts, and Mary Elizabeth soaked up this disco culture like a sponge. She was about seven years behind the current trends. She taught me the names of disco bands (information I promptly forgot), how to French-braid hair, and how to sew doll clothes. As a result of shuttling back and forth between Roy and Mary Elizabeth, I had grown up half rough, half refined. I could sew a complete wardrobe for my dolls or shingle a roof—but neither of these things could I do well.

The school year after Roy left, I developed the habit of spending my afternoons in the basement. I would return home, drop my bag in the front hall, and head straight down the stairs. I had pulled a camping cot out of the fruit cellar, covered it with a sleeping bag and a white sheet, and languished there, holding a book in my hand, not quite reading, not quite sleeping, just staring. Sometimes I watched old movies on public television. Mary Elizabeth visited me often. Some of my other school friends came as well. They sat on the edge of the couch, drank milky tea, looked uncomfortable, and soon left. But Mary Elizabeth stayed. One day, in early autumn, she showed up in her red culottes and a green-apple Izod shirt. A box of strawberry Pop-Tarts tucked under her arm, she perched on the back of the couch and stared down at me where I lay on my camping cot.

"Want one?" She held out the box of Pop-Tarts.

I shook my head.

"But they're your favorite."

When I did not reply, she reached across the sofa and held the box under my nose. I could see the white frosting with the flecks of pink sugar mixed in. I could smell the sweet pastry. I shook my head again.

"Suit yourself," she said and bit into one. "What are you watching?" she asked.

"*The Bells of Saint Mary's.*"

"Nineteen forty-five. Bing Crosby. Ingrid Bergman."

I craned my neck around to look at her. She was brushing crumbs off her culottes when she looked up and caught me staring at her. Her eyes widened. "What?"

"How did you know that?"

"I know a lot of things," Mary Elizabeth said and gave me a slow smile. Then she stood up, smoothed down her outfit, and said, "Okay, let's go. You're getting out of here."

I stumbled into the yard behind her and slouched against the back wall of the house. The day was terribly sunny. I blinked into it. Sunlight bounced off the side of the garage, the pavement, the grass. "Can we go back inside now?" I asked.

Mary Elizabeth grabbed my hand and pulled me down the drive and across the street. When we reached her backyard, she set down the box of Pop-Tarts and sprang across the grass. Her legs, dark and smooth, scissored out and slid together again as she landed a perfect roundoff at the base of her favorite oak. "Come on," she called over her shoulder as she grabbed for the first branch and hoisted herself up the trunk. She disappeared under a thick cover of leaves.

Every summer, Mary Elizabeth and I had climbed the oak trees that grew in a row around the Hendersons' back lawn. We spent entire afternoons up there, swinging from one tree to the next. By the time we were ten we had become so agile we could actually climb from tree to tree all the way around the periphery of her yard without ever touching the ground. Once adolescence set in, we gave up climbing trees, but that day Mary Elizabeth revived the lost tradition. Her head poked out from between the branches. "Are you coming, or what?" she asked, and then she was off again, climbing higher. The branches quivered. I stepped toward the tree. The grass rippled and shimmered beneath me. I reached up, grabbed the low branch, and pulled. My feet scrambled against the trunk. My legs trembled with the effort. I lowered myself back to the ground and let go of the branch.

"What if I fall?" I called up to Mary Elizabeth.

"Don't be silly, Alison," she called down to me as she climbed higher. "You never fall."

She was right. I had never fallen. I was an excellent climber, but I had become afraid of the most ordinary things. Things I used to do with ease, without a thought, now left me stunned and troubled, unable to figure out where to begin. *I will fall,* I thought. *I know it.* I could feel my legs buckling. I stared up the trunk. Far above me, Mary Elizabeth climbed higher and higher, singing my name.

"Come *on,*" she called from behind the shadow of the leaves.

I reached for a low branch, closed my eyes, and hoisted myself up.

When I finally caught up with her, Mary Elizabeth pulled two bananas from a side pocket in her culottes, handed one to me, and began to peel the other. She bit into hers.

"Where do you think he went?" she asked.

"Who?"

"Roy, silly."

I dropped my banana.

Mary Elizabeth never mentioned Roy. No one did, if they could help it. I had gone from calling that name dozens of times a day, from crooning it, screaming it, whispering it, caterwauling across the yard—Roy, Royden, Alroy, Roydie—to silence. Since the day after he died, when we sat in my room and spoke of the forbidden newspaper article, Roy's name had never crossed Mary Elizabeth's lips. I stared down at my lost banana where it lay in the grass.

"Do you think he went to heaven?" she asked, and she held out half of her banana to me.

I waved her hand away. "No, thanks," I said. I grabbed a piece of loose bark and started to pull. "Where else is there? Limbo?"

"No, the Pope got rid of Limbo. Remember?"

I pulled some more bark. "Right. The Pope."

She bit into her banana again and thought for a long moment. "He's in heaven. I'm sure of it, Alison Lavon." When she was very serious Mary Elizabeth used my middle name.

She folded her peel into a tight square and set it on the branch next to her left sneaker.

"How does it feel?" she asked.

"How does what feel?"

Mary Elizabeth glanced down at my shorts. "You know."

I knew right away. She was referring to my period. I shifted away from her on my branch and renewed my efforts to strip all the bark from the tree. It was unlike her to make any allusions to bodily secretions. I stole a look at her. Freckles spotted her nose. Her cheeks were rosy. I don't know how she had found out about my period. It had come and gone without much notice on anybody's part.

"How did the first one go?" she asked.

"Fine. I guess."

"When are you due again?"

"I already had it."

"So you're working on number three. When does it come?"

I frowned, pulled up some more bark. "I don't know."

"You have to keep track, how else are you going to be prepared?"

As the afternoon progressed we moved inside, to the Hendersons' dark, wood-paneled back room. We listened to eight-tracks and LPs of ABBA and Shaun Cassidy. Mary Elizabeth practiced her dance moves. She was teaching herself (and me when she could lasso me into it) how to disco dance. She practiced constantly. She was one of the smartest students at Our Lady of Mercy School for Girls—her homework was always impeccable—yet I never saw her do a stitch of work. Instead, she danced.

In the middle of her Bus Stop demo, I slipped away to the living room. I ran my hand along the ceramic shoes and picked up my favorite, an imitation French court shoe. But the little shoes no longer held the same magic for me. I had become fascinated with an ornament that sat on the upright piano: a butterfly encased in Lucite, stilled in flight.

I hated to leave my basement. But I would travel across the street; I would put up with the rounds of greetings, the hair tousling, the plying me with food, the dance lessons, just for a chance to stare at the Lucite butterfly. I felt for the little butterfly, how it struggled to get somewhere but instead was stuck in the invisible glue. I brushed the dust off the Lucite casing, sat down on the piano bench, and held the heavy, clear mass in my palm.

Mary Elizabeth appeared at the doorway, her hands on her hips. "You're never going to get the spin right if you don't practice."

I followed her back into the family room, and we went through the steps one more time. She was playing ABBA, "Dancing Queen," singing along in her high soprano, and for a few moments I caught on. I got all the steps right. Mary Elizabeth grinned. "I knew you could do it." And together we twirled and stepped and clapped and sang. Mary Elizabeth's older sister, Kelly, sauntered into the room, leaned against the doorframe, and watched us dance. "You're such goons," she said and cut off the eight-track. "I've got practice and we need silence."

Kelly was a singer. For the past four years she had landed the part of ingenue in all the high school musicals. Over the summer, she had formed a rock band. She was the only female among the motley crew of musicians. They practiced in the Hendersons' basement after school. Mary Elizabeth pretended not to care about what she called "Kelly's Stupid Band." But she wanted to watch.

She wanted to sing with them. "How about letting Alison and me watch you practice? Alison really wants to see you guys."

Kelly leveled me with one of her long, cold looks. She flipped her hair back, readjusted her feather earrings, and asked, "You really want to see us?"

I didn't. I was terrified of Kelly and her band. But I was not about to betray Mary Elizabeth. "Sure," I said.

Kelly looked at Mary Elizabeth, at me, and then back at Mary Elizabeth.

"Okay, jerk." She sighed in Mary Elizabeth's direction. "But only if you're totally quiet." Then she slung her hip out, opened the door to the basement, and disappeared into the darkness.

Mary Elizabeth and I sat in the red and green beanbags by the washer-dryer. The washing machine hummed behind us, the amplified and wild chord progressions shook the house. As we passed a bag of Doritos between us, Mary Elizabeth never once took her eyes off the band. Mostly they performed covers, but the guitarist Jimmy, a skinny, angular boy with a tiny patch of stubble on the tip of his pointy chin, composed sappy, earnest lyrics about love melting him into a heap on the floor. Mary Elizabeth leaned over toward my beanbag, pressed her mouth to my ear, and whispered, "Isn't he dreamy?"

I stared at her. "Dreamy?" I asked.

She waved her hand in my direction, tossed her hair off her shoulders, and said, "You're just too young, Alison Lavon. Someday you'll understand." Then she slipped her glasses off her face and slid them into her side pocket.

As we huddled on our deflated beanbags in the corner of the Hendersons' basement, Mary Elizabeth leaned forward and tried not to squint as she memorized every line, every vocal intonation, every gesture of Jimmy-the-Lead-Guitar-Player. And the more she leaned forward, the further back I sank.

12

By September, Mother and Father had returned to work. Every night when Mother came home from her secretarial job and Father from the factory, they sat down at the dining room table and wrote acknowledgment notes to the four-hundred-some-odd people who had sent sympathy cards. It took most of the autumn, all those evenings of doling out the replies, of envelope addressing and stamp licking. Bent over their work late into the night, their foreheads almost touching, they read the cards, shook their heads, and wrote.

When they had finished with the allotted replies for the evening, Mother pulled out her blue ledger and together they examined the household accounts. They whispered to each other. They hid their papers and smiled at me whenever I entered the room. Mother and Father had always been reticent. Now, they became even more secretive. My parents would not talk of insurance claims or accident reports, of lost dreams or current troubles. Instead they had mysterious codes, whispered phrases, private looks. I started listening around corners, waiting in hallways, pressing my ear against the wall.

"You could sue," I heard Mr. Wilson suggest to Father in a whisper one evening. From my perch on the stairs, I watched the two of them. Mr. Wilson was sitting on the hassock at the foot of the big green chair. He leaned in close to Father, his baseball cap held in both hands, his tennis shoes pressed into the dull weave of the carpet. "It was their fault," he continued. "Her husband had bald tires on the car. It would not have passed inspection. She should not have taken it out on the road, Roy."

"No," Father said. "We can't sue. He lost his wife."

* * *

I stood in the yard that night, my hands shoved deep into the pockets of my jeans. I had not thought to put on a jacket. My fingers curled around the greasy paper bag nestled at the bottom of my pocket. I clicked my tongue against my teeth, and like clockwork, Shadow appeared. We walked to the back of the yard.

By this time, two months after the accident, Shadow and I had developed a routine. Every night, just as the sky darkened, I stepped out onto the back lawn and Shadow appeared. She walked me to the fort, and there, lying on the ground outside the door, her muzzle resting in the dirt between her paws, she waited for me. I opened the door and stepped into the pitch-dark room. Once inside, I pulled the paper bag out of my pocket. That night, the bag held half a pork chop and a handful of soggy carrots. I dumped the contents onto a dinner plate I had stolen from the kitchen. Then I sat down in the molding easy chair by a window and stared at the sky.

You could sue. Bald tires. He lost his wife. These phrases rattled around inside me. I had no name for the feelings they conjured up. Like captions for a set of lost photographs, I knew what the individual words meant, but I didn't know what to attach them to. And my parents didn't know how to tell me. We had lost the thread of our own story. Grief takes that from you. It makes the familiar, the quotidian, turn strange.

As the strangeness grew up around us, I turned to books. I read voraciously, indiscriminately, everything from cereal boxes to roofing manuals to the complete works of Jane Austen. When I wasn't reading or languishing in my makeshift camp in the basement, I stared—just gazed into the middle distance. There were so many wasted afternoons. So many useless, listless, empty hours of staring and blinking and then staring some more. I passed entire days tracking the course of a single dust mote across the basement. I stared so hard, for so long, at nothing, I convinced myself that I could actually see the texture of the air, watch its atoms break apart and re-form. My eyes turned red around the rims and swelled up. And when I was done staring, I picked up another book.

I spent so much time reading in bad light, in the basement with the fluorescents off, in the fort by lantern light, under the covers with a flashlight. My eyeglass prescription increased four times over the next three years.

And when all the books had been read and all the dust motes had settled, I walked around the house and touched things. The velveteen smoothness of the couch, the hard curve of Mother's glass lamp, the sharp edges of Formica countertops, the rough wool of blankets. I ran my hands over these objects, pressed my fingers against the furniture, and waited to see if I could feel the pressure, the texture of the upholstery, the counter, the blanket pressing back.

There were nights I wandered the rooms of our house, keeping my eyes shut, wondering how far I could get without opening them, counting the steps from the kitchen to the front hall, from the front hall to the living room, from the couch to Father's easy chair. When I had finished counting steps inside the house, I unlatched the back door and walked into the yard. I gazed up at the starry sky. I waited for the long silence inside me to end, for God, for Jesus—my first and best friend—to return. I waited for the music of faith to find me again. And as the hoot owls and the crickets called and chattered, and the smell of woodsmoke from the first fires of the season crept out of the chimneys, inside I remained silent, stunned, incredulous. I waited for Roy to come back.

For my parents, it was different. It was to God that they turned. If there was doubt, if there passed a fleeting moment of disbelief, a slender passage of time when they entertained the possibility of God as a fraud, I did not detect it. They never stopped seeing Him in every aspect of life. Losing your faith in a world where God is all around you is a precarious business. When God shows His face on a daily basis to your friends and neighbors, it is, on some level, impossible to stop believing in Him. Instead I felt that God chose to exclude me from His world. Since I was the only one to lose faith, to stop hearing Christ's voice, I thought perhaps it was my fault that Roy had left us. I thought I was being punished for some unknown sin. I had learned early in my Catholic career that one could sin silently, in one's heart. One could even sin without ever discovering what one had done or why it was wrong. What had I done, I asked myself, to make God disappear and take Roy with Him?

13

ALL FALL THEY came, two at a time in square brown packages, landing with a thud on the front stoop: the encyclopedias. As soon as Mother heard the rev of the delivery van's engine, her head shot up and she jogged to the front door to retrieve them. The A–B volumes arrived in September. She borrowed a blue nylon external-frame backpack from the Hendersons' second oldest boy, unzipped its rusty front zipper, and slipped the A–B books inside the tattered main sleeve. Wearing Roy's work boots, Mother strapped the pack to her back and walked. She said she was preparing for a mountain hike, getting used to carrying extra weight.

On the day the encyclopedias arrived, the pack always came out and the new letters of the alphabet slid in between the folds of the frayed nylon.

"You have to work up to this gradually," she told me as she added the D encyclopedia to her pack.

I imagined that once she turned the corner, she would sit down, unzip her bag, and read those encyclopedias. But that wasn't her style. For her they were just weight, an accumulation of pressure. Her legs grew taut with the exercise. She started taking the car out on Saturday mornings. After loading the heavy pack into the hatchback of her Chevette, she drove to Lock Number 32, just southeast of the city, and hiked along the wooded paths by the canal. She said she liked to be near the water.

After a few weeks she started to make friends with the regulars, hikers and walkers who came early in the morning and trekked down the wide, easy gravel trail. Day hikers asked if they could join her. Cyclists stopped to ask her where she was going.

"I'm just practicing," she'd tell them. "I'm getting used to weight."

At home in the evenings, Father and I would sit in the living room and watch as Mother practiced putting on and taking off the pack. She told stories about the people she had met on the trail. Father looked up from his paper after the seventh male name was mentioned. "Vonnie, is it all men on this trail? Aren't there any women?"

"Men are more adventurous," Mother said as she grunted and strained, pulling the pack off her back and dropping it on the couch. "They hike the trails more."

She began suiting up again immediately, pulling the pack back on, timing her progress with a stopwatch that hung around her neck from a nylon string. Father got up out of his green chair and placed a hand on the pack's outside pocket. "Need some help?"

"I'm fine," she said, and she checked her stopwatch.

"About these men," he began.

She shrugged the pack into place as she interrupted him. "I guess they just find me irresistible." She giggled.

My parents had never been jealous of each other. Infidelity was an impossibility in their world. So when Father suggested that he join her on her hikes, he was concerned only for her safety. And when Mother refused him, she just wanted to be alone with her pack on the trail.

"Who knows where these men are from?" Father persisted the next morning on the front lawn.

"They're nice boys. I like young people," she said, waving him away from the car.

"They're young?" he asked. "Like Roy?"

Mother leveled her hazel eyes on his face and looked at him for the first time that morning. Her arm rested on the window of the hatchback. The pack lay on the ground, nestled against the back tire.

"No!" she said, a bit too loudly. Then she stopped herself. She looked up into the ancient beech that bent into our yard from the Lovells' front lawn. Its leaves always fell on our driveway in the first storm of autumn. She nodded. "Yes," she said. "Some of them are Roy's age."

She put her pack in the hatch, popped open the driver's-side door, climbed in, and drove away.

Saturday mornings Father stood on the front stoop in his stocking feet, the paper tucked under his arm. Mother waved, pulled up the hatchback, and tossed the pack in. As soon as the Chevette turned the corner, he darted back into the house, took the stairs two at a time, got dressed, bundled me into the camper-van with him, and drove to the Pittsford Canal trail. We headed off down the trail five minutes behind Mother. If she stopped to retie her boot, to adjust her pack, to talk to another morning hiker, we stopped as well, fifty yards back. Father kicked the gravel at his feet, stared into the bushes by the side of the trail, and waited. When she started walking again, so did we. We must have been an odd sight: a woman with a pack full of encyclopedias marching down the canal path with her husband and child just behind her, creeping along, watching her from a distance.

The leaves on the trees bristled in the autumn wind. They turned brilliant colors, bleeding reds and oranges across the azure sky. As the weeks went on, fewer and fewer of them clung to the branches. I liked the rustling sound as they crackled beneath our weight. I turned off the trail from time to time when we passed a particularly inviting pile of fallen leaves and crashed through them; their desiccated bodies flew up, caught the wind, and, for a moment, it seemed, were brought back to life.

Once, only once, Mother looked back at us. She paused in the middle of the trail and stood completely still. Father and I stumbled to a halt and watched her, waiting. Then slowly, she began to turn around. I looked up at Father to see what he was going to do. He grabbed my hand. I remember that huge blue pack moving aside as she turned, like some massive primeval glacier, slowly floating out. As it did her rosy cheeks peeked out from behind it and her face came into full view. She looked right at us. Her lips quivered for a moment, trembled to life, and then suddenly she broke into a wide grin. She waved. Father lifted his arm. He pumped his hand back and forth in the chill air like a bright flag.

He smiled, and for a brief moment, he looked truly happy. Then Mother turned around and the three of us continued down the long trail, Father and I keeping our distance.

My mother was not the only one who found comfort in constant exercise. Roy had been a runner. From fourteen, when he began, till the day he died, it was his passion—a silent, wordless, and continuous need for movement. He got shinsplints and blisters, he pulled muscles; the house was suffused with the smell of Ben-Gay. The back hall overflowed with running shoes, their soles eaten away by the pavement, tongues and laces frayed, mildewed; they were strung up in rows against the pressboard coatrack, reflector vests and all-weather gear draped around them. Each summer his white shins, his narrow shoulders, his long, ropy arms, all of him tanned to a deep brown as he ran. He was out the front door before I was even out of bed. He ran seven hundred miles that last summer alone, in and out of every side street, across the city and back. He had long ago chosen his role—the long-distance man.

I remember when it started: the last day of eighth grade at Saint Thomas More Elementary School, right after the graduation ceremony.

The nuns had arranged a mini-carnival, an afternoon of games and contests to entertain the young graduates. The main event was a race. The nuns had laid out a course that looped the building and skirted the edge of the grounds. They planned a contest to see who could run the farthest and the fastest. Each runner carried a green index card. Every time he rounded the building, Sister Jean punched a hole in the card. Roy outran all his classmates. I do not mean that he was the fastest runner; in speed he was beaten out by the Calabrese boy. But Roy just kept going. He could not stop running. As the school day came to a close and the buses arrived, he kept at it. By four o'clock it was just Sister Jean and Roy. Leaning forward, her green sweat suit topped by a dark blue wimple, Sister Jean thrust out her hand, the hole punch clasped between her thumb and index finger, and punched his card once again.

"Only one more lap, Royden," she said as he grabbed the card back from her. But she didn't have the heart to stop him. The afternoon bus left without him. I rode home alone.

When Sister Jean finally dropped him off, it was close to four-thirty. Mother and Father were both at work. I'd spent the afternoon sitting in the big green chair in the living room waiting for him to come home. When I saw the car drive up, Sister Jean leaning over the steering wheel and brushing the wimple back off her shoulder as if it were a fall of long hair, I went out to the front stoop to greet him. He was flushed, wild-eyed as he ran up the steps. He held the green index card as if it were a trophy. It was sweat stained, damp, and wrinkled—I failed to see the glory in it. To me, it was simply a dirty, used card covered in holes.

"Twenty-seven holes, Little Sister. That's twenty-seven laps," he said. He quickly did the math in his head. "I bet I ran over seven miles today."

His slender body had gained height over the last year. Although he was still a beanpole, slowly he was growing to match the size of his big head. As he spoke, a little sliver of hard flesh bobbed up and down at his throat—his Adam's apple had appeared.

"I'm going to go out for track next year," he told me.

"At McQuaid?" That was the boys' Jesuit high school he would attend in the fall.

He nodded. "They run together every afternoon in a group. I've seen them up and down Clinton—"

"*Every* afternoon?"

"Yeah, on Clinton Avenue."

I tossed his green index card in the bushes and walked into the house.

"Al!" He called after me, leaning into the rhododendron, fishing for the card. "What did you do that for?"

The following autumn he started high school. He joined the track and cross-country teams. He got up at 5:30 every morning to deliver the local newspaper, left for school, got home from track after 7:00, and disappeared into his room to do his homework. I saw less and less of him.

* * *

In November volumes E–F showed up, and Father sent away for a statue of Saint Jude from the Saint Jude Society in Chicago. For four dollars and ninety-five cents the society would deliver to your door a six-inch replica of this beloved miracle worker. The day Father pulled Jude out of the Bubble Wrap packaging and dusted him off, his shoulders straightened for the first time since Roy died. He held Jude out for me to examine.

"It's the Saint of Hopeless Cases," Father explained.

He looked me straight in the eye when he said it, and smiled. Then he carried Jude down the hall and set him on the kitchen table next to the weather radio.

Jude was made of tawny brown plastic fashioned to imitate the texture of carved wood. He looked suspiciously like the statue of Jesus that Father had ordered from the same mail-order religious catalog three years before. Unlike Jesus, who cradled a young lamb in His arms, Jude held a staff in his right hand. And in his left he supported a platter in front of his chest that displayed a profile of Christ.

Saint Jude sat across from Father at the kitchen table, and every night Father asked him a series of questions. He inquired after Jude's health and then offered him part of his meal. He held his fork out toward the statue, a morsel of meat perched on the tines, nodded toward the food, and asked, "Are you hungry, Jude?"

Jude held his platter over his heart and stared out at us.

"He's fasting," Father whispered, and he winked at me.

One night, soon after Jude arrived from Chicago, Father told me about the insurance investigation. I had just come up from the basement, where I had spent a few hours staring at the toys in the old toy cupboard. I found him sitting on the porch at the card table, his hands folded on the white embroidered tablecloth. It was just after two in the morning.

"Baby," he said, his eyebrows rising in surprise. "You're up!"

I nodded and slid into the folding chair opposite him. He

stared down at his hands, and without looking up, he said, "An insurance company is looking into Roy's death. To see if we had him murdered."

My spine tingled. I felt a buzzing in my brain. I sat up straight.

Father looked through the window screens at the night sky. His temple pulsed in and out. "I opened an insurance policy on Roy two days before the accident."

It was a promotional offer he had received in the mail. As a parent you could open a life insurance policy on your college-age child. The hook was you could secure this twenty-thousand-dollar policy with a starting fee of one dollar. Father, a man who believed in insurance, jumped at the offer. The application was in the mail, en route to the New York City office, and then the accident happened. As it was considered a completed contract once it had entered the U.S. mail system, the company had to honor Father's policy. With a one-dollar payment, he was poised to make good on a twenty-thousand-dollar claim. But the company was suspicious. They were not willing to hand over the money without a fight. They began an investigation.

"They think we planned it. To collect the money," Father said. "Or that he committed suicide for it."

He told me they wanted eyewitness reports from neighbors on the tenor of our family relationships. They wanted letters from doctors and teachers on Roy's mental attitude, deportment, and drug use. "I told them to keep their damn money."

"Can I write a letter?" I asked.

Father looked up at me. His cheeks were wet. The watery brightness made his eyes shine. They glowed, almost feline. "No, baby," he whispered. He made a small gesture, reached out toward me to pat my hand, but something distracted him, and for a moment his hand just wavered there in the air between us. He slumped back into his seat. His hands slid off the table and hung in fists at his sides.

I leaned against the edge of the table, pressed my arm into the sharp corner. It was a cold night, but I was hot, flooded with a warm, pulsing ache. "Murder?" I said.

"It will be over soon, baby," Father said, and he looked out through the porch screen.

It was then that I noticed Father had brought Saint Jude out there with him. In the pool of light from an old camping lamp hung on the wall, Jude stood silent, unmoved, leaning into the hard line of his staff. Father sat up again and slid forward in his seat. He stared right at me. He put his elbow on the table and pointed at me. "You must not tell anyone." His hand sliced the air as he spoke. "Anyone. About this. Do you understand?"

The insult of implying that we would willingly trade Roy's life for a bit of money, the embarrassment my father felt upon being investigated for insurance fraud, the audacity of this company, to doubt an honest, forthright, grieving man—all this escaped me. I knew only that my father was giving me something precious and terrible. And now he needed me to do something for him. He needed me to keep silent. I called it the Insurance Secret. It occupied the place in my mind shared by the Before-People and the fort visits and the new van and the forbidden newspaper article.

The sky darkened and the ground grew cold. The snow arrived and covered us in a deep blanket of white. It coated the grass and the trees. It dusted the front walk and the cars. The snows grew higher and higher till they tipped over the edges of the windowsills and the world went quiet. Sound could carry in that white world, bounce off the snowbanks, echo down the empty streets. But there was little sound that winter. No sleigh rides, no ski runs, no hot cocoa by the fire. There was almost no movement, except for Mother's hiking and shoveling. And the snowplows—they swept through the neighborhood after dark, their yellow lights flashing across the house. The next morning the world was rearranged, the seamless line of snow broken, drifts cut through, revealing the iced road underneath. I did not skate that year. In fact I did not skate again for years. The skates were retired to the toy cupboard in the basement, and there they would remain, gathering dust.

As winter progressed and the months since the accident piled up, I watched Mother on the driveway, the snow weighting her shovel. She always found a new patch of pavement to clear. Father tried to help. I asked if I could join her. But she said, "No. I like the work." She shoveled all winter. But sometimes, mid-shovel, she would stop. First the shovel would slow and then list to one side, and before you knew it the snow would have tumbled back down onto the clean drive and she would drop the handle. She would stare at the sun on the trees, or watch the neighbors' dog chase its tail, her shoulders slack, her hands hanging at her sides, palms open, ready to hold her lost child.

At night after the plows left, stray dogs started to emerge from the gully, roaming the streets and licking the snow-packed ground. They circled the houses with their pointed noses nuzzling into the stained snowbanks, ice chunks caught between the pads of their feet. Goaded on by the neighborhood dogs in their fenced yards, they knocked over garbage cans, dragging their contents through the snowbanks. And then they slinked behind the garage, back to the fort. By morning they had disappeared. Father woke first. His slippers skidded across the snow-crusted yard. He repacked the cans. He weighted the lids with heavy stones, but that did not deter the hounds.

After he had washed his hands, Father came to my room every morning, as sure and steady as the snow, the cold relics in his hand. *Bless her mind. Bless her throat. Bless her hands. Bless her voice.*

14

THE CROSS-COUNTRY team at Roy's high school dedicated the season to him, and for the first time in the history of the Jesuit boys' school, they won all-state. In the months before this momentous event, the boys rerouted their weekly long run to go right past our house, and on Wednesday afternoons, the house filled with red-cheeked, lank-limbed, mud-splattered boys. When the boys appeared at the top of our street and made their way, en masse, down that low, sloping hill, neighbors stepped out of their houses, stood on their front porches, and waved. The team moved as one unit, a perfectly tooled machine of flesh and breath. In their black-and-gold school colors, they looked like skinny, perfect bumble-bees as they jogged up the front steps and into our house.

Father set down the evening paper, and his tea grew cold on the side table. Mother brought out a tray of cookies and juice. The boys stretched out in the front hall, draped themselves over the couch, slouched around the dining room table. As they caught their breath and drank their juice, as they rested their long, ropy muscles and talked about their shinsplints, their intervals, the latest invitational, the house hummed with life. It was contagious. You could not sit in a room with those young boys at the height of their running careers on their way to State and not get excited.

When I passed through the muddy crowd of boys on my way from the living room to the kitchen—their long bodies towering above me, their perfect teeth, the high color on their skin—the odor of sweat and fallen leaves and damp earth and Ben-Gay wafted up around them. They filled the rooms of our house with a lost smell: the scent of Roy just home from a good run. As they lounged and caught their breath, as they bantered and my mother's laughter pealed out across the crisp afternoon air, I looked into my parents' faces. It was the one moment of the week when I saw joy in their eyes.

Then Mother and Father walked them to the door, arm in arm, laughing, calling each other by their pet names. Father gave the boys one final piece of advice. Mother called after them, "Come again, I'll make brownies!" And they stood in the doorway waving as the boys sprang into action, their long, graceful legs carrying them down the front steps, across the lawn, and out onto the pavement. They buzzed up the street, turned the corner, and were gone.

Mother returned to the kitchen. Father sat down again in his green easy chair and leaned back. For a moment he trembled. His entire body shook slightly, in unison, as if he were riding a train, as if we had caught him in the middle of a long journey. "All those boys," Father said from the depths of the old chair. "They'll live to be a hundred. They'll live forever."

We bumped around the house for a good six months, stunned, hungry, longing, waiting for the runners, unable to find the door back to our lives. I returned to school, grew two inches and lost ten pounds. Mother climbed Mount Marcy—twice. The new Saint Jude joined us at the kitchen table. But nothing really changed. Mary Elizabeth still mooned over Jimmy-the-Lead-Guitar-Player. I still sneaked out the back door every night and visited the fort. My parents said their daily prayers, and every Sunday we all dressed up and went to Mass, and after a while, even God's long silence did not seem that strange. We remained removed, one foot in this world, one foot in the next with Roy.

I checked his bed every morning. Just in case.

While I waited for Roy to come back, my parents waited for the Next Terrible Thing. It was unclear what shape it was going to take, but it was clear that it was going to snatch me away from them. I was in danger. Wherever we went, I was positioned between them,

Mother on the right, Father on the left, in church pews, at movies, in restaurants, on walks in the woods. I could not get away from them or their questions: "Where are you going?" "When will you be back?" They took up the habit of speaking about me instead of to me. They pressed their palms to my forehead, checking for fever. They pushed their fingers into the glands of my throat. "Feel this," Mother would say to Father, poking my neck. "Does that feel swollen to you?" Father would poke and frown and say, "I think she's getting sick again." "Do you?" Mother would ask. And then I'd pipe up. "I'm right here. Why won't you talk to me?" They would stare down at me as if looking through a foggy glass that, no matter how many times they wiped it, was never going to clear. They devised crazy rules, like: I was not allowed to cross the street alone. At fifteen, I had to have an adult hold my hand.

One afternoon Mother showed up outside my bedroom door, pulled the book out of my hand, led me down the stairs, and bundled me into the car. She took me to the emergency room and told the sallow-faced nurse who asked for a list of my most troubling symptoms, "She reads too much. You've got to stop the reading." A doctor tried to explain to her, as he walked us toward the exit, that there was no known cure for reading.

But there was one thing that, despite strict street-crossing rules and house arrest and prayers to Saint Jude and emergency room trips, was not going to go away. I was growing up. My braces came off. I turned sixteen. When Mary Elizabeth got her license, the first thing she did was take me to the mall and buy me a bra. She handed over the package and said, "This is way overdue." And even as my parents prayed that the Next Terrible Thing would not come, it did.

Part II

The Virgin on the Second Floor

15

TEN MONTHS BEFORE Roy died, I began my first job. It was the fall of my freshman year. I received two dollars and seventy-five cents an hour to answer the phone and operate the switchboard for the Sisters at Our Lady of Mercy Motherhouse, the convent attached to my high school. The nuns received few calls. Considering this, the size and complexity of the switchboard was stunning. Installed in a tiny room off the convent's main hall, the enormous machine was a maze of wires and levers. It took up over half of the room. To put a call through, I had to rearrange several patch cords in a four-row jack field. One wrong move and the line went dead.

On the fourth floor of the convent, the Sisters ran an infirmary for elderly and disabled nuns. During the first months of my tenure as switchboard operator, Sister Agnes James, who was strictly confined to the infirmary, began to break free from the nurses and escape. Her favorite destination was the switchboard room.

"Gotcha!" she cried.

I jumped in my seat and turned around. In the doorway stood an elderly woman. Her fine hair floated in a wild nest of curls. The top three buttons of her daisy-print housecoat had come undone, exposing the luminous skin of her neck. She had hoisted her cane onto her shoulder and pointed it at me like a rifle.

"Did I scare you?" she asked.

"No," I lied.

"You must be new. I'm Aggie," she told me, and she thrust a yellowed, arthritic hand under my nose.

I set down my book and offered her my hand. Despite her frail appearance, she had a strong grip.

"I give all the switchboard girls nicknames," she said, placing the rubber tip of her cane on the ground and leaning into it. "There's Smiley and Happy. You know them?"

I shook my head.

"You're a quiet one, aren't you? What will I call you?" She scratched her cheek and stared at the floor. Then she glanced at my hair. "How about Blondie! How do you like that?"

She leaned in. Her nose almost touched my cheek. I smelled oatmeal and antiseptic, and the almost imperceptible odor of cigarette smoke. "Well, Blondie. It looks like I gave them the slip again!" She beamed; her dentures glistened. "The warden hasn't called for me yet, has she?"

"The warden?" I asked.

"Sister Flo, in the jailhouse," she said and pointed at the ceiling with her cane. "How do you like that?" She chuckled. "The jailhouse!"

The phone rang. I picked up the receiver and plugged the patch cord into the fourth-floor jack, flipped three switches, pressed the intercom button, and said, "Praise be Jesus Christ, Main Desk." Sister Rose's voice, tinny and weak, came over the line. "Is Agnes there, dear?"

Agnes pursed her lips, brought her other hand to her mouth, and proceeded to mime locking it shut with a tiny invisible key.

"No, Sister," I said into the phone. "I haven't seen her."

"You're a good egg, Blondie," Agnes said after I hung up. She shifted her weight to the other side of the doorframe and leaned forward on her cane. "I really worked up a sweat."

"Are you all right?" I asked.

"Just a little vertigo." She winked at me with her one good eye.

Our Lady of Mercy School for Girls was the first of its kind in Rochester. Three orders of nuns had braved the wilds of western New York State and failed before Mother Mary Francis arrived with her small brood of Irish nuns in 1914. Indomitable, fearless, and practical, the Sisters of Mercy thrived in the harsh climate. For a while, all the nuns lived on the top floor of the school, converting classrooms into dormitories and a chapel. In the forties they secured the money to add a convent to the premises and finally the Sisters got their own home.

By the time I arrived in 1983, the sawdust stuffing in the auditorium seats was seeping out of the torn seams, the gym floor had warped and bowed in the middle, and on every wall, in every hallway, the powder blue paint chipped and buckled. The strangest and, to my young mind, most appealing part of the school was its basement. As the student body expanded, the Sisters were obliged to provide more and more classroom space. In the sixties they hired workers to clear the old basement, and there they carved out the cavelike rooms that served as language classrooms and student offices.

Father Ray, the resident chaplain, an affable, round, bearded man, proved to be the only priest in the tricounty area to hold his own at our rowdy all-female school assemblies. Father Ray and Sister Maureen (a young nun who spent half the year in Guatemala and replaced the traditional habit with khakis and sandals) celebrated the Mass together. It is strictly against Catholic Doctrine to allow a woman to concelebrate Mass, but no one complained. If the bishop of our diocese knew of the unorthodox practices that took place behind Mercy's walls, he said nothing.

In my freshman year, I watched rapt as Father Ray and Sister Maureen stood behind the plain wooden table that doubled as our altar in the auditorium. Sister Maureen grasped the chalice in her callused hands and raised it over her head as Father Ray sprinkled holy water on the altar and the student body. I remember sitting in the front row, tipping my head up toward the spray, the holy water catching my face, my white blouse. I loved the coolness of it, the weightless refreshment, even on dark winter days when the snow drifted up the auditorium's granite steps and swirled around our ankles.

The best part of my first year with the Sisters of Mercy was the switchboard job. In my hours in the tiny room, the radio whispering next to me, a book open across the worn oak surface of the desk, I imagined the Sisters living their silent lives above me. And then Aggie would arrive, whooping and hooting, caroming down the hall. On those long, empty nights, her frail and hunched frame shuffling toward me, the cane bouncing along the carpet, Sister Agnes James was a welcome sight. She would reach the doorframe and collapse into it, her face flushed with triumph.

"Hiya, Blondie," she'd holler in her booming voice.

On days when she was feeling particularly frisky, she would take out her glass eye and let me examine it.

On the first day of my second year of high school, at Mercy's opening Mass, Father Ray offered up a prayer for Roy's soul to go directly to heaven. Everyone had been informed of his death, but no one spoke to me about it. All this silence troubled me. It made the world seem strange again. Simple tasks like finding my way from the science lab to the library, or locating a chapter in my textbook, stumped me. There were days when I was so exhausted by the business of learning that I just shut my book, floated out of my seat, wandered over to the door, and stepped out of the classroom into the empty halls. I usually slipped out during math class. Sister Aquinas never stopped me. She just kept right on lecturing with her big wooden ruler, pointing and drawing out proofs on the chalkboard.

Invariably I ended up on the second floor, in front of Our Lady of the Broken Toes. Of all the religious icons that peppered the halls of Our Lady of Mercy, the shrine to the Virgin hidden in a shaded alcove at the south end of the second floor was the students' favorite. Set at the back of a dimly lit corner, she offered a rare moment of privacy, a hidden spot away from the watchful Sisters. This particular Virgin had suffered quite bit of wear during her long tenure in the stairwell. Her left arm had fallen off and been reattached at least twice. Her toes were almost completely gone, knocked off one year when she fell off her pedestal and landed face first. (Fortunately her nose was quite strong—never even chipped.) In my freshman year, each morning as I passed Our Lady of the Broken Toes, I would stop and pay homage. I crossed myself and ran my fingers along the flaking plaster. Its chalky powder rubbed off into my palms. I would raise my hand to my nose and breathe in the scent of the Virgin.

Staring up into her weathered face in my second year at Our Lady of Mercy, I could not tell how much I had changed, how the events of the summer had taken a toll. I was just pleased that the Virgin was the same. I would run my hand along her blue robe, press my fingers into the dusty plaster where her toes used to be. And then a fresh wonder would set in and I would gaze at my hand on her feet. I would try to remember what class I had just come from, and the machinations of thought would become too much for me. I would stop in my tracks, lean my body against the wall or a bank of lockers and slowly slide into a heap on the floor. And I cried. I don't think I understood why I was crying. It was a distant sound, a distressing noise far below me.

When Sister Daniel found me, she would pick me up and carry me to the nurse's office, lay me down in the shadowy back room on the vinyl couch, place a thin cotton blanket over me, and let me sleep it off. Those afternoons languishing in the nurse's office were the beginning of a new epoch in my life. Soon I would come to be known, in our small Catholic community, as the Girl Whose Brother Died. A strained cautiousness overtook my classmates whenever I walked into a room. The nuns tut-tutted and patted my hand. The teachers held back, careful with their criticisms. When I did not show up for classes, it was overlooked. When I handed in homework late, I was not scolded—unheard-of indulgences in our tiny, disciplined school.

Despite all this, I excelled at my switchboard job. I needed some piece of life to continue as usual. The Motherhouse offered me that. I patched through calls. I mended broken patch cords. I received visitors. I delivered messages. I hunted down lost phone numbers. But not once did I see Aggie's spry face. By the third week of the term, I was nervous.

I heard a rumor that one of the oldest Sisters in the convent, one of the founders, was dying in the infirmary. I tried to figure out if it was Aggie and if she really was that ill, but the Sisters did not dwell on bad news. No one would tell me anything about Aggie's prognosis. So I sat and waited. Every night I poked my head around the corner of the switchboard room, hoping to see her barreling down the hall, her cane waving in the air. For a month those halls remained silent. Finally, in early October, she appeared.

"Look at me, Blondie," she called, spewing cracker crumbs, as she careened toward the switchboard room, the hem of her daisy-print nightgown waving back and forth around her knees. "Free at last!" she cried and flung her cane wide.

I smiled at her. She had shrunk two inches and lost a few more pounds. Her white hair had thinned into a narrow plume that frothed up from the top of her head like a puff of steam. She wore a red cable-knit cardigan sweater over her nightgown. All of the buttons were missing.

I stood up to greet her. "Are you all right?" I asked. "I heard you were sick."

"Sick? Ah, Blondie!" She dismissed the idea with a wave of her yellowed hand. "Just a touch of vertigo and the old girls go Code Red on me. Chained me to the bed for a month!"

"Did they really?" I asked.

Sister Agnes tilted her head back and laughed. The cross around her neck shook. "Oh, Blondie, you're too easy," she said. She pursed her lips, pressed her cane onto the carpet, and shuffled into the room. She nudged me with the tip of the cane and asked, "How are you?" She paused a moment, her one good eye gazing up at me, rheumy and wet. "I heard about the boy," she said. She turned away from me and stared out the narrow window. "Your brother." She sat down on the wooden stool by the desk. "It's a hell of a world." She shook her head, rocked a bit on her haunches, and used her cane to push her back onto the seat. She stared out the window again. "A hell of a world."

She sucked on her teeth for a moment, and then she rose up out of her seat and said, "It's time you got a change of scenery." She marched down the convent's main hall. "Come on!"

I hurried after her. "We're not going far, are we? I've got to be able to hear the phone."

Sister Aggie stopped, spun around, and stared at me. She leaned forward, hunched over her spindly cane, and motioned for me to bend over toward her. "Fuck the phone, Blondie!" She grabbed my hand and pulled me down the hall. When we reached the end she stopped and pointed at a tiny cupboard door in the wall, about a foot square. "You know what that is?" she asked.

"Is it a laundry chute?"

She slapped her forehead. "Beauty *and* brains," she said. "But do you know what it's good for?"

"Laundry?"

She waved her hand in front of her face as if she were shooing a fly. "No, no, no. I guess I'm going to have to show you." Aggie stepped forward, popped open the door, stuck her head inside, and screamed. The aluminum sides absorbed most of the sound and left only a muffled echo of her voice. I stood dumbstruck and listened to her scream tumble down the long chute and into the bowels of the convent. She pulled her head out and brushed back the plume of hair. "Now you try," she said.

She gave me a nudge toward the opening in the wall. I stuck my head inside and looked down the silver shaft. Light from the hall reached about three feet down, and after that there was just inky blackness. I pulled my head out. "I don't know about this."

"Don't be a such a ninny." She pushed my head back inside. "Now scream!"

I opened my mouth and I screamed. I screamed until red spots floated behind my eyes and my knees grew watery. By the time I pulled my head out, I was laughing.

Aggie placed her long, weathered palms on my face, one on each cheek. "You're all right, Blondie, you know that?"

16

I RACKED UP MORE hours that fall at the convent switchboard—rearranging connector wires into the byzantine system of jacks, observing the private lives of the Sisters of Mercy—than I spent in the actual school itself. The narrow glimpses I caught of the nuns' lives from my perch in the switchboard room fascinated me. I thought that if I could be that close to the believers, perhaps I could find my way back to faith.

Instead I read *Pride and Prejudice* about five times. I played countless games of gin with Sister Agnes. By midwinter I owed her more than sixty dollars. She kept strict account of her winnings in a tiny notebook she hid in one of the pockets of her housecoat, extracting great pleasure from reminding me just how indebted I was to her. It was Aggie who told me about the Sisters' secret cookie stash, and about their late-night grocery runs. It was Aggie who taught me the dirty version of the Hail Mary, and it was Aggie who clued me in to the Sisters of Mercy's strangest secret.

Halfway through October I was switched to the afternoon shift. It was more responsibility; the Sisters were much more active in the afternoons than in the evenings. Whenever a Sister entered or left the Motherhouse, she was required to inform the switchboard girl. I kept track of the comings and goings on a yellow steno pad. Soon after I started on the afternoon shift, I noticed a perplexing pattern among the Sisters. When they came to the switchboard before leaving the convent, they were not dressed. It was not simply that they were venturing out without their habits and wimples. They just hadn't bothered to dress at all. Sisters arrived in their bathrobes and slippers, announced that they were just on their way out for a bit, wandered across the lobby to the heavy oak doors in the portico, and stepped out into the crisp autumn afternoon.

About a week into my new shift, Sister Aquinas, my notoriously strict math teacher, showed up outside my switchboard door in a bathrobe, pink flip-flops, and nothing else. The upper-class girls had nicknamed her the Bouncer because of her habit of policing the school halls and kicking out any boys who had sneaked into the building. The sight of her in a bright green terry-cloth robe, her naked, spindly ankles poking out underneath, was so shocking that my mouth actually fell open.

"What are you staring at?" Sister Aquinas asked.

I looked down at the steno pad. "Can I help you, Sister?"

"Yes," she said, tossing a towel over her shoulder and pushing back the shower cap that perched atop her steely gray curls. "I'm going out." She pointed. "Mark me down." I watched her walk toward the main doors. After she turned a corner, I could hear her flip-flops smacking against her heels.

Five minutes later, Aggie arrived, flustered and disheveled. She slouched against the doorway. "I lost my getaway stick!" she cried.

Somewhere between the infirmary and the switchboard room, she had misplaced her cane. I knew this was distressing. I glanced over at Aggie, mumbled, "That's too bad," and then returned to the window. Sister Aquinas was crossing the lawn in her green robe.

"Blondie! What am I going to do?"

"About what?" I asked, not taking my eyes away from the window.

Aggie leaned over, stuck her craggy face right up next to mine, and barked, "What's got your shorts in a knot?"

I pointed out the window. "Look."

Aggie rummaged in her pockets till she came upon her glasses, held them up to her face, and squinted out the window.

"What do you see?" I asked.

"The sycamore, the lawn, and oh, they really do need to weed that pachysandra."

"No. Over there." I pointed to the south corner of the lawn. "Sister Aquinas!"

"That tough old bird. What about her?"

"They've been coming here for a week now in their night-clothes, checking out and wandering across the lawn! I was too afraid to say anything, but I think they must have all lost their—"

Aggie put out her hand. "Don't they tell you anything, Blondie? Us nuns got a pool!"

Strangely enough, the convent owned an in-ground pool. Strictly off-limits to the students, the pool had been built in the sixties, the Sisters of Mercy's heyday. It was well hidden in a patch of woods on the southern tip of the property, behind the Virgin's Grotto. On autumn nights the temperature in Rochester could dip below freezing, but still the Sisters signed out every afternoon, touched their white, veiny hands to their bathing caps, and drifted off into the woods for a brisk, late-season swim.

I was astonished.

"Of course I'm too old now, but in my day, I tell you, Blondie. We'd jump in that pool as late as November, and what a thrill!" Aggie sucked on her dentures and shook her head. "The best thing we ever did, installing that pool." She leaned in toward me. "And"—she smiled—"I swam in the buff." She winked at me. "Nothing like it."

"You mean you swam out there in the cold with no clothes on, nothing at all?"

"That's what I said." She leaned back on the stool and spread her arms. "Naked." Then she grew serious. "You can't tell anyone about this. Especially your schoolmates." She shook her head. "It's a secret."

Another secret, I thought. But this time it was a delightful one. This time, I wanted to tell it to someone. Every time I thought of it, of Sister Daniel and Sister Rose and Sister Aquinas up there on top of the hill in their hidden pool, I could not help but smile. I kept trying to picture Sister Aquinas in a pool. I could not imagine her in a swimsuit. I had thought she was born wearing the habit.

While she scribbled equations on the chalkboard and piled on the homework, I wondered what stroke she practiced.

The hard thing was not telling Mary Elizabeth. She was a year ahead of me in school and had spent longer under the peculiar tutelage of the Sisters of Mercy. She loved to show off her superior knowledge of just about everything at Our Lady of Mercy School for Girls. The day Sister Aquinas appeared in a green bathrobe and Aggie told me about the pool, I finally had one on Mary Elizabeth, but I had promised Aggie I wouldn't tell.

All that term, through the long winter months, I managed to keep the secret. Then one day, in February, five minutes before first period, Mary Elizabeth arrived at my locker, picked a piece of lint off my cardigan, and asked how my homework had gone the night before. I told her that I still couldn't figure out the geometry proofs. She launched into one of her impromptu lectures on all-things-Mercy. I burst out, "The nuns have a pool!"

I told her about the Sisters wearing flip-flops and shower caps, about Aggie and Sister Aquinas and the green bathrobe. For a moment Mary Elizabeth was dumbstruck. Then she sighed, tightened her ponytail, and said, "They do not have a pool, Alison Lavon. You must have misunderstood."

"Oh, yes they do, and I know where it's hidden."

"Where?"

"Behind the Virgin's Grotto, in the patch of woods."

"Why would the nuns have a pool?" Mary Elizabeth asked as she checked her pink-pearl nail polish for chips. (The Sisters had just recanted on the no-nail-polish rule, and Mary Elizabeth was taking full advantage.)

"And," I said, "it only has a shallow end."

"So?" asked Mary Elizabeth.

"Well, don't you think that's a little strange?"

Just then a voice came from behind us. "That's because nuns don't float," it said.

We spun around and came face-to-face with a total stranger. Mary Elizabeth grabbed my arm. "Where did she come from?"

The girl spoke. "I'm Teresa," she said. "But you can call me Terry." She put her hand out for a shake.

She had delicate features, a tiny line of a mouth, a small straight nose, and wide-set eyes—they were the most curious color, the color of amber. She had made a halfhearted attempt to tame her wild hair, pulling it back away from her face, wrapping the long auburn blanket of it around the broken end of a paintbrush, and securing it at the nape of her neck. Around her neck she had tied a thin leather band, and dangling there at the end of it, just at the opening of her blouse, hung a gold crucifix. It was the shiniest crucifix I had ever seen.

"What do you know about a pool?" Mary Elizabeth asked.

"This is the first I've heard of it. But then, I'm new here." She leaned forward when she talked, her chin tipping up at the end of her sentences. The crucifix bobbed up and down at the base of her throat.

"You must be a freshman," Mary Elizabeth said.

"No, a junior, actually. Just transferred in."

"Where did you come from?" I asked.

"Greece," Terry replied. It was a suburb of Rochester, far from Mercy.

"Oh. Well, that explains it," Mary Elizabeth said. She looked Terry up and down, from her messy auburn hair to her paint-spattered oxfords. She tilted her head to one side and said, "Well, welcome." Then she gave me a nudge. "You better get going. You'll be late for European." She pushed herself away from the locker.

I grabbed her arm. "You won't tell anybody, will you?"

"Tell anybody what?"

"About the pool. You won't tell?"

She turned away. As she walked down the hall she called over her shoulder, "My lips are sealed."

The new girl and I watched her perfect ponytail bounce down the hall and disappear into Room 217. The bell rang, and all of the classroom doors burst open at once. Girls in blue jumpers with white blouses spilled into the halls. They yelled across the throngs to each other. Two girls tossed a Nerf ball over our heads. Several held open textbooks in front of their faces and read as they walked. As usual, the crush of the crowd pressed me against my locker. Terry stood on my right, somehow impervious to the pushing and jostling. The only indications of the chaos behind her were the stray tendrils of thick auburn hair that flew up around her face. She took one hand, tucked the hair behind her ear, leaned in toward me, and whispered, "Do they really have a pool?"

17

In February, when the Sisters of Mercy invited me to join them on a school-sponsored field trip to Canada, Father consulted the statue of Jude. It was the first time I was to leave home since Roy died. Mother and Father called the Sisters about a hundred times with a barrage of questions. It was supposed to be a French class trip to the French-speaking cities of Montreal and Quebec, but really it was just an excuse to trot us in and out of every cathedral, every basilica, every convent and seminary and chapel in the province. It was practically a pilgrimage. Still my parents were skeptical. Who would drive? they asked. How many stops would we make? Where would we stay? Who would chaperone? The nuns patiently answered every one of their questions, and finally my parents agreed to let me go.

Every hour, from the bus ride through Buffalo to the Canadian border, to the guided tours of Notre-Dame de Bon Secours, to Saint Peter's, to Saint Joseph's, to Notre-Dame de Montreal, to the midnight flashlight checks, the Sisters stopped and counted us. And every time, they made special mention of me.

"Where's Alison?" Sister Aquinas asked.

Then Sister Daniel touched my elbow and said, "I've got her right here."

We stayed at the Château Frontenac, in an attic dormitory that used to be the maids' quarters, and practiced our French on the bellboys. In the morning, Sister Daniel woke us up at six and bundled us into the front lobby.

"Ready for a day of sightseeing, girls?" she asked as she ushered us out onto the cobblestone streets.

The first day we went to the Basilica of Notre-Dame de Quebec.

The Rococo interior, with its ceiling of blue sky and clouds and its great golden dome, stunned me. I had never seen such a majestic church before. The Masses of my childhood took place in the scaled-down churches of suburbia—cement walls and felt banners for decoration or converted school gyms with a basketball hoop hovering above the altar. I stared up into shrine after shrine, the arched ceiling so bright and high above me that I could not make out its edges. I watched the sun stream in through the stained glass windows. The airy light caught the dust motes, and they lit up like stars. I slipped into a pew and ran my fingers along the cool and polished wood.

I wore a red wool beret on the trip. It had been a present from Mother. "A French hat for my French girl," she had said, slipping it on my head just before I got out of the car and walked over to the waiting bus.

Around the edge of the hat marched a row of navy blue checks, and at the very top perched a red puffball. It was a bit large for me, and it slipped off every time I looked up at the crucifixes. I developed a habit of putting my hand on top of my head to hold the hat in place. I remember feeling the pressure of my hand on the crown of my head as I looked up into the faces of Jesus. I felt untethered in Canada, so far from home, as if gravity had lost its hold on me. As I put my hand on my head and looked for the face of God, something close to prayer overtook me. It felt like a tender cutting in my throat—as if I had just swallowed a small piece of glass—and I thought that, finally, Christ had come back to me.

"God," I whispered. "God? Is that you?"

I stared up into the perfect robin's egg sky and waited for a reply. As I stood there whispering into the emptiness, Mary Elizabeth joined me. "Have you ever seen anything so . . . beautiful?" she asked.

I looked over at Mary Elizabeth's rapt face. She turned toward me. "Well, have you?"

* * *

The Sisters allowed the girls to venture into the city on their own for a few hours every evening. The curfew was nine o'clock, and before leaving we had to give Sister Daniel a detailed description of our itinerary. Mary Elizabeth told the Sisters that we had planned to go down to the main square and eat in a bistro. When Mary Elizabeth finished speaking, Sister Aquinas nodded her approval, and six of us filed out into the lobby. But when I reached the front door of the Château Frontenac, Sister Daniel grabbed my arm. "Not you, dear. You have to stay in tonight. Parents' orders."

I watched my friends push open the gold-plated door and step into the evening.

"I'm sorry," Sister said.

She took the elevator up to the top floor with me. There were twelve of us in one cavernous room. We slept in cots lined up against the walls. Sister followed me into the room.

"Which one is your bed?" she asked.

I pointed to a cot by the window.

"Oh, that's nice. You can look out at the city this way."

When she left she closed the door behind her without a sound.

I carried two things with me at all times: a grease-soaked paper bag and a prayer card. On days when I had to wear my uniform jumper and I had no pockets in which to hide my two treasures, I stored them in the front pocket of my backpack. When I knew I would be separated from the pack, I would take the prayer card with me, pressing its hard edge into my palm. Custom-made, designed right after Roy's death, it was a tiny, two-by-four-inch laminated remembrance card. On the front, the priest had placed Roy's senior photo, his name, and the dates of his birth and death. On the back were excerpts from the letters of St. Paul and the Gospel of Matthew. I took out the card that evening, propped it up against the base of the hotel lamp, and dialed home. It was the first of my nightly calls on the trip. Mother would answer the phone and call to Father. When he heard Mother's voice calling out, "It's Alison!" Father sprinted to the upstairs extension and arrived breathless, puffing into the phone. "Baby!" he cried. "How good to hear your voice."

I imagined the two of them, Mother on the green bench in the dining room, Father on the edge of their double bed.

"We went to the Séminaire de Québec today," I told them. "The priests have a butterfly collection, just cases and cases of them."

"Only three more days till you come home," Mother said.

I touched the plastic edge of Roy's photo where it leaned against the cut-glass lamp on the nightstand. There was a knock on the door. I set down the phone for a moment. Sister Aquinas stood in the hallway, a card with my room number held in her right hand, as a reminder. She smiled down at me.

"Just checking. You're okay? Good." She nodded, touched the ends of her wimple, pursed her lips, and left.

I returned to the phone.

"Do you think we should have let her go?" Father was saying.

"Yes," Mother said.

"Hey," I said, "I'm back."

"Why?" Father asked. "She's so young and it's so far away."

"She has to go sometime," Mother said.

"Hey!" I said again, louder.

"What is it?" Mother asked.

"I'm going to hang up now."

"Okay," she said. "Good night."

"Pray for us," Father said.

"Pray for us," Mother said.

They hung up.

I did not sleep any better in Canada than I did in America. At night, I slipped out of the room and wandered the halls of the old hotel. The halls of the upper floors were as deserted as the streets below us. After the first few nights, I grew accustomed to having the endless corridors with their maze of crooked passageways to myself. So when I came upon Teresa Dinovelli sitting in the alcove of a window, a sketch pad balanced on her knees, a slim flashlight held between her teeth, I was more than a little disappointed. I stepped back around the corner and watched her. She sat curled up with her back pressed against the molding. In her left hand she held a charcoal pencil. The only sound came from the nub scratching against the page.

I did not know much about her—just some rumors circulating among the girls. She had been at Mercy for only a month, but already the Sisters were saying she was the best physics student the school had ever seen. But she had no interest in physics. That was the scandal, according to the Sisters—to have such a gift and to throw it away. Terry did not want to calculate. She wanted to paint. She practiced figure drawing during physics lectures. When Sister Aquinas called Terry out of her drawing reverie, Terry always gave the right answer, without even looking up from her sketch pad.

I had also heard that she hated the uniform. She said she did not have to wear one at her last school. So she spilled paint on it. By the end of her second week at Mercy, her uniform jumper was splattered with green and brown and purple oil paint. She already had spent a week of afternoons in detention for this uniform infraction. Finally, the Sisters realized that detention wasn't doing her any good. In the end they overlooked her small acts of defiance.

I had seen her at work. Sometimes after I finished my shift at the Motherhouse I would sneak back into the school halls and stop by my locker. The route from the convent to my locker passed right by the art room, and often I saw Terry there, bent over a canvas, a paintbrush in hand. There were days when I passed the art room at three on my way to the convent and then returned to my locker at six and she would still be there, in front of the same canvas, the same brush in hand. And there she was again, hard at it, on the top floor of the Château Frontenac in a window seat overlooking the rooftop gardens.

After about five minutes, she pulled the flashlight out of her mouth and said, "Don't you know it's rude to stare?"

I stepped out into the hall. "Sorry." I pulled at the end of my nightshirt and stood there. "It's just that you startled me. I didn't think anybody else was up."

She looked down at her sketch pad and resumed drawing. "What are you doing?" she asked.

"Walking around," I said. "What are you doing?"

"What does it look like?" She would not look up at me.

I turned and started to walk back down the hall.

She jumped up, put her hand out, and grabbed a tail of my nightshirt. "Look. I'm sorry." She sat back down. "I can be a jerk sometimes." She picked up her notebook again. "I'm sketching."

"What?" I asked.

"The church we saw today."

"From memory?"

"Yeah. And I'm doing a terrible job of it, too," she said.

"I bet you're not as bad as you think."

"I bet you're wrong."

"Show me."

She closed the book and shook her head. "Maybe some other time." She looked at me. My braids were unraveling. I had crammed on my sneakers over my slippers. "You can't sleep either?" she asked.

"No," I said.

"Are you homesick?"

I thought about it for a moment. I shook my head. "I'm just a terrible sleeper."

"Me, too," Terry replied. "That's cool."

"You think so?"

"I think people who can't sleep have fascinating minds."

"Yourself included?"

"Sure," she said, and she grinned at me. Her dimples deepened. She leaned back, her shoulders pressing into the windowpane. I imagined it must be cold—the night air seeping through the thin glass, pressing up against her flannel nightshirt to the skin underneath—but she did not shiver. At school, she always tied her hair back, pulled in the curls and pinned them at the base of her head, but tonight it hung loose. It curtained down around her wide face and draped across her cheekbones. She wrapped her hands around the edge of her closed notebook, tilted her head back, and gazed at me. I avoided her eyes. Instead I looked down at her notebook. "Show me your sketches."

"No. I suck, really. There are things I know I'm good at—"

"Like physics."

"How did you know?"

"It's a small school. Word gets around."

"Okay. Like physics. But I hate it. And there are things I seem to have no talent for, like drawing. And I love it." She looked up at me. "What are you good at?"

"Reading."

"What else?"

I shrugged. "Nothing, really."

"You've got to be good at something."

I did not reply. I looked down at her sketch pad.

"You don't want to talk about it. That's okay. We'll talk about something else." She took her feet off the bench. "Have a seat," she said.

I stepped toward her and slid onto the seat beside her.

"You know," she said. "They say if you look long enough, you'll see the ghost of old Frontenac wandering around out there in the garden."

The last church we visited was the Oratory of Saint Joseph in Montreal. With the largest dome after Saint Peter's in Rome, Saint Joseph's stands atop a huge windswept hill on the west side of the city. The center flight of the three long staircases leading to the main doors is reserved for pilgrims who walk the steps on their knees. Saint Joseph's is an enormous complex, with four chapels, a gift shop, two escalators, and three museums, all clustered around an austere dome. Sister Daniel and Sister Aquinas ran themselves ragged trying to keep us all together in the mazelike structure. After four days of close confinement with twelve girls and two Sisters, I was exhausted. I missed my solitude. So as the group progressed toward Brother André's chapel, I hung back. I stood alone in the cavernous main cathedral and stared up into the empty granite dome. As I reached for my hat, I felt someone at my side.

"Why do you think they built it so high?"

It was Terry. Earlier that afternoon I had watched her from the terrace as she stood on the oratory's snow-covered front lawn and pitched snowballs against a tree. Sister Daniel left the group and ran down after her, took the snowballs out of her hands, and bustled her back up the stairs. Her cheeks were rosy from the cold and the exertion.

"To be closer to God," I said, and I held out a pamphlet on the oratory. "It says so right here."

"Do you believe everything you read?"

I folded the pamphlet and put it in my pocket.

"There's supposed to be a great view of the city from the terrace. Have you seen it?" she asked.

"Yes," I said. Then I glanced over at her. "I'll show you."

"Aren't you afraid of getting too far behind the rest?"

"Come on," I said. "It will only take a minute."

I stared up at the dome again, pulled my hat down over my ears, and headed for the double doors to the terrace. Terry was right behind me.

As the afternoon progressed, the wind had picked up. It was now whipping around the outside of the dome in great icy gusts. Terry stepped out into the cold and shivered. "Jeez," she said. "It's freezing here."

"Only the Sisters of Mercy would go sightseeing in Canada in February."

Terry laughed and pulled the collar of her coat around her neck. I walked ahead of her to the edge of the terrace.

"Come on. You won't be able to see anything from back there," I said. I pointed across the landscape. "There's the cross on top of Mont Royal."

Terry stared at the skyline. "It's getting dark already. I can't believe this! It's only three o'clock."

"You act like you've never seen winter."

"I know," she said. She stepped back for a moment and took in the whole picture. The cross on the mountain and the dome behind us and the pilgrims on their knees slowly making their way up the steps. "Did you ever read the Bible?" she asked.

"What kind of a question is that?"

"Well, did you?"

"Of course," I said, and I dug my hands deeper into my pockets, wrapping my fingers around the oratory pamphlet.

"I read the Bible once," Terry said.

"All the way through?"

She nodded. "Cover to cover." She squinted at the cross on top of the hill. Just then, the lights of Mont Royal switched on. The cross glowed against the horizon. "Did you ever read it like that?" she asked.

"No, just in pieces, during Mass, like everybody else. And at night with my parents," I replied. "It must have taken you forever."

"Not really. I'm a fast reader."

"When did you do it?"

"Last summer," Terry said. "I had a job at one of those photo booths in the middle of a parking lot over at the empty mall."

"You mean Southtown?"

"Yeah, there. We didn't have a lot of business, especially in August. Everybody was on vacation, I guess. We got maybe two or three rolls a day. So I read the Bible."

"Why?"

Terry looked down at the middle steps of the oratory. There was one lone woman on her knees making her way up the wooden stairs.

"I was looking for something," she said.

I stepped closer to her. The wind whipped her hair across her face, and for a moment I could not see her expression.

Then: "Heaven have mercy, I thought we had lost you!"

It was Sister Daniel. She stood behind us in her mismatched wimple and habit, a line of dust down the right side of her sleeve.

She stepped toward us and gently grabbed my arm. "What would your parents have done?" Her eyes widened as she considered the prospect. She turned toward Terry. "Teresa, you know Alison has to stay with the group." Sister Daniel peered at her over her bifocals for a moment and then softened. "You're new this year, so I will overlook it, but we must be very careful with Alison. Her brother died. She's the only one left."

"Oh," Terry said, and she stepped back. "I'm sorry."

"You go and join the rest of the group in Brother André's chapel," Sister Daniel said. "I'll stay with Alison."

I watched the back of Teresa Dinovelli's head grow smaller and smaller as she crossed the parking lot, climbed the stairs to the chapel, and disappeared behind a wooden door.

"Why did you have to tell her that?" I asked.

"Death is nothing to be ashamed of," Sister said. "You should not dwell on it, but you must not hide it."

I didn't mind if Terry knew about Roy, but I wanted to be the one to tell her. She was not exactly a Before-Person—she had never met him—but she was the only person I knew who didn't know about the accident.

I opened my palm and held it out to Sister. "Look. I bought a relic for my father."

She peered down at my outstretched hand and stared at the tiny silver pendant in the center of my palm. "That's a good one. Saint Joseph. The father. The protector. Your father will like that." She grabbed my hand. "I know the pastor here. We'll get it blessed for you."

Sister Daniel rushed me down another series of halls and passageways until she found the pastor's office. He was in and receiving visitors. Sister smiled. "Praise be," she whispered. "Go on." She nodded. "Show him what you've got." She knew the relic was worthless without a sprinkling of holy water and the Latin mumblings of the old man. As the pastor waved his liver-spotted hand over my tiny Saint Joseph, I thought of Terry in her Kodak photo booth in the parking lot of the empty mall, a cup of coffee in one hand, the Good Book spread across her lap, searching for some nameless thing.

After the Canadian field trip Terry became absorbed in the business of learning how to draw perspective. I dissolved back into the misty nether-time at home. I kept up the reading and staring and walking around touching things with my eyes shut. I saw very little of Terry for the rest of the year. But once that year she gave me something. A birthday present, for my sweet sixteen. It was three months late, but then she had barely known me back in December, when my birthday rolled around. Wrapped in plain brown paper, tied with string and a tattered paintbrush, was van Gogh's *Vase with Fourteen Sunflowers*. A cheap reproduction, tucked into a pressboard frame.

I remember the day she gave it to me because that night was the first time my parents openly disagreed with each other since Roy died. I was sitting in the basement staring at the painting when Mother came downstairs, sat on the edge of the couch, and fiddled with an envelope that she held on her lap.

She handed me the envelope. Inside was an application for a learner's permit. I stared down at the yellow form. She ran her hand across my bangs and touched my forehead. Her fingers were cold. "Fill this out and I'll take you down to the DMV," she said. She rebuttoned the top button of her Fair Isle sweater. Her hands trembled.

"Are you okay?" I asked.

"I'm fine. Just a draft."

I tossed the envelope back to her. It landed on the cushion by her thigh. "No, thanks," I said.

"Are you sure?"

"I don't want it."

"Alison—"

"I said I don't want it."

We stared at each other for a moment.

She sighed. "At least get your learner's permit."

I pulled the sleeping bag up around me. "We live a mile from school. What am I going to do with a driver's license?"

"Your father and I discussed it."

"Oh, God."

"We think you need to try this."

"Leave me alone."

She brushed her hand across my hair, glanced at the painting on my lap, and shook her head. Then she stood up, smoothed her slacks, and walked out of the room. The stairs creaked on every step as she made her way up to the kitchen. Later that night I heard Mother talking to Father in the living room.

"Royden, she doesn't want it anyway, so what are you going on about?"

I could not make out Father's words, only the murmur of his voice.

"If she doesn't want it then don't worry about it," Mother said.

As they talked I took down a picture of the first astronauts on the moon that Father had pinned onto the wood paneling four years after they bought the house. I put the van Gogh in its place. As I straightened it, gazing at the bright yellow of the flowers, Father's voice grew louder. It seeped through the floorboards.

"She can't!" I could hear his steps on the living room floor. He said it again. "She can't drive. I won't allow it."

I stepped back and gazed at van Gogh's painting. The wind picked up. It whipped across the eaves. Even through the sound of my parents' voices rising into the night, pitching higher and higher as they walked the floor above me, I could hear the wind whistling around the rickety old house. And then there were the sunflowers. I remembered reading—in one of the numerous books I picked up and put down that year—that van Gogh painted them in the south of France, that he went there for the light. It was supposed to be very different there, the light. The way it fell across the landscape, the way it caressed the hills. I looked closely at the flowers.

Tumbling out of the vase, the blossoms seemed impossible, too heavy for the stems. Van Gogh's sunflowers hung on the wall all through the dark winter. I stared at them on cold afternoons, and in the rains of the late spring. Tattered, unwieldy, wild with life, they were the strangest flowers I had ever seen.

18

SPRING ARRIVED, AND the three of us emerged from the house. As the snow melted, the neighborhood filled with water. It flooded the gutters. It dripped off the icy roofs. It ran down the road, collecting in pools at the ends of driveways. We squinted at each other, rubbed our eyes, and stretched, as if we had just woken up from a long sleep. I finished out my sophomore year of school without much fanfare and I was faced with summer—vast, empty months with nothing to fill them.

We did not go to Cape Cod. Instead we camped closer to home with the Henderson family. We pitched our tents by the stream at Stony Brook State Park outside Rochester, and every night we fell asleep to the sound of the water gurgling through the streambed. During the day Mary Elizabeth and I dove and paddled in the shallows. One night we ate fish roasted over the campfire. The Henderson boys had caught trout in the stream, and I remember the taste of it. The charcoal crust and the tender white flesh underneath, smoky from the fire. I ate only half my portion and slipped the other half into the bag in my pocket.

On our last morning there, my parents walked to the outhouse together. I watched their rumpled heads bob down the rutted road. Father bent over and picked up a stone for Mother. "Look," he said. "It's got a V on it. A V for Vonnie."

He leaned over, pressed the stone into her palm, and whispered something to her. She laughed—tilting her head back, it burst out of her. No runner boys. No hikers on the canal. Just my father, his handsome face leaning over hers as he smiled. "My Vonnie," he said, and he grabbed her around the waist and kissed her. They held hands all the way back to the campsite.

* * *

That fall, when I returned to school, I tried to talk Mary Elizabeth into auditioning for Mercy's children's theater with me. I stood outside her locker with the poster in hand.

"Please," I said.

She took off her poncho, hung it up in her locker, and pulled out a hairbrush. "No way," she said, and she started running the brush through her hair. "Kelly's the actress, not me."

Terry's locker was just four down from Mary Elizabeth's. Terry showed up every morning in the middle of my daily audition campaign, her book bag loaded down with textbooks. On day four, she asked, "What are you guys talking about?"

I shoved the poster under her nose and said, "This."

The play was called *The Caged Princess*. It told the story of a Japanese princess who was imprisoned in a tower. There was an evil stepmother, a dragon, a handsome prince, and three cousins.

"You're going to audition?" she asked, taking the poster out of my hand and staring at it. "It looks kind of stupid."

"It will be fun."

Terry glanced up at me.

"Why don't you audition with me?" I asked.

"You're not serious."

"Just try. It won't kill you to audition."

"I'm not so sure about that."

"You don't even have to prepare anything. Just show up."

Mary Elizabeth pulled her hair back into a ponytail, shut her locker, and walked by us. She shook her head and smiled at Terry.

We auditioned that afternoon along with six other girls and Susanna Spindale. Susanna was going to be an actress. She was known for her dramatic orations at all-school assemblies and her eccentric wardrobe. She was the only girl in the school who had altered her uniform jumper to look like a Jackie Kennedy original. When Mary Elizabeth and I first met her the year before, Susanna was wearing elbow-length opera gloves.

"Do those things fall within uniform code?" Mary Elizabeth asked, pushing her glasses up her nose.

"The rule book makes no mention of opera gloves, so I figure I'm safe," said Susanna, and she tugged the long sleeve of her left glove further up her arm.

Susanna Spindale was cast in the lead. Everyone who auditioned was given a part, so it was no great victory that Terry and I found ourselves playing ladies in waiting to Susanna Spindale's Princess. We had only two scenes, and by the fourth performance, we did not even have to watch the play to know our cue. Terry hated the costumes and the makeup and the girls who preened in front of the mirror and practiced their lines incessantly.

"But I do like the backstage," she said. Deep in the wings, we lay on our backs in the theater's storage lofts. Lounging atop piles of musty flats and torn velvet curtains, Terry gazed up into the blackness. "It reminds me of Colette. All those backstage scenes with the dance hall girls." She sat up on her elbows. "Have you read Colette?"

"Who?" I asked.

"Don't tell me you've never heard of her."

I did not answer.

"What's your favorite book?" she asked.

"*Pride and Prejudice*."

"That prissy little novel?"

"It's brilliant! And it's really funny. I'm sure it all just went over your head."

"Keep your voice down. You want to get us in trouble, again?"

I lay back down. "It is really good."

"I'm sure it is," Terry replied.

The next day she arrived with the collected short stories of Colette. "Skip the beginning section," she said. "Go right to 'Backstage at the Music Hall.' It's the best part."

I loved those stories. The dance hall girls, the quick-change artists, the magicians and the pantomimes. The shabby mystery of the vaudeville beauties—the exotic, verboten music hall. And

Terry was right. Our dingy, dust-soaked backstage with its antique scrims and ancient flats did evoke the Colette stories. I brought a flashlight and started reading backstage.

"Hey," Terry whispered the next afternoon. "It's almost our cue."

"Just one more page."

"Al, it's our cue!"

I threw the flashlight and the book into the velvet pile behind us. Terry pulled out a mirror and examined her makeup. Then she set the mirror down and examined my face. "You're a mess." She ran an index finger under my eyes, pinched my cheeks. "Lick your lips." I did. "Not so much! You have tiny geisha lips now." She leaned in toward me, the edge of her pinkie on the corner of my mouth, and fixed my lipstick.

"For a girl who hates makeup, you sure fuss over it a lot," I said.

Terry did not reply. She leapt down from the high rafters, landing silently on her Chinese slippers.

One afternoon, after a shift at the convent switchboard and before an evening performance, Terry convinced me to go in search of the nuns' swimming pool.

"I don't know, Terry," I said. "What about their privacy?"

"They live in a commune!" She threw a stick across the lawn. "If they were interested in privacy, they would not have become nuns."

"You're missing the point," I said.

"So what's your point?"

"I just don't want to disappoint them."

Terry grabbed another stick. "When's the last time you went out for some fresh air, switchboard girl?"

I shrugged.

"Exactly. We'll just go for a walk, and if we happen upon a pool, we'll check it out."

We took the long, low hill beside the Virgin's Grotto. As soon as we reached the top of it, Terry cut across the field and into the woods at the far end of the property. There was no path, and the underbrush was heavy. Pretty soon we were knee-deep in brambles. Terry's shoe got caught in a hole. Branches scratched my face.

"This is not what I call a little walk," I said, picking sticks out of my hair.

Terry pulled her foot free and kept walking.

Eventually, we came across a narrow dirt path. After about a hundred yards we found a high wooden fence.

"This is it," I whispered.

I crouched down, ran my hand along the boards till I found a loose one, and pushed it gingerly to the side. There on the other side of the fence, inside a long cement basin, lay a swimming pool. Through the crack in the wall I could see only a narrow slice of the middle of the pool, but I could tell the water was moving. After a moment a hand appeared, lapping across the water, then an arm, and then a mop of curly gray hair. It was Sister Daniel, doing the breaststroke.

"Look," I said.

Terry bent down and peered through the break in the wall.

"Jackpot," she whispered. Then she leaned in. "There's two of them!" She crouched down to get a better look. "It's only fifty degrees today. They're nuts!"

"Let me see."

She moved out of the way. I looked again through the peephole. Right behind Sister Daniel was a white mass thrashing through the water.

"What is it?" I asked.

"Look closer."

A shock of steely gray curls emerged from the water, and then two arms sprung out. There, gasping for breath, framed in swim goggles, was the face of Sister Aquinas.

"Holy Mother of God," I said.

"Let me see."

I slid over so that Terry could watch with me. "What is she doing?"

"The butterfly," Terry said, gazing. "And she's not half bad."

"The butterfly?" I started laughing. "Sister Aquinas's doing the butterfly!"

"Shhh," Terry said.

But it was too late. I could not stop. Terry grabbed my hand and pulled me back onto the path. We ran down the wooded trail laughing and pushing the trees out of the way. Before we knew it, the trail ended and dumped us out right at the mouth of the Virgin's Grotto. Two girls in white dresses walked up and down the stone steps. As we stared up at them, Terry whispered, "What's that?"

"You don't know?"

She shook her head.

"They're practicing for the May Court."

We crawled back under the rhododendron and watched the girls process up and down the rickety steps in their white heels. Terry put her hands under chin. "So what's the May Court?" she asked.

"Every year in April nomination forms are passed out to the juniors and seniors during homeroom. Didn't you get a ballot last spring?" I asked.

Terry shook her head. "I must have been sick that day."

"Anyway. They—that would include you, if you came to school more often—choose classmates they think most emulate the qualities of the Virgin Mary: piety, humility, and of course virginity. Then, on May Day the nuns hold this Mass, and the chosen queen and her court of ten virgins will march down the center aisle of the auditorium and sit onstage with the priests and the nuns for the whole Mass. It ends with the crowning of the Virgin. The priest crowns the May Queen, then the Queen takes off her crown and puts it on the statue's head. There are other categories, like Crown Bearer. She comes in behind the Queen carrying a wreath of white flowers."

"Crown Bearer?" Terry asked.

"It's kind of like being the first runner-up in the Miss America pageant."

"But there's no statue there now," Terry said. "Just a bunch of steps leading nowhere."

"They move Our Lady of the Broken Toes up there the day before."

"How do you know all this?" she asked.

"Everybody knows about it. You're the only person I've ever met who doesn't."

Terry looked back at girls on the grotto. "So who are they?"

"They're the O'Malley sisters. Those are the two youngest. There are eleven of them. All of them go to Mercy, or have gone. And they've all been in the May Court or they're going to be in it. There was one year when half the court was O'Malleys. It was like a takeover."

"I've never heard of them."

"Kim O'Malley is in your chemistry class."

"I didn't notice her."

"That's because she's only good at one thing—being in the May Court."

"You said this thing was in the spring. What are they doing up there now?"

"Practicing."

Terry blinked. "You've got to be kidding me."

"It's not as easy as it looks to walk on those grotto steps, especially in dress shoes. That's the reason the statue of the virgin has no toes."

Terry looked at me. "What are you talking about?"

"That happened the year Molly O'Malley was May Queen. She leaned over to crown Our Lady, slipped, and fell on top of her. She knocked over the statue and took down three of her court. Ever since then, the O'Malley sisters practice like crazy for May Day."

We watched as the girls ascended and descended the narrow grotto steps, their white heels sinking into the moss between the stones.

"This is a weird place," Terry said.

Just then Kim called up to her sister, "Not so high, Bridget, not so high." The wind whipped her words out of her mouth, and the two girls in white bent down over the rocky steps, leaning toward an invisible statue, straining to place an invisible crown on her head. As they did, their white calves peeked out between the folds of the soft muslin fabric.

19

IN OCTOBER, BETH Mier threw a Halloween party in her family's refurbished basement. We ate donuts off strings. We bobbed for apples in big Tupperware bowls set up along the Ping-Pong table. And then we collapsed on a musty couch. I wore red-and-white-striped baseball pants and a Boston Red Sox jersey. I had thought it was a costume party, but I was the only one in costume. Susanna Spindale turned off the lights. Beth Mier collected every candle in the house and piled them onto the lid of a steamer trunk. We sat on the dingy couch—bored, restless, lit only by Mrs. Mier's extensive collection of scented candles. We were too old for trick-or-treating and too young to let go of the spooky allure of the holiday.

"Let's tell ghost stories!" Beth suggested.

"What about the girl in the prom dress?" Jenny Silan asked.

"By the side of the road who stops the driver." Susanna slumped back on the couch. "We all know that one."

"Besides, it's fake," said Beth.

"I want a real ghost story," Susanna said.

"About a real dead person," Becky Leland said.

"Don't we know any?" Beth asked.

Susanna glanced at me. "What about your brother?"

Silence fell over the basement. I looked over at Mary Elizabeth sitting on the arm of the couch. Terry came down the stairs at that moment, a pitcher of cider in her hands, and stopped on the bottom step when she registered the silence. By now all the girls were staring at me. No one moved, except Terry. She set the cider down on the Ping-Pong table and sat on the floor next to Beth.

"What's it like? To have your brother die?" Susanna asked.

I sat up and looked at her. The gutsy Susanna Spindale, the one who asked the forbidden questions. The scratchy fabric of the old couch dug into my elbows as I pushed myself up and sat as tall as I could. A small part of me was glad for the question. I felt relieved that somebody was finally asking. They had held back, keeping their mouths shut because they knew better or their parents told them to. But once they started with the questions, they could not stop.

"Can you talk about him? Are you allowed?" Beth asked.

"My mother said you're not supposed to talk about him. That it will just make it worse."

"That's stupid," said Jenny.

"What was he like?" asked Becky.

"Was he cute?"

"You can't ask that!"

"Why not?"

"It's disrespectful."

Then the conversation turned.

"Can you communicate with him?" Mary Riccard asked.

"Can you call him up right now?" Susanna asked.

I looked down at my striped pants. I wanted to disappear.

"Let's do it," Susanna said. "Let's call him up."

She grabbed a box from the bottom of a stack of games on a metal shelving unit across from the couch and pulled out the board inside. There, spread before us on the basement carpet, lay a Ouija board.

Susanna grabbed my hand. "Al," she said as she pulled me toward the board. "Don't be scared. We're all here with you."

So there I sat next to Susanna Spindale, the Ouija board open in front of us, a crowd of girls gathering around me, all of them waiting for Roy. I gazed into the tattered board with its dark, beveled edges, its alphabet of answers. I looked over at the box and read, "A Milton Bradley Game."

Near the left corner, over the *A*, there was a coffee stain. The brown of the coffee bled into the fake parchment on the Ouija board. I wondered if the mark rendered the board ineffective, if a coffee ring could somehow short-circuit the magic.

Susanna leaned over. "Come on," she whispered.

Susanna was a strange combination of glamorous and childish. She was the first to hoard candy, giggle during silent prayer, and forget her homework on the bus. She sported heels with her uniform and spent many afternoons in detention for this uniform infraction. Dark shadows grew under her eyes, deepening as the day wore on. She wore them proudly, savoring the drama of her fragile constitution. A great protester of the school's seasonal coed formal dances, Susanna put together the most beautiful outfits, but she refused to ask a boy to accompany her and she turned down all offers. "I'm bringing my Ken doll," she once told me while I watched her brush her hair in the first-floor bathroom mirror. As she smoothed down her black hair with her opera glove she said, "I'll be the only girl at the dance who, when she grows tired of her date, can shove him in her purse."

I thought of the exchange about the Ken doll as I gazed into Susanna's dark eyes over the Ouija board. I liked Susanna. I liked her irreverent nature, her wild fashion sense, her dramatic aspirations. I wanted her to like me as much as I liked her. "All right," I said. "I'll do it."

Susanna smiled. "Shut your eyes."

I shut them.

She took my hand and placed it on the plastic triangle and guided me toward the board. "Don't open them," she said.

I nodded.

"Okay now. Just concentrate on Roy. Feel his presence."

I knelt in the half-darkness, the scent of Mrs. Mier's vanilla candles wafting across the room, my hands resting on a plastic divining triangle. The room started to spin, and even though I was already sitting down, already on the floor, I felt like I was falling. I felt a hand on my shoulder, and I heard a voice behind me.

"Al," it whispered. "Al." I opened my eyes and found myself looking into Terry's face. "It's okay," she said. She turned around. "You guys are really sick."

Susanna's eyes widened. "Why do you have to go and spoil

everything, Terry?" She grabbed the triangle from me and tossed it against the couch.

"Who wants carrot cake?" Mary Elizabeth asked, clapping her hands together. "Mrs. Mier made two of them."

But Susanna was not going to let up. "Wait a minute. Don't you think Alison should decide if we're done or not?" She touched my arm. "What do you say, Al?"

I pushed the board away and looked down at my hands. "He's dead and I don't want to talk to him."

"Let's go," Mary Elizabeth said. She stood up and headed toward the stairs.

Susanna slumped back. "Things were just getting interesting."

The cakes, huge sheets with cream cheese frosting, sat on the dining room table upstairs. Beth's mother cut me an enormous piece. I waved it away. "No, thank you, Mrs. Mier. I'm not hungry."

She held the cake out to me on the paper plate. "But you haven't eaten anything all night." With her free hand, she squeezed my upper arm between her thumb and forefinger. "You're thin as a rail."

Mary Elizabeth glanced over at me just then. When I caught her eye, she looked away.

That night at the party, I lied. I wanted more than anything to talk to Roy. I still knew, in those days, over a year after the accident, the number of months, weeks, days, hours, even minutes that Roy had been gone. At that moment, I calculated 15 months, 65 weeks, 456 days, 10,944 hours, 656,640 minutes. Every day, sometimes every hour, I calculated his distance from us, the number of moments that the world had gone on after he left. But I could not tell Susanna and the girls that. I could not admit, when she asked me to call him up, that I spent my time trying to do just that, to step out of this world, to meet him on the shining edges of life. I had every intention of calling him back. And when I did, I certainly would not bring him to some silly party, to a stupid basement room of giggling girls.

I still visited the fort almost every night. As the months passed, I set up a little study back there. I made a bookshelf, hammered it up on the back wall, above the doghouse-table. I combed the city's used bookstores and collected copies of the science books I found in his room. I brought out a camping lantern, candles, a sleeping bag, and his high school yearbook. I read his last journal, copied the pages out, imitating his handwriting. I taped the journal pages to the plywood walls. I sat in the fort while my parents watched the evening news, a plate of uneaten food before me, the dog outside whining into the cold. I realized that this would be our last fort.

I looked into Roy's face in photograph after photograph. In his senior yearbook I found him on the grainy edge of images. A skinny boy, soft-cheeked and lanky. Or mud splattered and fierce as he ran intervals at cross-country meets. He looked out at me from classroom desks, from dingy school halls, from track races, the easy grin, the serious, wide-set eyes, the narrow chin. An eighteen-year-old boy, standing on the edges of crowds in his rumpled corduroy jacket, the shirttails of his oxford pulled out, hanging down over his chinos, his soft, brown hair caught in the still, gray light of a November afternoon. As I stared at the photos, I tried to recall the conversations we had in his last year of life. There was one conversation I returned to often.

By his last summer, he was at the height of adolescence. He carried a portable radio with him everywhere, went through two four-packs of size-D batteries a week. The Who blared out of it. He spent hours in the backyard playing air guitar and practicing Pete Townshend's famous midair split. Roy was good at it. His long, mud-soaked legs scissored out over the lawn. The wind picked up, the evening train would call out from behind the back fence as Roy's face contorted with the energy of his silent chords. I sat on the porch, pitched pennies into a baseball cap, and watched his new moves. He didn't have much time for me that summer. We talked little, but there was one conversation I recall in detail.

It was late June. He was already working the grounds crew at the golf course in the mornings, but that added up to only about twenty hours of work a week. He needed another summer job to meet the expenses of his first year at college. He put off the job search as long as he could. He was a shy boy. Asking for work was a daunting task. Then Mother found him on the back lawn, flicked off his radio, dangled the car keys in front of him, and said, "Go find a job."

He went upstairs, showered, changed, and moments later, walked out the front door. A fresh white dress shirt, three sizes too big, hung off his narrow shoulders. He put a foot on the van's runner, turned back toward the house, and squinted through the screen door. "Little Sister?"

I sat up when I heard him.

"Are you coming or not?"

I sprinted for the van.

We toured the city, looking for summer work as a cashier, a waiter, a groundskeeper, anything. I saw parts of Rochester that I had never seen before. After four hours of driving around and searching, filling out application forms against the hood of the camper-van, sitting in parking lots, eating soft ice cream, and tossing a ball back and forth while he waited for the manager, Roy began to talk to me like he did when we were children. We had stopped outside a convenience store on the edge of the city, near Brighton, and once again, we were waiting for the manager.

He pulled out one of his favorite books. Leaning against the van, he asked, "Have you ever heard of the fourth dimension?"

I shook my head.

It had to do with your conception of time, he explained. "You know how pictures, photos are two-dimensional and the world"—he flung his arms out—"life, is three-dimensional. You've heard that?"

I said I had.

"There's a fourth dimension, which is time. Space and time are linked together indissolubly."

I blew my bangs off my forehead, leaned away from the heat of the engine. "Indissolubly?"

"Like this." He hooked his forefingers together. "They can

never be separated. If a place changes, then you know that time has passed, right? So if time changes, space must change as well."

I stared at him.

"You don't get it?" he asked, petulant, almost forlorn. It was as if my noncomprehension was a personal slight. He hooked his fingers together again and repeated it, "Indissolubly." He was quoting his favorite scientist, Hermann Weyl, but I didn't know that yet.

I remember the sound of his voice rising, cracking on the last syllable, his face growing flushed in the heat and the excitement, the deserted parking lot spread out behind us, and his hands, the nails bitten to the quick, two fingers linked together. "Indissolubly." After he died, I would imitate him. I would stand in our fort and roll the word on my tongue, the soft roundness of it, its opaque meaning. I believed that somehow it was the word that linked him to me, that stitched his fate to mine.

But I was not much of a scientist. The physics of it escaped me. What stayed with me was the moment when he linked his fingers together and said, "They can never be separated." Indissoluble, that is how I thought of the two of us. I stared into the faces of the scientists he loved, grainy, black-and-white portraits of Heisenberg, Einstein, Bohr, Weyl. I studied their lives and their work. In the fort I first stumbled upon something that soothed me. The act of contemplation, of study, of research became my new faith. I looked for the fourth dimension, the marriage of time and space, light and movement. I believed that there was a secret code in it, and if I could somehow break it, Roy would come back to me.

The night of the Halloween party, I visited the fort. On the dog-house-table lay an orange-and-brown plate with bouquets of daisies painted around the rim. I let go of the fur on Shadow's neck, and she dove for the plate. I opened the bag. Nestled against the dark, waxy paper lay one half of a meatball, a pile of spaghetti, and an enormous piece of carrot cake. I turned the bag over on the plate and shook it. The contents came out with a solid plop.

The crumpled bag had become my constant companion at meals. While the food was served, I slid my hand under the table and into my pocket. I pulled out the bag, unfolded it, and held it on my lap. I did this without taking my eyes off the table. I talked, I laughed, I followed every conversation, but all the while I was transferring the contents of my plate into the paper bag. As the meal progressed, I managed to get half of the food on my plate under the table and into the bag. No one ever caught me. No one ever noticed the food slipping under the table or the half-eaten meals. And for the first year, until the night Mrs. Mier mentioned it, no one noticed how much weight I had lost.

Saving food, the paper bag ritual, the nightly visits to the fort—perhaps it all would have faded as time passed but for this one fact: mysteriously, miraculously the food disappeared. The next day, when I returned to the fort, the plate had been licked clean. Some-one—or something—ate it. I saw this as a sign. A message from Roy. During the day, I was just a normal schoolgirl. I did my home-work. I went to work at the convent. I seemed to move on from this terrible tragedy. But at night, the distance between the living and the dead changes. At night, we persuade ourselves that the most impossible things are possible. At night, we believe. As I ate less and less and carried more and more food out to the fort, I was finding my way to the fourth dimension, to the secret door in time that would lead me back to Roy. And the ritual of it, the deep sat-isfaction I felt from taking my own nourishment and serving it up to memory, to my dead brother, sustained me.

20

MISS BEAL DID not own a car. She did not believe in them. Her button nose and apple cheeks flushed with cold as she entered the school every morning fresh from her daily two-mile walk. With her oversized aviator glasses and her long brown hair, she looked like Gloria Steinem. In my junior year I took her American history class. She was one of the lay teachers who taught alongside the nuns. As the years progressed and the Sisters aged, more and more of the classes were taught by lay teachers.

Miss Beal had unorthodox teaching methods. She dressed up as her favorite characters from the Revolutionary War (Paul Revere and John Adams). She had memorized the Gettysburg Address and was fond of acting it out, complete with top hat and beard. But more than anything, she was known for her provocative subject matter. The first semester went by without a hitch. It consisted of biographies of the Founding Fathers and statistics on the Civil War's bloodiest battles. But right after Christmas break, things heated up.

In January she informed us that to pass her class we had to participate in a debate. She passed her hat—a wide-brimmed felt fedora—around the room. In it were tiny folded sheets of paper on which she had written the debate topics.

"There will be three separate debates. I have already chosen the topics," she said as she sat cross-legged on her desk, her wide-leg pants falling over her cork-bottomed clogs. "You will be assigned to topics randomly. There will be no special favors for this one, people. The topic you get is the topic you will do. Got it?"

I pulled my scrap of paper out of the hat. Printed in Miss Beal's round, uneven handwriting, was my topic: Gay and Lesbian Rights.

* * *

I soon ascertained that there were no books on the topic at the school library. Miss Beal pulled me aside. "You might be better off downtown at the main public library," she told me.

That night, I asked Father if I could go into the city to the big library.

"What are you going to do there, baby?" he asked.

"Research," I replied.

There was a bus, but Father preferred to drive me. The next afternoon, he picked me up after my shift at the switchboard, and at six-thirty we entered the massive Rundell Library, which overlooked the Genesee River. The glass ceiling on the main floor was covered in four feet of snow. Dim pools of light from the ceiling lamps fell across the tile floor. My boots squeaked along the aisles as I walked up and down the rows of wooden card catalogs. Father sat in the foyer with a styrofoam cup of tea and the evening paper and waited.

I found few resources in the card catalog. But I wrote down the names of a handful of books with the keywords "Gay" or "Homosexual" in the titles. I copied out their call numbers. Then I went to the shelves. Not a single one of the books was on the shelf. I tracked down the reference librarian and handed him my list.

"I cannot find any of these."

He looked at the crumpled piece of paper with the six titles and the corresponding call numbers. He stared up at me, glanced at my braids, and then fixed his watery brown eyes on the Catholic uniform.

"We keep these books in the basement stacks," he said, and he turned away.

"Can I see them?"

He stopped and gave me another long look. Then he took a handkerchief out of his pocket, wiped the corners of his mouth, folded it twice, slipped it back into his pocket, and nodded, slowly. "Wait here," he said.

I waited. Five minutes passed, then ten. I set down my book bag. I pulled off my winter hat. Finally I sat down in a chair across from the reference station and stared at the metal door in the back wall where, a half hour earlier, the librarian had disappeared. Just when I was about to give up on him, the metal door creaked open and he reappeared, brushed the dust off his sleeve, and set five books on the counter. I leapt to my feet.

"This is all I could find," he said as he slid the stack of books across the counter.

I thanked him and found a place in the history section to read. I plodded through the books, taking notes, rereading Miss Beal's ditto titled "Five Steps to a Good Debate," and trying to figure out what we should choose as our platform, how we would win the debate. I stared out the window and down at the cars passing below. I took more notes, doodled in my journal, flipped through a few more books. A few of the books labeled homosexuality a psychological disorder. I wrote in my notebook, "possible psychological disorder," and the page numbers and the titles of the books. Just as I was about to gather my notes and look for Father, I came across a set of lithographs called *The Reading Lesson*.

They were from the second half of the nineteenth century. The artist who made them was not mentioned. In the first print two women in Victorian clothing are seated next to each other in a schoolroom. The one on the left holds the book. The one on the right leans over, her hand on the other's arm, and points to the book. I had seen plenty of prints like these. In fact, I loved this sort of thing—"Two Girls Sewing" or "Afternoon Tea." It reminded me of the characters in *Pride and Prejudice*, of Elizabeth Bennet and her gaggle of lively sisters. I liked to imagine myself in the prints, sitting next to the girls, sewing with them or reading aloud together. There was nothing unusual about this image. I wondered what this picture was doing in a book about the history of homosexuals.

When I turned the page and looked at the second print, I almost dropped my notebook.

In this one, the book lies open on the floor at the women's feet, discarded, flung aside, its pages rippling. The one on the left now sits in the other one's lap. And there, in sepia print tones, in Victorian dresses, with crinolines and bodices and hairnets and little white gloves, the blackboard bannered out behind them, the lesson long forgotten, the ladies kiss. And it was no schoolgirl peck on the cheek. Their bodices pressed against each other, arms clasped around each other, clutching at the folds of the dresses, they are holding on for dear life. The one seated on the bench, her face turned up, her hands on the other's back, presses the other closer to her. And the one on her lap, bending down to the other, her fingers raking through the other's hair, musses her perfect bun. I stared at the print. I blinked. I stared some more. At the bottom, there was a caption. "Circa 1857," it read. I did a few mental calculations. They had been kissing like that, passionately, shamelessly, for 129 years.

I felt blood rush to my head. I looked away from the book. I pulled off my sweater. I closed the book. I opened it again. I sat there holding the edges of the page and stared. I don't remember the name of the book. I don't remember the author or the subject, or any of the text for that matter. All I remember is the page number—page 247. And the year. 1857. I kept repeating these facts to myself, like a mantra, a secret code. *Page 247. 1857. 129 years.*

I looked around the library. The place was practically deserted. A woman two tables away sat next to a stack of Art Deco books, her head bent over a notebook. In the reading area, a man leaned back in a leather chair and turned the pages of *The Wall Street Journal.* Outside a light snow fell. The streetlights buzzed on and lit the slushy road. And, despite the kiss, the world marched on.

The librarian flashed the overhead lights. It was nine already. I put my sweater on, bundled the books into my arms, and headed toward the checkout desk. Halfway across the lobby something stopped me. I stood there, the lamps cutting off one by one around me, my braids unraveling, with an armload of books on homosexuals pressed against my chest. I was not a very savvy kid, but some moment of discretion, some morsel of tact or self-protection, or even shame seized me. I wanted to keep the books away from my parents. I turned and headed back to the reference desk, located the librarian who had helped me earlier, and smiled up into his watery eyes.

"Excuse me?" I whispered as I stumbled toward him. "Could you keep these books here for me?"

The librarian looked down at a pile of files he held in his right hand. "You can check those out," he said, and he waved his finger in the direction of the front desk.

"I know but—"

"They're not reference books," he said without looking up from his files. "What is the problem? Take them out."

"But I want to read them here."

He pulled a pink card from one of the manila folders, stamped it, and placed it back in the file. "Then bring them with you next time you come," he said. "Or leave them here and request them again."

"But that will take forever!"

He stepped back. "I'm sorry. That's our policy."

I cleared my throat and quietly set the books down on the counter between us. He looked at me and crossed his arms. The lights had been cutting off around us, starting with the ones on the periphery and moving to the overheads, and now the lamps on the study tables dimmed, and finally everything went dark except for the one lamp at his station.

"We're closed, now," he said.

I looked down at the nameplate on his desk. "Tom Rifton," it read. "Reference Librarian."

"Please. Mr. Rifton. Tom."

The clock ticked loudly. He set down his files, walked over to me, and examined my books.

"You want all of them?" he asked.

I nodded.

"I'm not supposed to do this," he said, and he opened a little cupboard behind him and slid the books inside. "Ask for me when you want them," he said. "If you don't show in a week they all go back to the stacks where they belong and you'll have to request them all over again."

I smiled up at him. "Okay. Thank you!" I said, a bit too loudly, then I started to walk away, got five steps from him, and turned back. "Excuse me?"

"What now?" he asked.

"When do you work?"

"I'm always here." He smiled wanly and returned to his filing.

I went to find Father in the lobby. A cool breeze rushed across the granite foyer every time someone opened the main doors. I found him sitting on a stone bench. His cup had slipped from his hand and his head nodded forward, his chin receding into the collar of his overcoat. He slept. The paper lay folded, untouched at his side.

I asked for a week of afternoons off from the switchboard, and every afternoon I waited for Father to get home from work at four-thirty. I met him at the door with his tea and then sat on the stairs as he drank it, my coat on, my book bag at my side, waiting for him to drive me to the library. After a few days, Tom got to know my schedule. As I entered the library, he pulled the books out of the cupboard and set them on the corner of his desk. I walked by, picked them up, slipped into one of the straight-backed wooden chairs, and pulled the chain on the desk lamp.

I suppose I learned a lot. I must have. I spent enough time there. But the truth is I don't remember much of it. I don't remember the names of the books I read or the kind of information I learned (outside of the biblical scholars, which, for obvious reasons, became the backbone of my platform for the debate). I don't remember what the other girls on my team did for research. I became completely absorbed in my private study of homosexuals. I told myself that all the research, the skipped work, the hidden books, the long hours in the library—it was for the grade.

One afternoon I asked Father to stop at the drugstore so that I could buy some index cards. They were yellow, with green lines, and I had already used up an entire pack. I put a different fact on each one, and then at night in my room I studied those cards, shuffled and reshuffled them, numbered them, stood at the end of my bed and imagined myself in front of the podium, imagined how I would approach the debate. I pictured the rows of girls in blue jumpers with blue kneesocks, and Sister Daniel and Sister Aquinas and Sister Barbara all standing in the back as I spoke.

The week before the debate, Terry began showing up at my locker with articles copied from magazines and slim volumes of poetry. It was stuff she said I'd never find in the library.

"Thanks, Terry," I said. "That's really nice of you." I stared down at the little pile of books. "But how did you know I was even studying this?"

"I heard it from some other girls."

"What other girls?" I asked.

"Al, it's all over the school what Miss Beal gave you as a topic."

I slammed my locker shut. "She didn't give it to me. I picked it out of a hat."

Terry didn't say anything. I held up one of the books and glanced at the title. "*Sappho Was a Right-On Woman?*"

"It's about feminism in the seventies."

"What's that got to do with gay and lesbian rights?"

Terry smiled. "You'll see."

I pulled my math book out of my book bag.

"How did your trig homework go?" Terry asked.

"Fine." I tossed the book in my locker. "Did you know Walt Whitman was gay?" I asked.

Terry laughed. "Yeah. I think I heard something about it."

Later that week Terry left a book explicitly about homosexuality with my homeroom teacher, Sister Rose. I don't know what she was thinking. I guess she couldn't wait. Her bus got in fifteen minutes before mine. She had run up to the third floor and handed the book over to Sister.

"This is for Alison," she had said.

Sister Rose wrapped the book in tissue paper and slid it in her top right-hand desk drawer. When I arrived, still flushed from the cold morning air, Sister pointed at me as I walked in the door. I knew this meant to come up to her desk.

"Yes, Sister?"

"Terry left something for you." She slid open the drawer, pulled the book out, wrapped the tissue paper around it tightly, and handed it to me. I began to unwrap it immediately. She put her hand on my arm and looked into my eyes. "Leave it for now," she said.

That winter I took up the habit of sitting in the bathroom between classes. I read, perched on the toilet, my uniform skirt pulled tightly beneath me, a book propped on my knees.

21

I SPENT THE NEXT Saturday at the library, and as usual, Father drove me and waited in the lobby, but that afternoon he didn't drive me home afterward. Instead he drove deeper into the city. He showed me the neighborhood where he grew up. He could not show me the house or the street, for they had both been demolished in the sixties. When the inner loop was built it tore through the heart of his neighborhood. But he showed me the alley and the mile walk from his house on Delevan Street to Saint Joseph's Church.

"I was an altar boy," he said. "Every morning I got up at six to help the priests in the sacristy before school."

He told me about the meals he ate with the priests, the stern nuns who trained him in the rules of the altar boys, and the heavy woolen robes they wore. As we walked the mile walk between the alley and the church, I tried to picture my father as a little boy. There were few photos from his childhood, but I knew he had looked a lot like Roy. Except his hair was darker, his skin paler. He was terribly thin—a wisp of a boy in sweater vests, his hair combed back, his woolen knickers worn to a dull shine. I looked up at him as we walked along. He took my hand and tucked it into the palm of his own.

In the year and a half since Roy died, Father had traveled downtown to a church called Saint Anne's, where he attended Novenas every month. He offered them all up to Roy. For those nine nights when he made his way through the beads of his mother's rosary with the priests, his head bowed, kneeling and standing and folding his hands together, all to honor God, he was happy. He would come home after the Novena a little giddy, filled with stories about his mother, about his childhood, awash with nostalgia and Bible quotes. Those Novenas fed him, buoyed him up in difficult times. And when I was sad, when I was lost, he wanted that same surety of faith, that same hope in the light of God for me. But I could not join him. So in those days the one place Father and I met, the one place that he and I loved to go together, was the past. I longed to hear everything about his childhood. The days of trolley cars and formal wear, of scapulars and delivery boys, of candlelight and nightly radio broadcasts, it all enchanted me.

My fingers were freezing, and I longed to shove my hand deep into the wool-lined pocket of my coat, but I did not want to let go of his hand. Despite the joy of looking back at the lost time together, I had always felt my father's childhood was sad. He lost his father when he was two. His sisters were so much older than he was. He was alone a lot. It was before Social Security. His father died in 1933 and the widow's pension was not established until 1939. They barely had any money. After his father died, the family was forced to move downstairs and rent out the second floor of their house. In his high school yearbook under his photo, where you list all the clubs, all the honors, and all the sports you participated in, my father's page remains blank. I asked him once, "Why didn't you do anything in high school?"

"I did! I worked," he said. "I worked as a delivery boy every afternoon and night, and I had to attend services and be an altar boy on the weekend."

But Father always smiled when he talked of his childhood. As we walked away from the alley and toward Saint Joseph's I asked him, "Were you sad?"

"When?"

"As a child? Were you lonely?"

"Oh, no! We were the kings of the neighborhood!" he said. "Everybody loved your grandma. Anytime the butcher had a little extra meat, we got it. And the druggist always had a piece of candy for us."

During the rations of the Second World War, when no one could get their hands on sugar or coffee, when there were long lines for the basics like butter or eggs, my father's family had it all. The grocer, the butcher, the baker, they all knew the widow Smith, and they all looked out for her. The amazing thing is that she did all this, she ruled the neighborhood, became the most popular lady in downtown Rochester (according to my father), without ever leaving her house. As a child she had survived polio and was left with a crippled leg. She walked with crutches. As she aged, the condition worsened. The only time she left the house was to go to church on Sunday. She must have been a winning lady. And my father, the looker, the relic carrier, the Novena sayer, he took after her.

We made it to Saint Joseph's Church by dusk. It was not exactly a church anymore. Saint Joseph's had burned down years ago, in the late sixties. The wooden structure had been completely destroyed. There was no hope of saving the church. When the fire was finally extinguished, when the last ember had been doused and they'd cleared out all the debris, all that was left standing were two beautiful Medina stone arches and the stone steps leading up to them. Nobody had the heart to tear them down, so they planted grass and some trees and turned the burnt-out church into a park. It was there, on the site of the former church, that Father brought up the subject of Roy.

"You understand he's dead, baby," he said.

The light was behind him. I could not make out his face, but I was not sure that I wanted to. He had not talked directly about Roy dying since the summer day in Provincetown, and I was not eager to revisit the subject.

"What?" I asked.

"He's not coming back."

I picked up a stone and tossed it from one hand to the other.

"Baby, it doesn't matter how much you study or how good you do at school, he's gone. He's waiting for us in heaven."

"How do you know?"

"I talk to him."

"What does he say?"

"He's saving seats for us."

"Seats?"

"In heaven."

"Oh."

"So, baby. Don't work so hard. You're going to get sick. All these trips to the library, all this late-night studying—"

"That's what you think this is about?"

"Don't go chasing answers, baby. Sometimes it's best to just accept. Sometimes it's better not to know."

I looked down at my hands. Then up into the dull gray sky. I took his hand again, and we walked back to the van.

He tucked me in that night. It had been a long time, years, since he had done this, and I was clearly past the age. He waited in the hall until I was dressed for bed, then tapped on the door, came in, and pulled the covers up to my chin. "Are you warm enough?" he asked.

I nodded. His face was the last thing I saw before I fell asleep that night and the first thing I saw the next morning when he came in and blessed me with the relics.

22

WE LOST THE debate. Despite forty-five cue cards, despite thirteen quotes from biblical scholars, despite Germaine Greer and Simone de Beauvoir and Simone Weil. Despite revealing the sexuality of Walt Whitman, Gertrude Stein, and Oscar Wilde, and the questionable sexuality of everyone from Shakespeare to Emily Dickinson, we lost. Or I should say I lost. My teammates, Jenny Silan and Beth Mier, jumped ship halfway through. It must be said in their favor that I never told them of my week of study, I never joined them for a study session, and I never discussed strategy with them.

"We need to declare complete and total emancipation for gays and lesbians, including the right to marry and the right to adopt," I whispered to Jenny and Beth at the beginning of the period.

"Are you crazy?" Jenny asked. "Do you *want* to lose?" Jenny had the highest GPA in the school.

"This is not like you," said Beth.

"We have to do it this way," I said.

"All right, but if we lose this debate I am going to hold you personally responsible for my falling GPA," Jenny said, and she marched up to the podium to announce our position.

Jenny gave her three-minute speech about the history of legal rights for minorities in the United States. It was very good. Well measured, evenhanded, and convincing, up to a point. The other side delivered a piece about special privileges. Then I got up and gave what must have been a very convoluted speech. In three minutes I covered homosexuality in the Greek tradition, the history of homosexuality in America, and gave a laundry list of famous people who, all things being even, probably were gay.

Somebody said, "It's a sin." And someone else mentioned the Bible, and soon girls stopped raising their hands. They just called out their opinions. The volume in the room began to rise. I glanced over at Miss Beal. She did not seem to notice the growing tension. That's when Jenny switched sides. She said losing would kill her grade for the class. When Jenny broke ranks and changed teams, Beth soon followed, and I was left alone. I gave a brief speech about Sodom and Gomorrah and how God punished the people of those two towns not for their sexual proclivities but because they were impolite. (I did not make this up. This is a documented study.) A girl I hardly knew, a girl who never spoke, raised her hand. In her two and a half years at Mercy, Bethany Peters had never raised her hand and offered an opinion on anything. Now she had something to say, and the room went silent. I nodded at her. Bethany lowered her hand, looked me in the eye, and said, "It's disgusting. All gays ought to be lined up in front of a ditch and shot."

It was not just what she said but how she said it—like she had been sitting on this one thought, this one terrible image for her entire high school career, and now, finally, she had found the right occasion to say it, and the right person to say it to. She folded her hands on her desk and kept her eyes on me. The class held their breath for a moment. Then slowly, I heard them shift in their seats. They all turned toward me and waited. They wanted to see what I would say. I held on to my pile of cue cards and stared into Bethany's shining blue eyes. I felt my face grow hot. I tried to think of something to say. I thought if I opened my mouth right then, I would start to cry, but I did not understand why. Miss Beal sat quietly through all of this. She seemed to find everything, from the sudden desertion of Jenny and Beth up through Bethany's comment, quite compelling. But she did not step in and help me.

Then Stephanie, the musical prodigy of the school (she already had a full piano scholarship to Eastman School of Music), raised her hand and offered me an out. "You don't actually believe any of this, Alison," she said. "You just want a good grade, right?"

I remember pressing the meat of my palm into the edge of the stack of cards and feeling the sharp corner biting into my hand. "I believe every word of it," I said.

After that, it seemed nobody had anything else to say. Jenny grabbed the chalk and conducted the final count. I lost, 23 to 1. I voted for myself.

When it was over, when the bell rang and the girls had gathered their books and filed out of the class as if nothing had happened, Miss Beal approached the podium and patted me on the shoulder. "Good job."

"Good job? I lost!"

"I figured you would."

"You mean you set me up for this?"

"Not you, specifically. Remember, the topics were assigned randomly. But the truth is I think it's good that you lost."

"My father's freaked out, my friends all think I'm crazy, we didn't even follow the five steps to a good debate, and you're happy?"

"You've been quiet for too long. This got you out of yourself."

I liked Miss Beal. I liked her wry humor, her quick laugh. I liked the way she paused before she answered our questions, as if she really thought about things, really cared about our opinions. But at that moment I was not happy with Miss Beal. Even though I found the strength to defy most of my classmates that day, I could not screw up the courage to tell Miss Beal what I thought of her debate topics or her getting-out-of-yourself speech. But she could tell.

"You'll see. It will all work out." She flashed me a quick smile, returned to her seat, picked up her briefcase, and started to walk away. Then she turned back toward me. "By the way. A plus."

During the years when Roy and I attended middle school at Saint Thomas More, there was a group of boys who met every morning at the top of our street. This was before my brother started running. It was at the height of our fort making and gully wandering. These boys had formed a club of sorts, and they fancied themselves rather tough. They called themselves the Fighters. For the most part, they engaged in relatively harmless pursuits. They went fishing, they played street hockey, they collected frogs and tortured them. They rode up and down the street, bare-chested, their T-shirts tucked into the waistbands of their shorts. In winter, they liked to throw snowballs at passing cars. In early autumn, they ended their days by riding around the neighborhood catching the early-evening air on their sweat-warmed faces and harassing the Catholic schoolkids.

During the summer, Roy and I had always managed to avoid them, hiding in the backyard, working on our fort, or slipping into the gully early in the morning, long before they were awake. But when school started up again, our bus dropped us off at the top of our street, right in front of the Fighters' main meeting place.

I don't know what started them that particular day. Maybe their fishing poles had been confiscated by a scolding mother, or the school day had gone on too long, or they had gotten detention or failed spelling. For whatever reason, their own fragile pride tripping behind them, they descended upon us. Their bicycle tires spinning, they skidded into us. The dust and stones off the gravel road rose up around them. They taunted Roy. Their bottoms held high over their banana bicycle seats, they leaned over the handlebars and yelled, "Roy-the-Toy-Boy."

The polyester of my thin plaid uniform skirt stuck to my legs, and I shivered in the cold. Roy untucked his powder blue oxford shirt and let the tails hang loose over his navy blue uniform pants. "Roy-the-Toy-Boy!" they cried. Their faces grew red with their own daring. They circled as we made our slow descent toward home.

Roy acted as if he did not see them. He looked straight ahead, removed his required Catholic school clip-on tie (an object of particular embarrassment), and slid it into his pocket. "Roy-the-Toy-Boy," they called, circling us all the way down the street. Roy's knuckles grew red; the color on his cheeks deepened. I could not tell what he was thinking.

When we got to our house, Mother was on the lawn. She had heard their voices and come out to see what the commotion was. She started walking toward them as they approached, cycling across her lawn. They did not see her, or they did not care, because even then, at such close range, in our own yard, the taunting continued. "Roy-the-Toy-Boy," they called. My brother did not even look up at Mother. He just kept walking. He kept his eyes on the driveway, and when he reached it he started walking down it. The Fighters finally saw her. She walked right up to the biggest of them, grabbed his handlebars, and said, "You leave him alone."

When he did not answer, she pulled hard on the handlebars, twisting them down and to the right. The rider fell in a heap on the ground, his legs tangled in the bicycle's pedals.

"Alroy," she called. She looked behind her, searching for him, but Roy was gone. He had already disappeared into the backyard. I stood by Mother. She turned back to the collection of boys on their bicycles. "Get out of here," she yelled. "Get off my lawn."

They picked themselves up and mounted their bicycles. When they did not move fast enough, she stamped her foot on the ground. They scurried away, pedaling furiously up the street. Mother smoothed her hair down, placed a hand on my shoulder. "He's got to learn to defend himself," she said. But she said it so softly that I was not sure she was talking to me. A moment later, when I slipped out of her grasp and followed my brother into the backyard, she did not notice.

I found him in the fort. It was our third fort so far. With this one, we had accomplished leak-proof roofing. I pushed open the fort's creaky door. He sat in the molding armchair in the corner, chewing on his thumb.

"We're going to form a club," he said without looking up. He pulled out a piece of paper. "And there are going to be some rules." He grabbed a drafting pencil off the overturned doghouse. "First, there are no girls allowed." He glanced up at me. "Except you." He wrote down the first rule. "Second, no kid from the neighborhood, or from school, or from church can ever, ever join our club." He wrote down the second rule.

I sidled up next to him, squatted down, and watched the paper as he wrote the list of rules. "What's the club going to be called?" I asked.

"We don't need some stupid name. We know who we are."

"Who are we? I mean, who's in this club?"

"There's me and there's you."

"Who else?"

"Isn't that enough?"

Winter came. The Fighters spent less and less time outdoors. It was too cold to stand around and wait for the Catholic school bus to arrive at the top of the street. And they never dared to enter our yard again. Roy and I kept up our club. Despite the cold, we spent our afternoons playing cards in the fort, the deck splayed out across the surface of the overturned doghouse, our winter hats pulled down over our ears. When spring arrived, Roy pulled out his drafting paper and began plans for the next fort.

The night of the debate, I took a deck of cards out to the fort. On one of the shelves I found our tattered copy of *According to Hoyle*, the book of card games. I remembered that chilly winter with Roy—the winter of hiding from the Fighters, of cards in the fort. We taught ourselves almost every game in the book. Hearts, rummy, blackjack, bridge, euchre. For the games that required more than two players, we doubled up, each of us playing two hands. But the one game that we couldn't figure out was poker. We read and reread the section on betting, tossing our dimes and pennies onto the overturned doghouse, but it never quite turned out right. We never could get the hang of it—if you should drop, when you call, how you raise. When I tell people this, they laugh. "The rules for betting are easy," they say. "It's getting the cards right that's hard." But still, all that cold winter and well into the spring, it was betting that eluded us. I dealt the cards again that night—

two hands—and I played both. When it came time to start the first round of betting, I tossed a quarter onto the doghouse. I looked at my hand. I looked at the other hand. Since I knew all the cards, it should have been clear to me who was going to win, but this was poker. I was never sure.

23

I LOVED GOING OVER to Terry's house. It was warm and loud and filled with paint supplies. The whole family painted. The Thursday after the debate, Terry met me at the door in a pair of brown overalls and a large button-down oxford that looked like a hand-me-down from an older brother, except she had no brothers, just sisters, three of them. She held a paintbrush with one hand and with the other she grabbed my arm and pulled me into the warm, dilapidated kitchen.

"What took you so long?" She grinned so broadly that I could make out the gap between her third and fourth teeth. "We're painting," she said.

I nodded at the paintbrush. "No kidding."

She mussed my hair, took my coat, and showed me the walls. This was not your average paint job. The bottom two feet of the walls were riddled with bright, waxy lines of color—crayon marks. A five-year-old girl stood in the corner wearing a pair of overalls just like Terry's. The left strap had slipped down her back and dangled around her knees. A black crayon in her fist, its tip pressed against the white wall, she scribbled furiously. When she saw me, she dropped the crayon and climbed into my arms.

"I'm painting the night," she told me, yelling loudly, as if she had grown used to raising her voice over a pitch of noise. Her name was Thisbe. She was the youngest.

The middle section of the walls were coated with so many different colors of paint that they must have bought every shade Dutch Boy had made that season. The colors spread across the expanse of white in bright strips of greens and yellows and blues, all overlapping with no discernible pattern.

The third sister, called Tasi, was in seventh grade. A gymnast, she wore a leotard, the bodice of which was speckled with yellow paint. Tasi, I learned, liked to pretend that she was a Russian princess, one of the last of the Romanov line. The first time I met her, she pulled me aside and whispered, "I'm the lost princess. They call me Anastasia. Tasi for short."

She showed me a bent, stained black-and-white photograph in which a serious, pale-faced child stood in formal nineteenth-century dress.

"Her name's not Anastasia. Don't let her fool you with those stories," Zoe, the second oldest, told me, and she glanced at the photo. "Though it does look like her, doesn't it?"

Two years younger than Terry, Zoe had started at Mercy the previous fall. An earnest, plainspoken girl, she appeared to be the most normal of the bunch.

The top section of the walls was Mrs. Dinovelli's domain. When she was not cooking, Mrs. Dinovelli could be found perched on the top rung of a stepladder, Birkenstocks clamped to her feet, her elbow out, paintbrush in hand. She wore an old paint-stained apron around her waist, and her hair hung in a loose, sloppy bun at the nape of her neck. Her work was a combination of Children's Bible illustrations and Matisse. Often she found a way to slip in quotes from the Old Testament along the upper edge of her brightly colored images. That afternoon, as Terry and I gazed up at her, she rubbed her neck, arched her back, and sighed. "Michelangelo might have gone blind painting the Sistine Chapel, but at least he got to lie down while he worked."

She was unlike any other mother I had ever met.

Looking back, it seems as if it was always spring in that house. It was always warm and filled with noise, the sun moving higher in the sky, our shoes and socks off for the first time that season, the door propped open, children running in the breezeway, their scabbed knees peeking out from under their shorts, rosy with the chill. But it couldn't have been that warm. It was only February and spring was six weeks away.

* * *

Terry and Zoe slept in the cellar in makeshift bedrooms behind the furnace. Mr. Dinovelli had slapped the rooms together for his daughters when they reached puberty. They offered a small measure of privacy in the crowded house. Half the walls were mere two-by-fours to which Mr. Dinovelli had stapled industrial plastic. The girls draped the blank spaces with heavy fabrics—a hodgepodge collection of their grandmother's old skirts, yards of wax-stained velvet, Indian prints, and old tartan-plaid wool blankets.

On sunny afternoons when the sun was too bright for us, Terry and I scampered down the cellar stairs, past the dusty furnace, the piles of toys her younger sisters had discarded, and Mr. Dinovelli's workbench, to the small partitioned-off section of the basement that was her bedroom. It was always dark there. The light was artificial, except in the last moments of the day, when rays of the setting sun cut through the one high window. A soft layer of dust settled on everything that entered her subterranean room. It was carpeted with a matted orange shag throw rug. The closet door, made of a rough, unfinished pressboard, gave me splinters whenever I touched it. Long fluorescent tubes glowed cold and eerie under the mottled glass covers on the drop ceiling. An old mattress lay on the floor, and a metal desk hunched in the corner. Two of its legs had gone missing, and Terry propped it up with milk crates. In the opposite corner, she had placed a chair with large carved arms and a torn leather seat—we called it "the throne." At the head of her bed stood her most prized possession: a tall pinewood bookcase. The shelves were jammed with books, mostly secondhand paperbacks and old textbooks. There was a system to the chaos; any book you mentioned, Terry could lay her hands on it in seconds.

One afternoon Terry showed me a secret compartment in the ceiling. I lay on my back on her mattress and watched as she climbed the shelves of the bookcase. She hung on to the top shelf with one hand, and with the other, she pressed one of the foam-core partitions up, out of its casing. She tilted it to the side, and out from the hidden spot in the ceiling poured sheets of paper. The pieces floated down and fell around me, landing like falling leaves. I sat up and grabbed one of them. They were paintings, watercolors in earthy browns and peaches. Just shade upon shade of colored lines moving in and out of each other.

"They're Rodin studies," she told me. "From his sculptures."

I spread the paintings across the bed. There were about twenty of them. "You made all of these?"

"Yes."

"Why do you hide them?"

"Look closer."

As I stared into the pale wash of color in one of the paintings, two bodies began to emerge from the sea of shapes. The two figures were pressed up against each other. They were kissing.

I looked up at her. "They're both women."

Terry nodded.

"I lost the debate."

"I know. I was there."

"You were? How?"

"I skipped chemistry."

"Miss Beal gave me an A anyway. As a consolation prize, I guess."

"An A plus. I heard that too." She glanced over at me. "You know all those people you've been studying?"

"What about them?"

"I'm one of them."

My hand froze, clasped on the edge of her watercolor. I could hear her breathing. I watched her chest rise and fall in that darkened room and said nothing. I knew there was an answer to this statement, an answer that she was hoping for, but I could not quite figure it out. I didn't understand what she wanted from me. I remained silent. We sat there on her bedspread, side by side, not looking at each other. Finally, she sat up and started to gather the paintings into a pile.

"So you won't need my help anymore," she said.

"What do you mean?"

"You're done with your report. You won't need any more books from me."

"Terry." I put my hand on her arm. She brushed it off. She would not look at me. I helped her gather the paintings. When she climbed the bookshelf, I stood and handed the pages up to her. She slid them into the hidden compartment and pushed the ceiling tile back into place.

We went outside. It was an unusually warm day for February. Terry pulled out a ladder from the shed in the backyard and propped it against the side of the garage. We climbed up to the roof and let the sun wash over our faces. Terry pulled the ladder up behind us. It was the only place we were certain we would not be interrupted, the only truly private spot in the Dinovelli home. Terry brought a novel along. It was Evelyn Waugh's *Brideshead Revisited*. She began to read to me. We did not even get through the first paragraph before the girls showed up. I looked down at the three sisters. They stood in the melting snow on a narrow strip of yard by the chain-link fence. It must have been about four o'clock. The bulldog next door barked and snapped through the fence, and I worried that he would catch a piece of the girls if they weren't more careful. They were oblivious. Thisbe and Tasi leaned against the fence, pushed their matching visors up off their foreheads, and pleaded, "Let us up!" and "Put the ladder down." Zoe hung back. She had more dignity than to beg.

"The girls want to come up," I said, motioning toward the lawn.

"The Three Musketeers." Terry sighed and crawled over to the edge of the roof and called down to them. "Go away. You're not getting up here today."

"Why?" Thisbe called. She stuck her thumb in her mouth.

"Let them up," I said.

"I spend my whole life trying to get away from them."

"Come on, let them."

She crossed her arms and turned away from me. I put my hand on her shoulder, but she would not turn back around.

"You don't have to live with them every day," she said.

I knew she was right, but I could not help myself. I crawled over to the ladder and lowered it. Thisbe put her arms out, and Zoe helped her guide it to the ground. Then, one by one, they climbed up. Thisbe came first, and immediately upon reaching the roof, sat in my lap. Tasi arrived next. She wore her gymnastics costume under her coat (her mother had pinned her new blue contest ribbon to her collar). She stepped off the ladder onto the roof and petted her ribbon, watching the two long strands of blue ripple in the wind. Zoe came up last. She pushed her dark curls behind her ears and huddled on the edge of the roof by the ladder. I had all the Dinovelli sisters around me. The run-down house on the edge of Rochester, with the three clinging sisters, seemed huge and so alive. I thought Terry Dinovelli was the richest girl in the world.

Terry was a moody girl. She could brood for hours when she didn't get her way, but something softened her. She forgave me for letting her sisters join us. She tucked her head and, somersaulting across the roof on those slippery tiles, rolled right into me. The girls yelped and cried, "Be careful, Terry!" and "Don't fall!" Zoe called her a fool for taking such risks. In many ways Zoe was older than all of us. But I didn't care. Terry was beside me. I could smell her hair in the twilight and the sharp scent of rosin on her fingers. She pressed her arm against mine. She pushed Thisbe out of the way and lay her head in my lap. I looked out over the darkening streets.

The house was on the edge of a city neighborhood, not quite urban and not quite the rolling expanse of the suburbs. Narrow yards displayed pink plastic flamingos. Ancient cars, propped up on cinder blocks, rusted in the driveways. We could see, over the tall beech trees, where the seamless line of yards ended and the city began. The sun fell into the smog behind the distant skyscrapers, disappearing into the haze, and the evening chill set in. It was freezing up there on the roof in early February, but none of us wanted to leave. Sounds we usually couldn't hear reached us: a mother calling her child home for dinner, the mew of a hungry cat, the long wail of a car horn. As each new sound broke into our conversation, we fell silent for a moment. The night rose, and we watched the line of white headlights moving toward us on the distant inner loop. The houses around us disappeared into the darkness, and for a moment we floated there above the city lights, the Dinovelli sisters and me.

24

I DO NOT KNOW what possessed the Sisters of Mercy to open a school for girls. Service to the poor, not education, was their intended vocation. It was clear that, while education may have been their profession, service was their passion. The nuns were always piling us into vans, Sister Aquinas at the wheel, and taking us to shelters and soup kitchens and prisons. Morning announcements were peppered with pleas for volunteers. I made up cots in homeless shelters, talked to inmates in the county jail, read the Catechism to elderly women in nursing homes, and sang songs with schizophrenics at the state hospital, all before the age of sixteen. In the dimly lit basement hall of Saints Peter and Paul's Soup Kitchen, in the back alleys behind the bus station, in the urine-scented wards of the state mental hospital, I saw, firsthand, that it was possible to lose everything and still go on.

Every morning during homeroom announcements, Sister Daniel asked for donations for her Valentine's Day party at the state mental hospital. Sister worked all year to make sure that every patient got a gift at the annual event. She had been at this a long time and knew the formula for a harmonious party. The trick was to take a hodgepodge of donations and transform them into three hundred identical presents. Every patient had to get the same thing. Otherwise fights broke out.

Sister spent every winter collecting sample-size perfume bottles, soaps, baby powder, other toiletries, and cigarettes. Cigarettes were a prized possession on the mental wards, and Sister had long ago given up her fight against smoking among the patients.

"It's their money in the hospital," she rationalized. "They are not allowed to have any real money. This is all they have," she said, and she held up a pack of Virginia Slims. "They don't really smoke them."

Of course they smoked.

During the first half of February, Sister Daniel's school store (located in the basement of the convent) was transformed into an assembly line. A local bakery donated three hundred cake boxes. The toiletries were separated by type and poured into empty garbage cans that Sister had scrubbed clean herself. She set up a cafeteria table, and girls passed the cake boxes down the table. Each of us added our assigned item: three cigarettes, one bottle of cologne for the men, one bottle of perfume for the women, baby powder, candy, shampoo, et cetera.

"Make sure you give everybody exactly the same amount," Sister said. She circled the table as we packed the boxes, poking through the neatly stacked piles inside, counting items. "One, two, three," she whispered over and over again as she kept track of the cigarettes in each cake box.

Two years ago the orderlies had to break up a fistfight between two men—one had received three cigarettes, the other four. "Oh, Mother of God, what a rumble that was," Sister Daniel sighed as she bunched up her shoulders.

Sister Daniel placed a strong emphasis on hygiene in the hospital presents, and we understood why as soon as we entered the large rec hall. The stench was almost unbearable. Our hands went up over our noses, and we stopped in our tracks. Sister ignored our coughing.

"No dawdling, girls, we've got presents to distribute," she said as she marched ahead of us. She pointed out that the conditions were in no way a reflection of the patients themselves. "It's not their fault, girls. It's terrible how they are treated."

The cake boxes were tied with ribbons: pink for the women, blue for the men. The patients sat at long tables, with a nurse stationed at the end of each one. We each took a box off the cart by the door and brought it to the table. Attitudes toward this event varied among the patients, but the overwhelming response to these cake-box presents and the swarm of girls in blue jumpers that accompanied them was bewilderment. Sister instructed us to go through the box of assorted treasures and examine its contents with our patient. If you really looked at every cake of soap and tube of toothpaste, unwrapping the presents took a good hour.

Mary Elizabeth did not like to sit with the patients. Instead she helped Sister clear the tables of wrapping paper and ribbons.

"Excuse me, excuse me," she said, bending between the tables, sweeping up the fallen wrapping paper. "Whoops, looks like you dropped that, didn't you, sir," she said to one man who had lost his dentures. She pulled a pink Kleenex from her pocket and fished the upper bridgework out from under the table, scooping it into the Kleenex. She set the false teeth on the table in front of him.

She sidled up to me halfway through the hour. "Which one's yours?" she asked.

"Second from the end. Schizophrenic." I pointed to a tiny woman in a stained yellow cardigan, a poof of white hair floating above her pink scalp. She ignored the contents of her cake box. Every time she moved her head, the cloud of hair swayed.

"How do you know she's schizophrenic?"

"She told me."

"She doesn't seem to like her gift," Mary Elizabeth said. "Who can blame her? Bunch of second-rate cosmetics." She tightened her ponytail and peered at the contents of the cake box. "But if she doesn't want this Oil of Olay, I'd hate to see it go to waste."

Mary Elizabeth picked up the pink bottle. I slapped it out of her hand.

"Mrs. Arthur, are you sure you don't want to try some lotion?" I yelled, leaning close to her face. "It's Oil of Olay!"

"She's not deaf." Mary Elizabeth grabbed my hand. "We'll be right back, Mrs. Arthur," she hollered. As soon as we got around the corner, she slumped against the wall. "It's hot in here." She fanned her face with her hand. "There's something I've been dying to tell you." She rummaged around in her purse, pulled out a lipstick, her address book, a pocket dictionary, and finally she found what she was looking for. "You are not going to believe this." From the bottom of the bag, she retrieved a small piece of paper and handed it to me.

"What does it say?" I asked.

"Read it."

I unfolded it and inside in a scratchy hand was written, "Call me," and a phone number. "What's this?"

"Jimmy's phone number."

"Jimmy-the-Lead-Guitar-Player?"

She nodded slowly.

"You mean he asked you out?"

"Well, not exactly. Not officially. But sort of. My dad's directing a play at the public school and . . ." She waved her hand in front of her face. "It's a long story, but look!" She pointed at the scrap of paper. "His number!"

"Mary Elizabeth, that is—"

"I know! I haven't told anyone but you."

"Does Kelly know?"

"No! And don't tell her."

She brushed a stray hair out of her face. She did look happy. She was practically glowing.

"Girls," Sister Daniel said, coming up behind us. "What are you doing?"

Mary Elizabeth shoved the paper in her purse. "Nothing."

"Good." Sister smiled. "Then you can take these trays of cookies into the cafeteria."

We ended the evening with a small concert. We moved the tables to the side of the room and ran through a repertoire of Valentine's Day love songs with the quaint hand gestures that Sister Ann had taught us. Mary Elizabeth and I were both sopranos, and because we were the same height, we stood next to each other in the middle row. Mary Elizabeth smiled and moved her arms gracefully. She could make any performance, no matter how ridiculous, look glamorous. In between verses she leaned over and whispered in my ear, "Come over early on Saturday and we can cook s'mores over the stove, then make our Jimmy plan."

"I can't. I promised Terry I would go to the movies."

"Oh."

The song ended. We bowed and stepped off the risers.

"It's just that we always spend Saturdays together," Mary Elizabeth said.

"I'll call you afterwards."

"Okay." Mary Elizabeth brightened. "Call me as soon as you get home from the movies."

Sister Daniel entered with the trays of cookies. She plugged in a cassette player. Soon the smooth alto of Doris Day rose across the room.

"Look at me, I'm cutting capers. I'm on a spree, I'm cutting capers," the radio sang.

Mrs. Arthur put down her Oil of Olay and looked around the room to see where the music was coming from. Sister Daniel danced toward us with a tray of cookies. As she passed us, Mary Elizabeth grabbed a heart-shaped cookie, broke it in two, and offered half to me. "Want it?"

I shook my head. She shrugged and popped the cookie in her mouth. Somebody bumped the lights up. Mary Elizabeth squinted. I shaded my eyes with my hand. The music swelled.

"Mingle, girls. Mingle," Sister Daniel said, and she began to dance across the room.

25

TERRY GAVE ME a picture postcard of Colette. In this photo Colette wears a man's suit. She sits in a white, straight-backed wooden chair, one leg tossed rakishly over her knee. You can see the scuffed sole of her elegant dress shoe, its slender heel poking out from her trouser leg. In her right hand she holds a cigarette. Two tendrils of smoke rise up from its end. As she looks back at the camera, only half her face is visible. I taped the postcard to my bedroom wall and stared at it for hours as I sat at my desk ignoring the essay I had to write for Mrs. Pinkerton's class or the trig problems I had to solve for Sister Aquinas. I longed to be backstage at the music hall. Through the keyhole of my imagination I stared at muzzy half images of girls at their dressing tables. A dimpled elbow, a knee, a shoulder would jut out into the light and disappear again behind a wall of shadows. I imagined Colette in the wings as she took a breath, stuck out her chin, pushed the curtain aside, and let the stage take her like a great mouth of light. I had never wanted to wander far from the Sisters of Mercy's placid blue walls, but something in Colette's face, in her eyes, in the curve of her elegant nose and trim mouth caused me to long for the world.

One afternoon as Terry and I walked from the cafeteria to the first-floor classrooms, in the hallway between Sister Aquinas's trigonometry class and the principal's office, she told me that Colette had a lover.

"You mean she was with another guy, besides her husband?" I asked.

Terry shook her head. Then she leaned in toward me, laid her hand on the wainscoting by the classroom door, and said, "It was a woman."

She moved her hand off the wall and pressed her fingers into the waist of my uniform skirt. "They kissed," she said, "onstage."

"They kissed?"

Terry nodded.

I looked down. I stared at the pattern of black and white tile on the floor. The tiles began to shimmer. Their outlines faded, and they blended into one another, transforming into a field of gray light. Something that had been floating loose inside me for years rose up. It broke through to the surface of my mind, and as it did the air itself split apart into dozens of glittering sequins. I started to lose my balance. I felt Terry's breath on my cheek. Everything I had read and felt and not understood, everything Terry had tried to tell me, came rushing in at that moment. I saw Colette onstage, her long arms bending, as she lowered herself onto the supine body of another girl. They kissed. Two girls kissed. And I thought, *Do you have to be French to do this?*

The bell rang. Sister Aquinas opened the door to her classroom, adjusted her wimple, and clapped her hands in the air in front of her face. "Hurry up, girls. You'll miss the Hail Mary."

"Look at me," Terry said. She put her hand on my uniform collar. "What do you think I've been trying to tell you?"

I leaned in toward her, and just as I touched her, Sister Aquinas's voice bellowed out behind us again. "Girls, girls, girls!"

Terry jumped back. She looked up into Sister Aquinas's face, then she grabbed her backpack off the floor and sprinted down the hall to Latin class.

I ducked out from under Sister's arm and ran after Terry. I called her name, but she was so far ahead of me that she could not hear me. She slipped into her classroom, the oak door shutting just behind her. I could feel my heart beating. Sister Barbara walked by.

"What are you doing loitering in the hall, Miss Smith?"

"I don't feel well," I said. As I said it I realized it was true.

Sister Barbara felt my forehead. "You do feel hot," she said, and she gave me a pass to visit the nurse. Mrs. Kelley was out, but I let myself in and lay on the vinyl couch in the back room and waited for Latin class to end.

26

NEXT PERIOD, I convinced Terry to skip gym with me.

"Where are we going?" she asked.

"You'll see."

I grabbed her hand and pulled her toward the stairwell. When we reached the second floor, I slipped into the hidden alcove, and Terry slid in behind me. Wedged behind Our Lady of the Broken Toes, I asked, "What were you going to say to me?"

"About what?"

"About Colette."

"When?"

I pushed my hair off my forehead. "You know what I'm talking about."

"Oh," she said, and she pulled at a chip of paint on Mary's blue gown. "Nothing, really." She looked at me. "How do you like the new book?"

We were reading an obscure novel by Colette.

I nodded. "It's okay."

We stood there for a long time and tried not to stare at each other. Blue light streamed in through the stained glass window, played across our white blouses, and landed on the tattered back of the statue of Mary. The strap of Terry's backpack still hung over her right shoulder. She let it slide down her arm, and it landed in a heap on the floor behind her. We were less than two feet apart. I closed that gap.

I felt her breath on my neck. Then I pressed my mouth to her forehead, her cheek, and finally my lips trembled against hers. The kiss struck me like a slap, like hitting water from a great height. I backed away from her. The wind picked up, and a branch of the sycamore tapped against the glass. Somewhere down the hall, Sister Faith called out, "In the Name of the Father, the Son, and the Holy Spirit. . ." A door slammed. Terry jumped. I caught her arm and stepped toward her again. I pressed my face into her neck.

"Come home with me on the bus," she said.

"I can't. I have to work in the Motherhouse."

"Come after."

"All right."

"And bring your tent."

"My tent?"

"Yes." She nodded, and she grabbed her bag. She was gone.

I stood there, behind Our Lady of the Broken Toes, for the rest of the period and stared at the blue light as it shimmered against Mary's long back. That first kiss burned into me. It woke me from a long sleep. For this first time since Roy left I wanted something.

Part III

The Next
Terrible Thing

27

I ASKED MOTHER TO drive me over to Terry's house.

"What do you need to see her for tonight?" she asked.

"I just do," I said.

Mother set the paper down and looked over at Father. He leaned back in his easy chair, put his unlit pipe in his mouth, and bit down on it.

"On a school night?" she asked.

"Please."

She stared at me for a moment. "All right, but finish your homework first."

After I had written an essay for Mrs. Pinkerton and washed every dish in the house, I waited by the door while Mother found her shoes and then her glasses and finally her keys. She noticed the orange tent. "You're not sleeping outside, are you?"

"No."

"Then what are you doing with the tent?"

"Terry's going to waterproof it for me," I said.

"I could do that," Mother said, and she reached for the nylon sack.

"I want Terry to do it." I hoisted the tent bag over my shoulder and went out to the car.

I stared at Mother across the wide cab of the van on the drive to Terry's house. Her hand played over the steering wheel, and she moved the van so gently, took every curve and stop with such ease that I could barely feel the road rushing under us. When we arrived and pulled into Terry's deserted drive, the house was dark.

"Are her parents home?" Mother asked.

I slammed the door and yelled over the running engine, "I think so."

It wasn't until I ran up the steps and rang the bell that I remembered I was still wearing my school uniform.

She answered the door holding Thisbe. Hovering behind the screen door, her T-shirt untucked, one hip slung out, she tried to steady her squirming little sister. Her hair fell across her forehead. She had cut it short the week before and was not used to the new style. She tried to tuck her hair behind her ear, but now she had none to tuck. Her hand hovered at her temple for a moment, and then she caught the latch with her outstretched fingers, flicked it up, and pushed the screen door open with her foot. Her jeans were splattered with paint.

"Have you been painting?" I asked.

"Are you kidding? I've been baby-sitting."

Thisbe put her arms out toward me, and I took her. She clung to me like a monkey, her hands clasped around my neck. "Terry said we all had to be in bed by the time you came." Thisbe straightened her arms and leaned back to get a better look at me. "But I wanted to stay up and see you."

"And now you have. So will you please go to bed?" Terry attempted to pry Thisbe off me.

We tucked her in together. First I read her a story and then Terry read her one and finally she settled down, her arm clasped around the Dr. Seuss book, her mouth half open, her hair splayed out on the rose-print pillowcase.

Terry grabbed the tent from the front hall, and we went out to the shed in the backyard. She rooted around among the rakes and shovels until finally she pulled out a spade.

"This will have to do." She tossed it to me.

We pitched the tent by flashlight. I held the light while Terry drove in the stakes with the back of the spade. She fiddled with the main pole. It kept collapsing on her.

"Damn," she said.

"Let me," I said, and I stepped in and secured it with one good shove. As the roof of the tent slid into place, Terry raised her eyebrows. "Tent poles are my specialty," I said.

When it was set and the bedding was in place and the tent window had been opened to air it out, we stood on the lawn in the dark and stared at the orange tent.

The night had turned cold. I crossed my arms over my abdomen and held myself. I glanced over at Terry. Her hands pressed against her sides, she shivered. We stood in the middle of the mud-soaked, pitted backyard with the cinder-block back steps to the porch rising up behind us and the summer garden just emerging from under the winter snow. I thought of all the time I had spent with Terry over the last year and a half. All the nights on the phone, the afternoons in the used bookstores, the bike rides, the backstage talks, the secret meetings behind the grotto. From the moment we met we were blindly, foolishly careening toward this night, and all along I never suspected it. I wondered if she had. I wondered how much she knew and for how long, and I wondered if she had ever kissed anyone before. But I was too afraid to speak. The wind picked up. I saw the sleek gray hide of a cat slither behind the hedge and disappear into the neighbors' yard. The stars wound their slow path around the sky, and we stood there scared and shivering, unable to look at each other.

In the coming months, in conversations outside movie theaters, on long car rides, at school dances, and in cafeteria lunch lines I would be asked, "Have you ever kissed a boy?" And I would shake my head and stare into the middle distance or grab a tray in the line or my ticket at the theater and say, "Let's go in." If they had asked differently. If they had said, "Have you ever kissed someone?" Or "Have you ever been kissed?" how different the answer would have been. For that night I kissed every part of someone's face. I tasted the metal of someone's earring in my mouth. I memorized all the colors of someone's skin: the forearm against the neck, the soles of the feet—those white rivulets of callused flesh, the ruddy hues of someone's tan hands, someone's flushed, glowing cheeks. I kissed someone's neck. I kissed the crucifix that dangled down below the collarbone and took Christ's tiny gold feet in my mouth. I took off someone's shirt and let someone take off mine, one button at a time, pausing at the breastbone, the plastic of the buttons clacking against the teeth, I let the warm cotton fall open into waiting hands. And I touched, with a shock that thrilled me so much it made me shudder, my naked chest against someone else.

I bent down and unzipped the tent flap—the noise of it, the long mile of that zipper, its metal teeth unfurling across the night air. Terry climbed in first, smoothed back the sleeping bags, tugged at the corner of the wool blanket. I crawled in behind her and sat next to her. A bloom of light from the kitchen window fell over the tent, and an orange glow caressed Terry's face. Whenever we pulled away from each other, our breath floated between us in the chill night air.

28

EVERY SPRING THE English department chartered a bus and drove up to Ontario's Stratford to see a Shakespeare play. As field trips, especially those involving Canadian borders, were hugely popular at Mercy, Mrs. Brown devised a scheme to ensure that only the most dedicated students would attend; she invented the Mercy Shakespeare Read-A-Thon. To participate in the northern journey, you first had to be willing to go door-to-door in your neighborhood and ask for money in exchange for the promise that you would read Shakespeare continuously for twenty-four hours.

There were two schools of thought on reading Shakespeare at the Mercy Read-A-Thon. Some believed that the time should be used to further our understanding of the texts we covered, and with that in mind, the English teachers Mrs. Brown and Mrs. Pinkerton liked to pause at key moments and engage us in discussion about the story and the characters. However, there was an equally strong camp, made up entirely of students, who felt that quantity not quality was the real business of a Read-A-Thon. They believed that, in order for our sponsors to feel like they were really getting their money's worth, we had to cover as many plays as possible in the twenty-four-hour period.

"Remember your sponsors pledged by the hour, not by the play," Mrs. Brown reminded us as she passed around trays of cookies. "This is not a race."

Despite these frequent reminders, speed became the be-all and end-all of the event. We read in shifts and slept in shifts, taking over the convent's two front parlors, which flanked the enormous entryway. The one on the right, the more formal of the two, became the reading room, leaving the smaller, left front parlor for our occasional sleep sessions. About eight hours into the Read-A-Thon, after we had made our way through *As You Like It, Twelfth Night, Richard III, All's Well That Ends Well, Pericles,* and *Two Gentlemen of Verona,* Mrs. Pinkerton suggested we try something a little different.

"How about *The Life and Death of King John?*" she asked, and she beamed at us over a plate of cookies. "That one's good and bloody."

King John proved to be a difficult text. We stumbled over the language. We were completely unfamiliar with the characters and the story. Mrs. Brown, who always bailed us out at these moments of confusion, had been called home to see to her sick daughter right as we commenced reading the first act. Mrs. Pinkerton, distracted by the cookies, offered us no insight. By 2:00 A.M. most everyone had fallen asleep, and those of us left awake voted against finishing the lengthy and, to our young minds, incomprehensible play. However, the vetoing of *King John* did not go smoothly for one reason: Susanna Spindale. Susanna questioned our dedication to the project and threatened to withdraw from the whole endeavor if we didn't finish the play.

"What kind of Shakespeare scholars are you?" she demanded, the sleeves of her overlong Elizabethan nightdress flapping about as she paced in front of the enormous stone fireplace.

"Come on, Susanna. Let's just move on. Nobody's following it anyway," Mary Elizabeth said.

"I'm with Mary Elizabeth," Terry said through a yawn. "Who cares about *King John?*"

"Who cares about *King John?*" Susanna asked. "Well, I do!"

"Terry's right," Mary Elizabeth said. "The play's really not that good anyway. What do you think, Alison?"

Before I got a chance to answer, Susanna started in on Mary Elizabeth.

"How dare you question Shakespeare's genius?" Susanna cried, and she grabbed her Riverside unabridged edition and stormed out of the room.

"Whose idea was it we read *King John* in the first place?" Mary Elizabeth asked.

Mrs. Pinkerton leaned over and whispered in my ear, "Call me when this blows over." She grabbed the empty cookie plate and trotted off to the convent kitchen to bake more oatmeal cookies.

Mary Elizabeth ran out after Susanna and caught up with her by the abandoned baptismal font in the stone entryway to the Sisters' chapel. Despite efforts to keep it down, their words bounced off the granite walls and echoed through the empty halls.

"You are such a purist," Mary Elizabeth said. "Can't you just lighten up for once?"

"I cannot believe that you, Mary Elizabeth, are asking me to lighten up!" Susanna said.

I turned to Terry, who was lying on the Sisters' blue velvet Victorian sofa drawing on her forearm with a felt-tip marker. "Do you think I should try and stop them?"

"Nah," she said, and she pulled a cookie out of the pocket of her pajama top and bit into it. "Actually, I kind of liked *King John*."

"Then why did you agree with Mary Elizabeth that we should stop?" I asked.

"I like it when Susanna gets mad," she said, and she smiled up at me.

In the end Mary Elizabeth's peacemaker instincts saved the day. She convinced Susanna to switch to an old standby, *Romeo and Juliet*. There was one condition: We had to agree to let Susanna read the role of Juliet in its entirety. This was a considerable sacrifice as Susanna was incapable of simply reading any dramatic text. She could not look at a script without feeling an overwhelming compulsion to act it out to the fullest extent of her ability. Susanna's lengthy pauses and breathy, heartfelt renditions may have done Shakespeare proud, but they did not make her popular at the Mercy Read-A-Thon. Nevertheless, we all settled in for the long version of *Romeo and Juliet*.

Two and a half hours later, just as Susanna was gearing up to swallow the sleeping potion, Terry picked up her paperbound copy of the play (which she had been using as an eyeshade), leaned down from the sofa, tapped the edge of my Riverside, and said she was tired.

"Let's cut out of here for a while and get some sleep," she said.

When we got out into the drafty hall, Terry walked past the sleeping parlor, took a sharp right, and headed toward the staircase.

"Where are you going?" I asked.

"Why don't you give me a tour, switchboard girl?" she said.

She was wearing a blue flannel nightshirt over her faded, paint-stained jeans. The tops of her bare feet glowed white against the dark oak floorboards.

"Actually, I've never been off the first floor," I said.

"Really." She opened the glass door of the grandfather clock and pulled on the gold chain. "Haven't you always wondered what their rooms were like?" she asked.

"No," I said.

Terry smiled. Her dimples deepened. "You're lying."

She grabbed the banister and started climbing the stairs, two at a time. When she reached the first landing, she turned around. One eyebrow arched up on her square forehead and quivered there. "Are you coming?" she asked.

29

WE TOOK THE second flight of stairs together. By the time we reached the top landing, she had curled her fingers into mine and I felt the heat of her palm. We stood there, the breath rushing in and out of our mouths, and stared. Terry took a step. The floor creaked. She stepped back, and we stood in silence a bit longer, waiting for our eyes to adjust to the darkness. Slowly the hall floated into view, and for the first time, like a long-held secret, the Sisters' living quarters came into focus. The hall was filled with doors. The line of doors stood open at the same angle, stoppers slid under the heavy oak, like a row of twenty mouths, silent, waiting for the word of the Lord. The walls were powder blue (the Sisters of Mercy's signature color), and in the dim light they took on a dusty gray hue. They were trimmed along the floor and around the ceiling with the same dark cherrywood as the banister. The beveled doors hung on their brass hinges an inch above the floor. Down the center of the hall ran the same faded runner that covered the stairs and the landing. Against the far wall, on a tiny three-leg table, sat the phone. Under the phone, atop the table, lay a white doily, and to the right was a straight-backed chair. I was transfixed.

For three years I had sat in the tiny closet of a room on the first floor, stared into the opaque metal of that enormous switchboard, and wondered what was on the other end of my connector line. So this is where they receive their calls. This is where Sister Faith and Sister Barbara and Sister Aquinas and Sister Jaikle and Sister Pat and Sister Phillip and Sister Daniel and Sister Robert—all of them—received my pages and call transfers.

I let go of Terry's hand and walked over to the phone and stared at its round, bone-colored dial. I read the numbers, one through nine and the zero. I sat in the straight-backed chair and put my hand on the phone. When I looked up, Terry was staring at me and smiling. Then she was next to me, and her hands were on my shoulders.

She led me down the hall, and we peeked into room after room and saw them all sleeping, the Sisters of Mercy, in their narrow single beds, under brown cotton bedspreads. Terry read the names off the doors, whispering in my ear, "Sister Ann, Sister Bushouse, Sister Daniel, Sister Augustus, Sister Barbara."

We stopped in front of that room. It was empty, the bed still made.

"Where's Barbara?" Terry asked.

"Spending the weekend at Saint Peter and Paul's Cot Shelter," I said.

Sister Barbara was the dean of discipline. I was lucky enough to have had very little contact with her. The bad girls spent just about every afternoon in Sister Barbara's dark, curtained office at the end of the guidance wing. Terry had passed her share of afternoons in one of Sister Barbara's plush chairs, reciting her Catechism for the dean. If she caught you with your kneesocks rolled down to your ankles, she'd stop you right there in the hall and bellow, "Drop and give me twenty!"

It was not uncommon to have to step over girls performing their push-up penances in the hallways between classes.

The curtains in Sister Barbara's bedroom were drawn.

"Come on," Terry whispered. She dropped my hand, started toward the door, and stepped inside.

As she disappeared into the darkness, I leaned against the doorframe and waited.

"Get in here, Al."

I followed her.

"Look, she has the same statue as your dad," Terry said, and she pointed at a five-inch plastic statue of Saint Jude.

I examined it. Inscribed on the pedestal were the words "The Saint of Hopeless Cases." But this Jude was slightly smaller than

Father's. And he had a jaunty, youthful flair, not the worn, emaciated look of Father's Saint Jude.

Terry sat on the bed. "Do you think they sleep in their habits?" she asked.

"No." I sat down next to her.

As I gazed at the outline of Terry's face, all of the empty nights I had spent on the deserted first floor of the convent, all the times I had passed this wide stairway with its ornate cherrywood railing and longed to climb those stairs, everything that I had ever denied myself, the years of Lent and confession, the past two years of hunger and half meals, the extra penance, the Hail Marys, and God's long absence, all of it trembled inside me. I gathered all the pained, practiced goodness and tossed it away.

I kissed her. I started to unbutton her nightshirt.

She pulled away from me. "Are you crazy?" she asked.

I shook my head and kissed her again.

It was my idea to stay in the room. It was my idea to get under the covers. And once under, our feet slipping between the cold smoothness of the sheets, I put my arms around her. I felt a fluttering in her back, just above the shoulder blades, like two tiny wings. It was the first time I ever felt her tremble. Terry was experienced at misbehaving. She knew how much you could get away with. She knew when you had to stop. Her mistake was in trusting me, in making me, even on that one night, the night in the nun's bed, the moral compass. It wasn't because of what we did in that bed—not because, for the second time in our brief affair, she let me take off her shirt and, in turn, she took off mine—but because of what happened next. I suppose it would have been fine in the end and perhaps I would never have lost her, if it weren't for our one fatal mistake: her warm, solid body tucked into the curve of my own, we fell asleep.

When I woke up, the grandfather clock was chiming and the sun had just begun to rise. Terry was still asleep. Her shirt was off. We had kicked the blankets onto the floor. Then I noticed it.

"Terry." I shook her. She turned to me, her eyes in narrow slits.

"What?"

"They've been here."

"Who?" She sat up and rubbed her eyes.

"I don't know, but look at the door."

Terry blinked for a moment and stared at the door. "What about it?"

"It's closed," I said. "It wasn't closed when we got here."

Terry fell back on the pillow. "So?"

"So—someone's been here."

"It's drafty. It was just the wind."

Still, Terry hopped out of bed and dressed in a hurry.

30

I FOUND TWO NOTES on my desk when I entered my home-room on Monday: a sealed envelope sitting in the upper right-hand corner and a piece of pink notepaper folded in half placed in the center of the desktop. I unfolded the pink note and read: *What happened to you at the Read-A-Thon? Inquiring minds want to know. xoxoxo, M.E.* Then I tore into the plain white envelope and read its contents. *Please report to guidance ASAP.*

When I arrived at the guidance wing, I found that my files had been transferred from Sister Lawrence—a timid, flighty woman who had insisted I drop French and take three semesters of home economics—to a laywoman named Mrs. Phillips. She had a reputation for being tough talking and no-nonsense. If you could stand her, she really worked for you—if you wanted to go to college and you had the grades, she pushed for you. She sported a mass of brittle, bleached blond hair, and she painted the same frosty pink lipstick across her mouth every day. She did not quite manage to keep the lipstick within the lines of her lips. I could not take my eyes off that smeared blotch of pink under her nose. She took the folder from my hand, read the name off its edge, and said, without looking up, "So you're the Smith girl."

"Yes, ma'am."

She took off her glasses and pointed at the hard-backed chair between her desk and a stack of file folders. "Sit."

I sat on the edge of the chair. She put her glasses back on.

A chain-smoker, Mrs. Phillips kept a tiny square air purifier on her desk and held a lit cigarette in front of its mesh face at all times. The smoke was sucked up into the contraption. Still the room remained hazy, as if all the purifier managed to do was distribute the smoke more evenly. After years of double packs a day, her voice had lowered to a croak. Girls who had her as a counselor called her the Frog.

She lit a new cigarette, crushed out the old one, leaned back in her desk chair, and stared at me. "How are things at home?"

"Fine."

Mrs. Phillips tapped her cigarette against the edge of the ashtray. "How are your mother and father? I know you suffered a terrible loss just—" She paused and looked down at my record again. As she glanced across the first page, she continued. "Almost two years ago, wasn't it?" She continued to read as she spoke. "Your brother died," she said. She paused and read a little further. She stared at me over the rim of her bifocals. "In a car accident."

"Yes."

"How's that going?"

"Going?" I asked.

"How is everyone?"

"Fine, thank you."

Mrs. Phillips nodded and tossed the folder on her desk. "Right. Everyone's fine." She grabbed her glasses off her face, pinched the bridge of her nose. "Look, I don't much go in for these inquisitions. You're going through a hard time. We both know that, so let's just get right to it. What are you up to with Teresa Dinovelli?"

"What?"

"They caught you. It was Daniel who found you. She went in to borrow a book from Barbara and got the shock of her life."

"Oh, God!"

"It's a little late for that." Mrs. Phillips gave me a stern look. "Personally, I don't much care what you girls do as long as you keep up the GPA, but the Sisters think you're confused, which you probably are, so you and I have to talk about it."

"Where's Terry?"

"You're not going to talk, are you?" she asked.

"Where is she? Don't call our parents. Please?"

"I'm not calling anyone's parents. I'm just going to tell you to watch yourself. Not with the Sisters; they are the most harmless bunch I've ever worked for, but this Teresa is trouble."

"Why? She's a very good student. She's in the fourth division of Latin and she—"

"Yes, she's gifted. I can see you're taken with her, but Teresa is also . . . passionate. She's got a lot of funny ideas. This happens sometimes with these Mediterranean types."

"Mediterranean?"

Mrs. Phillips nodded and reached for her pack of cigarettes. "Mediterranean." She opened my file again. "Now, on to other subjects. Can you tell me why you have taken three semesters of home economics?"

I walked out of Mrs. Phillips's office, a hall pass crumpled in my hand, closed my eyes, and leaned against the wall. I pressed my cheek against the cool plaster and thought, *Mediterranean*. The word kept running through my mind, and all I could see was a bright blue sea, warm water, and long stretches of sand. I was not very good at geography; I had never been overseas, but I knew where the Mediterranean was, and it was not in the suburbs of Rochester. In my sophomore year, Mrs. Gedge had pulled down the map of Europe and smacked the fraying parchment with the rubber end of her pointer and said, "The Mediterranean—birthplace of civilization." I put my hand on the wall next to my cheek, and just as I was about to slide down it, a voice bellowed behind me.

"Miss Smith!"

I jumped, opened my eyes, and stared into the face of Sister Aquinas.

"What are you doing out of class?"

I held my hall pass out for her to examine.

She peered at it. "All right. Run along."

Then Sister Barbara marched down the hall, her hand on Terry's shoulder. They passed by. Neither of them looked at me. Sister Barbara stopped, opened the door to her office, and shoved Terry inside. I tiptoed up to the door and tried to listen at the keyhole, but I heard nothing. The room was quiet. I didn't know what to do with myself, so I went to class. I suffered through American history and physics, and finally, when the last bell before lunch pealed through the halls, I grabbed my books and sprinted to Terry's locker. She was not there. I remembered that she had a free period. I went to the art room. It was deserted. So was our hiding place behind the grotto. I skipped the bus and waited for Terry in the grotto. She did not show. Finally, at half past four, I walked home slowly, my book bag bumping up against my thigh all the way down Penfield Road. The afternoon sun was shrouded in clouds, and the sky was muted in cool brown-gray light. When I got to the top of my street, it started to rain.

I walked up the front steps into the house and heard water running. I followed the sound of the rushing water all the way to the kitchen. I remember that short walk from the front door to the kitchen, through the dining room, my eyes on Mother's back as she stood over the sink and let the water fall across her hands, the steam rising on either side of her, a dish towel over her shoulder. She did not turn around and greet me as she usually did. That should have been my first sign.

"Mom," I said.

She froze.

"What's wrong?" I asked.

"It's a sin," she said. "You know that."

"What are you talking about?"

"It's a sin. God says so."

"Did somebody call you?"

Mother nodded.

My book bag slid to the ground. I stood there, silent, waiting to see what would come next.

Mother turned back to the dishes and shook her head. "I cannot believe they let you study that."

"What?" I stepped toward her.

"I don't understand that school. Why would Miss Beal—"

"Wait. Who called you?"

"Miss Beal. She told me all about the debate and how proud she was of you, but I don't understand. How can we be proud of . . . that?"

"Miss Beal called? Not Mrs. Phillips?"

"Who's Mrs. Phillips?"

I laughed. "Oh, it doesn't matter," I said, and I leaned over to hug her.

"Don't touch me," she said. She had a plate in her hand. She lifted it and threw it hard against the counter, where it broke, splintered into four pieces. Then she said it: "Don't you know lesbians will burn in hell?"

For a moment everything went silent. The birds in the backyard stopped singing their afternoon song. The water in the drain gurgled and then fell still. The refrigerator lost its familiar hum. I heard nothing. Not the clock on the wall, not the sound of my own heart. The world hushed, and that phrase, lesbians-will-burn-in-hell, reverberated in my head. When I think of that afternoon now, Mother's face clouds in my mind, and then the entire image burns over into a field of white. Just her voice comes through. I hear her sigh. I hear the quiver in her throat as she said it, lesbians-will-burn-in-hell, and then the world goes quiet. I smell the warm, salty sweat of her skin and the lily of the valley lotion she wore, but that is all. I cannot see her. My mind raced over all the photos I had seen of her through the years. The childhood ones, where she stood alone with her scabbed knees, the cornfields, miles of them, bannered out behind her. Her wedding photo. She wore a slim Audrey Hepburn–style dress. Pictures of her as a young mother in her orange bikini, her hair in pigtails. But I could not see her face as she looked into mine that afternoon, the anger it must have held, the disgust.

I ran out of the room. Mother ran after me. She caught me around the waist just as I got to the front door and pulled me back into the house.

"Let me go," I said.

She pressed me up against the wall, held me there, her hands still wet from the dishwater, pushing into my shoulders. I could hardly breathe. I wrested my arms loose from hers. I stumbled down the front steps and into the yard.

"Alison," she called. "Don't run away from me. Don't you dare run away!"

The rain was falling hard now on the new grass and the branches of the sugar maple. I looked back. Mother stood in the doorway, her hands resting on the frame to steady herself. And then I ran.

31

I RAN DOWN THE hill, straight for the gully. I ran for a good mile, until I saw the first beds of redtop along the riverbank. I headed right into the river, crashing through rising water. The rain was thick. It had turned the sky gray. It poured down from above, and the current rushed below me, tearing at my shoes and socks. On the other side, I pushed past the underbrush in the orchard, and finally I caught sight of it: the abandoned house.

I remembered Roy in the foyer of the house, his hand on his baseball cap, a band of sunlight splintering through the torn wall and resting on his face. How glorious it was then, the perfection of that half world, the stillness of it. We sat in it and walked through it for entire days that season. Once we even rigged up a makeshift flight of stairs out of old packing crates and a broken bed frame, and together we climbed to the second story. Under a fallen bureau in the back room, we found a child's toy chest. We decided to move the bureau. It creaked and moaned as we lifted it off the chest and pushed it back. The house shook when the bureau fell backwards, and for a moment, as it shuddered and listed to one side, we thought the abandoned house was going to come down around our ears. But then the house fell into stillness, and Roy lifted the lid off the chest. We examined the lost child's toys. Roy pulled each one out as if it were a rare artifact. He lined them up along the splintered floorboards.

The most impressive toy was a big metal top, the kind with a handle pump sticking straight out of it. When you pushed it in, the brightly painted ball spun and spun. This top was shaped like a globe, with a map of the world printed on its sides. We watched the little world spin on its axis between us. Roy made up a game. We would stop the top with our fingers, and whatever country we landed on, that was the country where the abandoned house's family would be. Roy, his knees up, splayed out, the top resting between the soles of his work boots, went first. He reached out toward the spinning globe, pressed the pad of his finger against the world, and it stopped. He leaned over and read off the name of the country.

"India," he said.

"India?" I imagined the abandoned house family in saris and sandals, trading in their car for an elephant and disappearing into the dust on a narrow, rutted road.

"I want to go there," Roy said.

"To India?"

He nodded. "When I grow up."

"Aren't you afraid of dysentery?"

"What's that?"

"It's when you can't stop going to the bathroom. Everybody who goes to India gets it."

Roy picked up the metal top and stared at the map of the world. "I don't care," he said. "I want to go. I'm going to go everywhere, see everything." He set the top back down, pushed it over toward me, and said, "Now you go."

I grabbed the handle and gave it a push.

The years since that day had not been kind to our house. Most of the furniture had been carted away or stolen; the wallpaper lay in shreds in the dirt. The second floor, the master bedroom and the child's room with the heavy bureau and all the abandoned toys, had collapsed in on itself, fallen through the floorboards, and in the process, crushed most of the first floor. Had I not known it all those years ago with Roy, I would have been hard-pressed to see it as a house.

I stepped back out into the rain and sat in a broken chair on what used to be the front lawn. I wondered what Roy would have thought of Terry. Of the debate. Of what a fool I'd been, going up to the second floor of the convent. I wondered if Roy ever did anything that bad over at the boys' Jesuit school. I had never tasted beer, never tried a cigarette, or stayed out all night. Roy did all that. He was a good boy, a hard worker, but I knew he had tried those things the last summer of his life, and I was glad he had. He never got to India, but at least he tried a few things. I wondered if he had ever kissed someone. And I thought about what Mother had said, *Lesbians will burn in hell.* Hell was a real place for us, as real as the next neighborhood. In our insular Catholic world, hell practically had its own zip code. Every year in school we had to write an essay about what hell was like, how it looked, the people who ended up there, what it would be like to spend eternity in that fiery pit. I did not want to go to hell.

I thought of Father saying, *Sometimes it's better not to know.* And for the first time in my life I doubted my parents. I remembered the day after the accident when I sat on the porch and Mr. Wilson came out to see me and told me that I was not allowed to read the newspaper article. Instead I was supposed to pray. I had read so much over those twenty-some-odd months. I had combed the shelves of the library, had read and reread every book in his room, but I had not read the most important thing, the last thing about Roy. Everyone else had read it, everyone else knew not to mention it to me. My parents had kept it from me, to protect me. I wondered if they were wrong about that, too.

When I showed up on the Hendersons' front doorstep, Mary Elizabeth answered the door. Her lip gloss was shining in the gray rainy light. She smiled down at me. She smelled like plastic fruit, like a giant grape Scratch N Sniff.

"Oh it's you," she said. She tilted her head to one side, and her dark curls bounced and swung around her rosy face. "Why didn't you just come in around back as usual?"

Then she looked down at me: the mud-splattered jumper, the sopping shoes. She grabbed me by the sleeve. "Get in here."

32

WE STOOD IN the foyer of the Henderson home, an exact replica of the one at our house across the street, and I asked her the question.

"Mary E."

"Yes?"

"Do you still have the article?"

She nodded.

"Can I have it now?"

Mary Elizabeth looked down at her hands. Then she poked her head out the front door, looked right then left, stepped back, closed the door, and turned the bolt. "Follow me."

We walked out of the front hall through the dining room, through the kitchen, and into the den, where her father, in one dim corner of the cluttered room, had fashioned a study. Mary Elizabeth opened the bottom drawer of the beige Formica desk with chipped edges, pushed aside three legal pads, and unearthed an outdated Rochester yellow pages. She pulled it out, balanced the book on one arm, and opened it to the Rs. As the thin yellow pages fell aside, a crisp white envelope appeared. Mary Elizabeth gazed at it for a moment. She plucked it out of the book's seam, turned it in her hands once, checked the seal to make sure it was still intact, and stretched her hand out toward me, the envelope balanced in her palm.

As the rain subsided outside and I caught my breath, Mary Elizabeth looked down at the cheap dime-store envelope. The raw light from her father's metal desk lamp washed across the wide plain of her cheeks. Like the visage of a virgin martyr in the *Saints' Lives* that we read as children, light bounced off Mary Elizabeth and softened across the dingy playroom.

She held the envelope in her gaze as I reached out and took it from her waiting palm. As I pushed aside my wet cardigan and slid it into the front pocket of my blouse, she kept her eye on it. Mary Elizabeth watched the envelope slip into my pocket as if she were watching a coin fall into a wishing well, one that, no matter how hard you tried, you could not imagine what wish it could possibly grant you. She started to speak, her eyebrows knit together, and she changed her mind. It was the only time she faltered, the one moment of doubt in Mary Elizabeth's endless sea of calm.

She turned away and asked, "How about some cocoa, Alison Lavon?"

The next winter, for my birthday, she would mail me, from college, a gold locket. Inside it would read: "To A.L.S. from M.E.H." On the back she would have the engraver inscribe the words "All My Love." Mary Elizabeth: loyal, pious, dogged, and scrupulously honest.

That day, in spring 1986, in the back room of her childhood home, Mary Elizabeth flipped her heavy black curls off her shoulders, let them fall down her back, and insisted I take off my wet things. She gave me a towel for my hair and made me sit at the kitchen table. She brought me a mug of hot liquid, with a spoon plunged in it.

"It's Swiss Miss with mini-marshmallows," she told me, and we stared into the chalky brown cocoa together.

She backed up, planted herself on a tall kitchen stool. I listened to her spoon rasping against the smooth porcelain and waited for her to give me advice. But for the first time she had none for me. She said nothing. After my hair dried, she released me. She let me go home. She stood in the doorway of her family's house and watched me walk away under her umbrella, which she insisted I borrow.

It wasn't until later, in the middle of the night, that I pulled out the envelope that held the article. Its creases already stiff with age, it was a simple news item, written by a rookie reporter, printed and forgotten by the end of the day. A blip of daily news, a tiny two-column, eight-inch speck of journalism. I read it by flashlight under the covers.

Democrat and Chronicle
JULY 28, 1984

2 DEAD IN FIERY CRASH IN PENFIELD
POSTAL-TRUCK DRIVER TRIES TO SAVE MAN
"ALL I COULD DO WAS WATCH HIM DIE"
by Craig Gordon

An 18-year-old groundskeeper at Penfield Country Club and a woman whose identity had not been confirmed were killed early yesterday in a fiery two-car crash on Penfield Road.

Royden J. Smith Jr. of Brighton died of smoke inhalation and thermal shock, a spokesman for the Monroe County Medical Examiner's Office said late last night. The woman has not been identified because doctors have been unable to obtain a positive identification based on medical and dental records. Both bodies were burned beyond recognition.

A passing motorist failed in an attempt to save Smith from flames shortly after the crash, which occurred about 5:55 A.M.

"It was like somebody napalmed the two [cars]. . . . All I can see is this guy shaking his hands, like he was trying to put himself out," said motorist Raymond F. Cino of Webster. "All I could do was watch the guy die. It was a very painful thing. I tried to save the man. I just regret that I wasn't able to."

A 1972 Dodge with bald tires apparently spun out of control while traveling west on rain-slicked Penfield Road near Panorama Plaza, colliding with a 1977 Dodge van driven by Smith, who was apparently eastbound on the opposite lane, a sheriff's department spokesman said.

Both vehicles crashed into a guardrail. Gasoline spilled from the van's ruptured tank and was ignited by sparks, and the car and the van were engulfed in flames when police arrived.

Cino, a postal-truck driver from the main post office on Jefferson Road, tried unsuccessfully to pull Smith from the burning wreckage.

Cino was making a delivery to the Penfield branch office when he passed the accident scene. At first he feared it was a trap set by people to rob his truck. Then he saw the van's driver.

"I went by and saw his hands flailing, and I said, 'This is no trap. There's a guy inside.' I knew he was alive when I saw his hands," Cino said.

Cino threw on a jacket and gloves and ran to the burning van. He said he could not see inside the car because of flames and smoke.

"I was running up the hill praying that the [van] didn't blow up," Cino said. "I wasn't worried about the car blowing because it had blown already."

Cino said that the van's rear door was jammed, and the windows were buckled and broken from the heat.

He punched out a window in the side door and opened it, but the van's roof had also caved in, keeping him from reaching the driver.

"Black smoke came rolling out of the fire," he said.

Police arrived shortly after Cino was forced back by the blaze.

33

My GREAT-UNCLE Andy got his hand caught in a combine when he was ten. He was on the family farm in Iowa, harvesting corn when it happened. It was a terrible accident. Blood splattered across his clothes, the corn, the other workers. It took them hours to extract Andy from the machine. In the end, the doctors managed to save his hand. But they could not save the thumb.

"They made me stay in bed for a week with a huge white bandage wrapped around my hand," Andy says, when he tells the story. "When they finally took it off, my mother gasped, pressed a dish towel to her mouth, and backed out of the room. But I couldn't see what all the fuss was about." When he went back to work in the fields, the men kept him away from the machines. He was only allowed to follow behind the crew and pick stray corn off the ground.

"It's a pity. A boy so young," the neighbors all said. But Andy didn't know what they were talking about. Whenever he looked down at his hand, he saw it as whole, intact, the thumb wiggling there at the side of his palm just like it always had.

Six months later he was tossing a ball around with his brother in the frozen fields and he noticed he kept dropping it. "I didn't know what was going on. My hand felt funny, uneven, like it was weighted wrong." Then Andy looked at his hand and finally, almost half a year after losing it, he understood that his thumb was gone. It took all that time for the news of his lost thumb to travel from Andy's hand up to his mind, for it to settle in there and register. It was not until then that he felt the pain of it. And when he did he sat down in the field of winter wheat and he cried.

The night I read the newspaper article, I finally understood. I remember the newspaper crinkling under the weight of my shocked hand. *He's gone*, I thought. *He's really gone*. In the intervening years, between the publication of the article and that night, I had not thought about its content. Every time I pictured it, my mind froze. I remembered Father curled over on the hall rug calling Roy's name, and being told to look for the answer in prayer, and I thought no further. I knew that even speculating on what secret the article might reveal, even wondering about this hidden information would be disapproved of, would be considered a sin. And so I had not planned in any way for the actual content of the piece. I knew only that the act of reading it was a defiance, a deliberate rejection of my parents' orders not to read. And then I read it. I cared little for defiance then. In my hand I held irrefutable proof that he was not coming back to me. But that was not the greatest blow. What took hold of me, what I have never been able to shake since, is how much Roy suffered. The horror of it hit me, the thing they wanted to keep from me: that he was trapped, pinned in a burning car, trying to get out. I heard Raymond Cino saying, "All I could do was watch him die."

I lost my breath, and as I gasped and trembled, I felt like I was suffocating. I thought that I was going to die. *Roy has come back*, I thought, *for me*. I clasped my hands over my mouth to quiet my rasping breath, and I waited for luminous transformation, a magical ascension out of this world; I waited for death. But death did not come. It was a simple panic attack, and like all attacks it passed and left me limp as a dustrag, soaked in sweat, and very much alive.

When my breathing finally slowed, I could not sit still. I wandered through the rooms of the house the way we had in the months right after he died. I remember every corner, every crack, every surface I touched that night. The red-and-blue comforter on his bed, the big closet that held our baseball gloves, our childhood toys, the green marbled wallpaper of the front hall, the iron door handle that would not latch, the silver-plate crucifix. My ears had been ringing since the day the police officers arrived to tell us Roy was gone. But for a few hours the ringing stopped and the night filled with voices. I heard a mockingbird in the low branches of the maple outside the window, the ticking of a clock on the bedside table. The wind picked up and buckled in the cold March night, and I heard the icy rain pattering against the side of the house. The creaking in the eaves, a low ticking in the walls, the hum of the refrigerator. It was as if the house had come to life, whispering its secrets to me, confessing.

I went into Mother and Father's unheated room and watched their breath roll in and out, their chests rise and fall in the gray light of the moon. The years receded from them when they slept. Softened around the edges, curled up like tiny shrimp, their hands tucked under their chins, their white skin laid out against the white sheets, they slept. For a small sliver of time, as I sat in Mother's wicker rocker hugging my knees, they became my children—scared, hungry, bereft, and young, too young for all that had happened to them. I remembered Mother's face when they came for us a year and a half before, when the officers showed up at the door and she knew right away, before they even said a word. How she had begged them not to say it; she clutched her chest that late July morning and said, "Please, please, no."

How can they sleep? I wondered. *When he burned to death a half mile from here?* But of course they had known for a year and a half. They had known all along, and they kept it from me. *How can they forgive God, when he died so terribly?* I gazed at them, the secret-keepers, the whisperers, the bearers of dangerous memory. I wondered why they had excluded me from so much, from his last minutes and the story of Raymond Cino and the fire, from grief itself.

Father stirred in his sleep and rolled over onto his back. I could just make out his strong English nose, his white Irish skin. As I gazed at him, I remembered the relics he blessed us with, Roy and me, every morning of our lives. All those childhood mornings lined up inside me like a long succession of blessings and benedictions. Roy sleeping in the other room, Mother downstairs, the coffee brewing, and Father arrives again and again with those disks of gold and blood and bone. Pressing the cold metal against our foreheads, our hands, our throats, naming every part of us, like Adam, claiming his domain, naming all the animals.

In that moment I understood all that we had lost. I understood also why they had kept so much from me. They wanted me to be untouched by it. They wanted to protect me, but more than that, they wanted some piece of innocence to remain intact. They wanted one thing in their life that was pure and untroubled, unstained by tragedy. If they could pull that off, if they could keep me safe from the harsh realities, maybe they could hold on to the dream of the perfect family in the Garden of Eden.

When I was a young child, Father used to say, "God loves you so much. Anything you want, baby, God will give it to you." He would pat my shoulder, place one hand softly on my head, lean over, and whisper in my ear, "Just name it." I talked to Roy about this, about the idea that God would give us anything we wanted. It scared us. We used to whisper about it under the sheets after Father left for work and I had padded into Roy's room, crawled into bed with him. We used to dare each other, "Name it."

"No, you name it."

In the end, whenever we asked God for anything, we made sure it was something that our dad would be able to give us—a new baseball glove, a ride to the playground, a good campsite at the beach.

That night I knew. My father was wrong. God would not give us anything we named. He could not.

Mother woke. Her head popped up off the pillow. "What are you doing?" She gasped. "Baby?" she called.

"It's okay," I said. I stood up, tucked the blanket tight around her. "Go back to sleep," I whispered.

I pulled on a pair of jeans and pushed open the heavy front door. I walked to the end of our street, and when I reached it, I kept walking. I went east on the main road, hugging the curb, walking along the lip where the asphalt fell away into a narrow ditch. I shivered in my thin nightshirt. I had not bothered with shoes, and I felt the gravel biting into the soles of my feet. Trees lined the road, crowding against the ditch. The wind blew. Rainwater cascaded down from the wet branches.

It was easy to find: the guardrail was still split, a tear in the metal where the 1972 Dodge with bald tires and the 1977 Dodge van broke through. A half mile from our house this broken fence lay there, torn, useless, marking the spot, the door in time that Roy had slipped through. It was the only visible sign left. I sat down on the railing and ran my hand across the rusted fragments. Shards of rough metal broke off in my fingers.

As I sat in the cold, my hands grasping the rusted metal, I saw Roy on his last morning, running out to the van, dodging the rain, his hands on the wheel as he backed down the drive and took the first turn at the top of the street. I saw the rain drumming on the steel roof of the cab, the windshield wipers sobbing their arcs across the wet glass, and struggling up the hill a 1972 Dodge, the bald tires sliding across the road. I saw Raymond Cino, the stranger, his hands out toward the heat, the bright gasoline fire. I walked over to the spot where Raymond Cino must have stood, his face tan and shining, as he gazed into the hot light of the fire and watched Roy die. I tried to imagine what it must have looked like to the two of them as the world went up in flames, went bright, impossibly bright, until everything around them glowed as if the sun were caught inside the van and Roy felt the heat rise around him, felt the fire sear his skin. I tried to imagine what made Raymond Cino stop trying, stop reaching for my brother, what made him step away from the fire.

Even now, in my mind, I follow Roy into the van. I climb into the passenger seat beside him and wait for a '72 Dodge to cross the yellow dividing line, for the explosion and the fire and finally for Raymond's hand to burst through the side window. The fire hovers around us, catching our feet, our hands, our hair. I walk into the flames as far as my mind will take me. I have been told that it is not the fire that gets you, it is the smoke. It poisons you long before the flames have reached you. The smoke fills your lungs, and you go light-headed. Slowly, the bright outlines of the world fade, the objects around you flicker and dissolve. And you give yourself away.

34

THE NEXT MORNING I found myself in bed, the article hidden under the sheets, and Father at the door with the relics in his hand. He whispered a short benediction and then made the sign of the cross, his hand waving across the morning air. He held the first relic to my forehead, and I felt the sting of the cold metal against my skin as Father began the blessing. *Bless her mind, Bless her throat, Bless her hands, Bless her voice.*

He slid the first relic back into the folds of the threadbare handkerchief, picked up Blessed John Neumann, the second, and began the series of blessings all over again. No matter what happened, no matter how far I fell from grace, no matter what sort of trouble I brewed up, Father was always there, 6:15 A.M., the relics tumbling out of his pocket onto the snow-white handkerchief, to offer his morning prayer. As he leaned over and placed the second relic on my forehead, I pulled my arm out from under the covers, reached up, and pressed the flat of my hand against his arm. For the first time in seventeen years of morning blessings, I stopped him.

"Baby?" he whispered. "You're awake?"

I kept my hand in place. "What are you doing?" I asked.

He blinked twice, stared down at the weave of the fabric on the moss green bedspread. Then he looked up into my eyes. He moved his hand back, folded his fingers over the relic. I watched its filigreed edge disappear in the meat of his palm. "I'm blessing you. Like I do every morning."

"Why?" I asked.

Father smiled. He touched the knot in his tie, pulled it into place, and cleared his throat. He shrugged and let out a little laugh, just one short, voiceless gust of air, and then said, "It's what I do." He smiled.

The newspaper article crinkled beneath me.

"I just want you, I—I just need you to be safe," he said.

I leapt out of bed. "What if I don't want to be safe anymore?"

Father stared at me. He began to respond, but then his gaze landed on my arm. "What happened to you?" he asked.

There, running the length of my forearm, from wrist to elbow, was a long gash. I must have scraped it along the broken guardrail the night before. I looked down at it and tried to remember when it had happened, but all I could recall was images of the fire, and Raymond reaching toward the burning van. I shook my head. "I don't know," I said, and I stepped toward him. "It's fine. It doesn't hurt. Daddy, I'm sorry. You can finish the blessing."

He shook his head. "It's all right," he said. "You don't want it." He slipped the relics and the handkerchief in his pocket. "You're all I have left," he said. "Baby. Remember that." He touched the cut on my arm. "You better have Mother look at it." And he bowed out of my room.

I dressed quickly and ran after him. But he had already put on his rubbers and his overcoat, already walked to the end of the driveway and stepped into the dark interior of the waiting car, his daily car pool ride. I stood in the doorway, my school uniform jumper on backwards, my socks slouching around my ankles, and watched the car grow smaller and smaller as it struggled up the hill, rounded the first corner, and disappeared.

I closed the front door and found Mother at the foot of the stairs. She was wearing a pink bathrobe, her hair disheveled from the night. "Isn't the zipper supposed to be in the back?" she asked.

I pulled my arms through the sleeve holes and shimmied the jumper around. I followed her into the kitchen, stood in the doorway, and stared as she put the kettle on, pulled the orange juice out of the fridge, and found the cereal bowls.

"What are you looking at?" she asked.

I shook my head and slid into my seat at the table.

That was it. She never mentioned the fight or my flight into the woods or the call from Miss Beal. Over the next several months she never mentioned that statement, *Lesbians will burn in hell*, again. Mother was playing Kremlin.

I ate the oatmeal she had cooked for me, drank my juice in one gulp, grabbed my bag, and headed out the door a half hour early.

"Aren't you going to wait for Mary Elizabeth?" she called after me.

It was cold, a raw, wet spring morning that sank into my bones. There was a mist on the grass, thick as clouds. It had settled in for the morning, no hope of burning off. Cars drove by, their engines working against the wet morning air. A bird sang in the tree above the Lovell house. I passed Mr. Henderson where he stood on his front stoop, the morning paper in hand.

"Aren't you going to wait for Mary Elizabeth?" he asked.

I cut across the Wilson lawn, threw my bag over the back fence, and sneaked around the corner to the marshy gully, taking the back way as far as I could, till I had to cross the main road. The soggy grass oozed around my penny loafers. A lonely crow cawed.

When I reached school, I climbed the stairs to the second floor and went straight for Terry's locker. She was not there. I checked her homeroom. It was empty. I was too early. I wandered down the darkened corridors—the Sisters had not yet arrived and turned on the lights. I stumbled into my own homeroom, the dew dripping off my shoes, my book bag still packed and my jacket on. My desk was clear, no summonses to the office, no missives from Mary Elizabeth, just a lonely slab of Formica empty and waiting for me. I slid into my seat and put my head down. Sister Rose arrived ten minutes later and flipped the light switch. The overhead fluorescents buzzed to life, and the room filled with a shaky, green-tinged, friable light. I closed my eyes to it. My book bag slid off my lap and landed on the floor with a thump. Sister Rose jumped.

"I didn't see you there." I heard her rummaging in her pockets for her glasses. "Is that you, Alison?"

I did not reply.

"You're early. It's only seven-thirty." Then: "Dear? Are you all right?"

I did not look up. There was no part of me that wanted to ignore this convent cherub, and considering my current situation it was not a good time to lose track of my manners, but I could not lift my head up off the desk. I could not figure out how to pull myself back to an upright position and offer her a respectful good morning and a reasonable explanation of my presence there. Sister Rose waddled out from behind her desk.

"You poor dear," she murmured. She rubbed my back with her frail hand. I warmed under her touch. I found the strength to sit up. I looked into her face, the curly hair peeking out from under the edges of her wimple, the wire-rim glasses perched on the end of her upturned nose. Her eyebrows knit together and met at the center of her forehead. Her eyes, ancient and watery, enlarged by the thick lenses of her glasses, flooded with concern.

"You've been crying."

I nodded.

"What's wrong?" she asked.

"Don't you know? Doesn't everybody know?"

"Know what?"

I burst into tears.

Even this sudden and unwarranted display did not ruffle her placid calm. She smiled, folded her hands across her bosom, sighed, and tut-tutted. Then, slowly, like this was the most ordinary occurrence in the world, she reached her hand inside her habit, and from a hidden fold, she pulled a linen handkerchief. She placed it in my hand and guided it up to my nose and said, "Now blow."

It was the softest hankie I had ever touched. I looked at the scrap of Irish linen with its hand-stitched border and its sprig of embroidered violets in one corner, a blue cursive OLM stitched in the opposite corner. It was crisp and white and perfect and clean. It even smelled like the Motherhouse, of cedar and violets. I pushed it away and, shaking my head, croaked, "I can't. I can't use that."

"Why? What's the matter with it?" Rose stared at her hankie, examining it for flaws.

"It's too good," I cried. "I don't deserve it!" I pressed my snotty nose and wet cheeks into her shoulder, and I let loose, sobbing against her. She patted the damp mane of my hair.

"It's as bad as that?" She bent down and gazed into my eyes. "I've got just the thing for you," she said, and she took me by the hand and led me down the hall.

In the alcove, just before the stairs, she stopped and genuflected in front of Our Lady of the Broken Toes. Her round body slowly folded, one stocking knee dipping down, touching the cold tile floor. She crossed herself. As she bent forward, her face disappeared behind the edge of her wimple and I lost sight of her. She whispered into her palm, the hankie still dangling at the end of her fingers as she offered a private supplication to the Virgin. And then slowly she pushed herself back up to standing. Her eyes crinkled in happy satisfaction. She looked like she had popped a delicious chocolate into her mouth. Stepping back, she took my hand and tipped her cherubic face up toward my ear, whispered, "Now, you," and she gave me a little nudge in the direction of the Virgin. I stepped forward.

"Just ask Mary." Sister Rose nodded toward the statue.

My classmates were starting to arrive, trudging up the wide stairways at either end of the hall. Gusts of damp air rushed up the stairwell and swirled around Our Lady of the Broken Toes. I shivered and knelt down in front of the Virgin. The air grew thick with echoes of morning business: lockers opening, book bags being unzipped, the soft voices of the girls calling to each other across the half-empty hallways. I looked back at Sister Rose. She nodded. I turned around and gazed up into the statue's face.

There she stood, the Virgin, frozen in time, in a rosy-cheeked moment of perfect benediction, her slender shoulders wrapped in the dusty folds of a powder blue cloak, her long arms bent at the elbow and held out, the fingers tapering to two points. I supposed when they first made her, when she rolled off the assembly line or emerged from her cast, she was glorious. But now, dust covered, dingy, her pink cheeks and rosy lips cracking in the dry air, she looked a bit forlorn. I closed my eyes, folded my hands together, and waited. Nothing came to me. Not the Lord's Prayer, or the Hail Mary, or any of a number of brief benedictions that I had been required to memorize over the years. Nothing. God was silent. And so was I.

All I could see was my brother's face, the terror he must have felt in those last minutes in the burning van.

I shook my head. "I can't," I whispered, and I started to cry again.

Sister Rose waddled over to me and put out her hand. "It's all right."

I unlaced my fingers and placed a hand in Sister's outstretched palm. She led me down the two flights of stairs, back across the first-floor hallway, and into the nurse's office. When we arrived, Mrs. Kelley jumped up from her post and grabbed my elbow.

"What do we have here?" she asked as she put a hand across my forehead and led me to the examination table. Mrs. Kelley had a wide, rough face. She smelled of Pond's cold cream and lemon Pledge. She was barrel-chested and strong-armed, and I was a little afraid of her.

"It's all right. No need to examine her," Sister said, and she guided me toward the familiar back room with the bottles of antiseptic and the Band-Aids.

"It's the Smith girl?"

Sister nodded.

"What's wrong with her?"

"She's sick with sadness again."

"I thought we were past that. It's been over a year since—"

"Relapse," Sister Rose said, and she waved the nurse away.

Sister guided me into the resting room. She found the fluffy white blanket on a high shelf, stood on tiptoes in her black utility shoes, and pulled it down. She tucked it around me where I lay on the vinyl-covered couch, and in her tremulous voice she whispered, "Shhhh. Shhhh."

Upstairs my classmates arrived to an empty homeroom, slammed their books down, removed wads of gum from their mouths, and pressed them to the undersides of desks. They pulled up their kneesocks, tugged down their short uniform skirts, and looked around for Sister Rose, faithful homeroom monitor, distributor of lemon drops, knitter of bright green afghans. If she didn't arrive soon, they would pull out nail polish and eyeliner and begin to whisper and lean across the aisles, bending in toward each other. Their chairs would squeak beneath them and their books would tumble onto the floor and they would get up from their seats. Someone would bring out a Nerf football, and someone would go long for it, and before you knew it, the room would erupt in chaos. Their voices would rise out across the cool morning air, float down the halls, and the pitch of noise in the room would grow until all the Sisters in all the homerooms would pause in the midst of morning announcements, tilt their heads to one side, and listen, trying to locate the source of trouble.

Mrs. Kelley paced back and forth on the other side of the door, calling, "If you would just let me examine her, Sister," and the girls in her homeroom made their way toward bedlam, but Sister Rose took her time. Her hand on my forehead, her voice in my ear, her blue habit blending with the blue of the wall behind her, she leaned over me and whispered *shhhh* till the sound became a sigh and the sigh entered my dreams and I drifted off to sleep. As I fell into a dull, aching slumber, I heard her utility shoes squeak across the tile floor. I watched, through half-closed eyes, as her hand reached for the doorknob and she stepped out into the hallway. She shut the door behind her and the sliver of light at the edge of the door grew smaller and smaller till the room fell into darkness.

35

I WOKE AN HOUR later, swimming in sweat, my uniform blouse clinging to my back. I sat up, looked around at the shelves of folded white towels, the glass cupboard with its vials of secret remedies. Mrs. Kelley appeared at the door, her hands planted on her hips. I slumped back on the couch and pulled the blanket up to my chin.

"Good, you're up." She marched over to the bed. "I noticed you have a scrape on your right arm. We'll get you fixed up and back in class, where you belong." She leaned down and started rummaging through a low cupboard to the right of my cot. "Now where did I put that antiseptic?"

I felt dizzy. I touched my head and looked around me. Over a year had passed since I first found myself in that cramped, airless room. Sister Daniel had found me the first time I broke down, curled up in a bathroom stall on the third floor, and carried me here and laid me in this secret resting room. While I gazed at Mrs. Kelley's rump, in the white uniform, I tried to piece together what had happened that morning. I felt a sting on my arm and looked down and saw the cut. Then I remembered Sister Rose's face, the powdery white cheeks, the furrowed brow, and I remembered why I had rushed to school. I had to find Terry.

Mrs. Kelley poked her head up, waving a bottle. "I think I got it," she said. She grabbed the handle of the cupboard and began to pull herself up. I made a break for the door, flung it open, and burst out into the hallway, pulling my shoes on as I hopped across the slippery tile floor. I could hear Mrs. Kelley yelling behind me, "Get back here!" As I banked the first corner, I saw her standing in the middle of the deserted hall waving a large brown bottle of hydrogen peroxide.

I looked up at the hall clock. It was nine o'clock on B day, so Terry would be in chemistry. I slipped down into the basement under the convent and went to the room where Sister Robert held her science classes. I peered in the narrow window next to the door. Terry was not there. I ran up to the front office. The secretary was out. I slipped around the counter and rifled through the papers on her desk until I found the attendance log. Terry had checked in that morning. She was somewhere in the school. The secretary arrived, snuck up behind me, and pressed a taloned hand against the logbook. "There you are," she said.

Miss Peach rarely moved from behind her desk, unless it was to nip over to the guidance wing and pour herself a cup of coffee. She took a sip from her mug, which said, "Have you hugged a secretary today?"

"I believe you have some unfinished business with Mrs. Kelley."

"Okay," I said. "Give me a pass and I'll go see her."

"Oh, no," she said, and she waved her finger at me. "I'm not letting you out of my sight." She flipped the switch on her ancient intercom machine and leaned over the tiny speaker. "Kelley. I got the Smith girl here. You want to come get her?"

"How did you find her?" Mrs. Kelley's voice crackled out of the speaker.

"She just showed up," Miss. Peach said, and she eyed me.

I turned my back to her, slumped against the edge of the desk, and crossed my arms. I felt the sting from the cut where it brushed against the rough nap of my sweater. Miss Peach shooed me away from her desk, her red fingernails flying. "Don't get your dried blood on my papers."

When Mrs. Kelley arrived two minutes later, she actually grabbed me by the ear.

"I promise not to run away again if you let go of my ear," I said as I hopped alongside her.

"I'm not losing you twice in one day." She dug her fingers in deeper.

Once Mrs. Kelley got me bustled into the back room, once she had the door closed and latched, the antiseptics out, the gauze unfurled on the table, and my arm spread out between us, the long cut facing up toward the bare bulb in the ceiling, she softened. She dabbed the wound with her fresh towel and clicked her tongue in a manner that I imagine I was supposed to find soothing. She shook her head. "How did you get this?" she asked.

"It's a long story," I said.

"I've got time." Mrs. Kelley smiled at me, revealing a gap between her front teeth.

"Don't you think I ought to get to class?" I asked.

She pursed her lips, grabbed the big brown bottle and guided me over to the sink. "This will sting a bit," she said and poured half a bottle of hydrogen peroxide down my arm. I shivered and grit my teeth, but I would not cry out. So she poured the rest of the bottle on my arm.

"See that," she said. She pointed at the line of bubbles fizzing around the cut. "That's all the germs, burning off." She stared at me. "A stoic one, are you?"

After Mrs. Kelley had bandaged my cut, I took the pink slip from her outstretched hand, trudged up to the third floor to Mrs. Pinkerton's English literature class, slipped in, and sat down. I listened as Mrs. Pinkerton examined the depths of Gatsby's love for Daisy till the lunch bell rang. I ran down to the cafeteria, checked the lunch line, scanned the tables, looked in the hall where they kept the apple vending machine—no Terry. I went to the art room. Empty. I closed the door, and in the sweet quiet of the deserted room, I stopped. I leaned against the storage cupboards and slid onto the floor. I wrapped my arms around my shins and put my head on my knees.

The next thing I knew Terry was kneeling in front of me. She wore a smock over her uniform. It didn't help. The collar of her white blouse was stippled with purple paint.

"Hi," I said.

She got up, looked out into the hall, closed the door, ran over to the windows, and pulled the blinds. She came back and sat next to me. "You shouldn't be here," she said. "Did anybody see you?"

"I don't know." I sat up. I shoved my hand into the pocket of my jumper. I thought that I had put the newspaper article in there before I left the house that morning. But my pocket was empty. I opened my book bag and started going through it, hoping that I had slipped the article into a notebook. "I have to show you something," I said. I looked through my English notes, my physics textbook, my American studies notebook. The article was not there. I pictured the article lying, crinkled and worn, in between the folds of my blankets on my twin bed at home. I wondered if Mother would go into my room and find it. "I thought I put it in here somewhere."

Terry put her hand on my arm. She took the notebook out of my hand and pushed my book bag to one side. "What happened yesterday, when they called you into guidance?"

I reached for the bag. "I have to show you—"

Terry put out her hand. "Tell me what happened yesterday."

I slumped against the cupboard. "They switched me to Mrs. Phillips."

"The Frog?"

I nodded. A few moist strands of hair clung to her cheek. "How much trouble are we in?" I asked.

She leaned against the cupboard and pressed her head back into the door. "'We' are not in trouble."

"What do you mean?"

She picked up a pencil off the floor and tossed it. "Never mind. I'm out of here in less than two months." She looked over at me. "What did they say to you?" she asked.

"The usual. 'How are your mother and father?'"

"That's it?"

"There was one thing."

"What?"

"What do you know about the Mediterranean?"

"They asked about your family and told you about the Mediterranean?"

"And they told me to watch out for you."

Terry ran her hand through her hair, pushing the bangs off her forehead. "You're a lucky little shit, aren't you?"

"I don't know." I thought of the article and the broken railing and the fire. I glanced over at Terry. "They blamed the whole thing on you and you let them."

She nodded.

I grabbed the edge of the table and stood up.

"It's going to be okay," Terry said. "We just—we can't hang out for a while. At least not at school."

"I'm going to Sister Barbara's office, and I'm going to tell her the truth."

Terry leapt to her feet. By the time I reached the door she was ahead of me. I grabbed the doorknob. She pushed my hand away. "They're not going to believe you."

"Why not?"

"Because I'm a troublemaker and you're the girl whose brother died."

I stepped back. I stared at her. I thought about that term, the-girl-whose-brother-died, and I realized that all this time everyone knew how he had died in the fire. That's what they meant when they said the-girl-whose-brother-died. Except for the rhythmic clang of the heater, the room was silent. I walked over to the windows and put my hand on the curtain cord. I touched the cut on my arm.

"Just don't say anything. You'll only make it worse for me," Terry said.

She walked toward me. I stepped away from her.

"You had to know that this"—she pointed to herself, then to me—"was not going to go down with them."

I slumped on the edge of a table.

"Al . . . ," she ventured.

I pushed her away. "Leave me alone."

Terry stood up. She picked up her brushes and took them over to the sink to wash them off. She dried them with a paper towel, pulled out the utility box where she stored her paints, and laid the brushes inside. She latched the box shut, grabbed the handle, shoved it under her arm, and picked up her books with the other hand. She walked toward the door, and when she got there she stopped.

"This is not the way to do it," she said.

"Then how?" I stood up and turned toward her.

She was gone.

36

At dinner, Father stared into Jude's plastic eyes and shook his head. "She doesn't like it anymore," he said. "She doesn't like the blessing." He would not look at me. Mother, on the other hand, could not stop looking. At one point she reached across the table, brushed my bangs out of my eyes, and said, "You're my good girl, aren't you?" I was stunned. I watched her as she withdrew her hand from my forehead. Her coppery skin had faded over the winter months. The collar of her T-shirt slipped and exposed the smooth arc of her throat. For a moment, I saw a flash of her in summer, wearing her orange flowered bikini on the beach. She was the first in the water, the fastest runner, and the only one of the four of us who could land a perfect roundoff. Sometimes she made fun of Father and his saints, his superstitious rituals, his morning blessings. But more than anything, more than fun or knowledge or even truth, my mother valued goodness. It was the most important thing in her life. It was the only virtue. When she said, You're my good girl, it was not an assertion so much as a plea. She was begging me to make it so.

When Mother left the table to get the catsup, I slipped cube steak and carrots off my plate and into my pocket. After dinner, Mother and Father retired to the basement and watched the evening news. I slipped out the back door into the yard.

A chain-link fence ran down its south side. Opposite that, the Lovells had constructed a wooden fence—so high you could not see over it. It afforded our narrow, closely set yards a small measure of privacy. At the very back, beyond the fort, hovered a bank of tall evergreens. Broad-limbed and drooping, they rendered the dark yard even darker. I wore an oversized schoolgirl blouse and a pair of baggy jeans bulging at the pocket. For months I had hoarded food, hid it, saved it, squirreled it away, done everything with it but what I should have done—eaten it. And all the late-night reading, the research into the fourth dimension. What a fool I was, I thought, for thinking there was some message from him, in the arrival of the Encyclopedia Boy, in the disappearance of the food.

He was just a boy with bad luck. It was just a slippery road, and a set of bald tires. I shoved my hand in my pocket, fingered the morsel of cold meat, the cut carrots. My stomach rumbled. Blood rushed to my head. I grew dizzy. I remembered the funeral, the scalded brightness of the day, the long line of cars, the seven Jesuit boys who carried the coffin. Those boys, the pallbearers, Tim, his best friend, and Bob and Chips and Greg and Peter and John and Bill, holding their dead friend, carrying the coffin out of the hearse to the gravesite, laying him in the ground. They wore rumpled, ink-stained corduroy jackets, even in the heat of summer. Their hair hung down to their collars. They kept their heads down during the service. They held their hands, balled in fists, at their sides. They would not look at me. We were all so young.

I walked deeper into the yard, past the garden with its broken tomato stalks. I walked behind the garage, brushed aside the dead branches, stepped up to the door of the fort, and pushed it open. I unloaded my pocket onto the plate, and I sat there, looking down at my uneaten dinner. Shadow showed up. She stared at the plate of food. I knelt down and set it right in front of her. She would not touch it. She ducked her head and paced in the doorway. I had barred her from joining me on my nightly visits to the fort soon after Roy died, and for over a year, every night, she lay outside the door, her muzzle on her paws, blinking into the blackness and wait-ing for me. She could not believe that I would change the rules on her. I tore off a piece of meat and held it out. "Come on," I said. "It's not a trick."

She sniffed my hand. Her pink tongue darted out; she tasted

the morsel. Gingerly, she opened her mouth and took the steak out of my fingers. I pushed the plate toward her. She was on it immediately.

"You might as well eat it all," I said. I sat back, pulled the sleeping bag up around me, and looked out into the darkness.

37

THE FOLLOWING WEDNESDAY afternoon, I knocked on Sister Barbara's office door. After a moment her voice boomed out from behind the heavy oak. "It's open." I grasped the brass doorknob, the door creaked open, and for the first time, I gazed upon the rich, dark interior of the dean of discipline's office

I soon realized the room, with its Chippendale furniture and dark wainscoting rising up the walls, was one of the most handsomely furnished in the old convent. Sister sat at an enormous oak desk in its center. The curtains were drawn on the windows behind her, and the only light came from the brass banker's lamp on her desk. Sister Barbara glanced up from her paperwork, gave me a quick once-over, and then resumed her business.

"I thought you might stop by." She pointed her pen toward a velvet-covered chair beside her desk.

I sat down.

"What can I do for you?"

"I want to resign."

Sister Barbara took off her glasses. "From school?"

"No, Sister. I hope you don't think I should leave school."

"Then what do you mean?"

"From my job at the switchboard."

"The switchboard?"

"I answer the phone in the Motherhouse. I have for three years now."

"So you do. And you want to leave us?"

I nodded.

"What for?"

"I found a better-paying job, at the public library." This, although it was not the entire truth, was not a lie. Sister set down her pen and stared at me. "And," I mumbled, "because under the circumstances it seemed like a good idea."

She laced her fingers together, leaned back in her seat, and stared up at the ceiling. "So you're through with us, Miss Smith."

"I just want a different job. That's all."

"You'll finish out the week and then you are released," she said. She stared at me. "Have you been seeing Mrs. Phillips?"

"I saw her once. I don't much care to see her again."

She nodded. "You have been so quiet and well-mannered, and then you pull this. You're an inscrutable child."

"If you say so, Sister."

"It doesn't matter what I say, Miss Smith, now does it?"

She did not wait for an answer. She picked up her pen, put on her glasses, and went back to her paperwork. I slid off the velvet chair and tiptoed out of her room.

On my last night of work at the switchboard, Aggie stopped by with a deck of cards. She had a new card trick to show me.

"I hear you're leaving us," she said.

"Yes. I got a job at the library, and it's better money."

"Bullshit," she said. She smacked the deck against the desktop.

"It *is* more money," I whispered.

"It's because they caught you with the girl."

I stared up at her. "How do you know about that?"

She grinned. "Nothing gets by me, Blondie."

I shook my head. "I don't know what you must think of me."

"What do you care?"

"Of course I care."

"Then why are you leaving me?"

"I'm not. I'll come visit you."

Aggie sat down on the stool across from me and waved her hand in front of her face. "No you won't. Don't fool an old lady, Blondie. You've had one foot out the door for a year now."

"No, I haven't. This just came up and I had to—"

"I know it's news to you, but I saw this coming."

She set the deck of cards on the desk, slipped her hand into the pocket of her housecoat, and pulled out a crumpled piece of paper. She unfurled it and held it up for me to read:

To Aggie. From Blondie.

IOU $97.33.

For gambling debts.

"Aggie, you know I don't have that kind of money."

She tore it in half and tossed the scraps of paper on the desk. "Don't say I never did you any favors." She leaned forward on her cane and stretched one long, craggy hand out. She touched my cheek. "You're okay, Blondie," she said. She stood up, hunched over her cane, and walked out.

I watched her make her way down the hallway, past Big Ben, the grandfather clock, past the main foyer to the narrow passageway by the laundry chute. She stopped for a moment, in front of the cupboard door, opened it, stuck her head inside, and screamed.

38

THE SUBJECT OF SEX ran through the school like an underground river. Girls whispered about it in bathrooms, eyed each other in the locker rooms. It was the unspoken end of almost every sentence. Everybody wanted to know how it was done, who had already done it, where they would go to do it.

The Sisters tried to keep the story tightly guarded, but by the end of the first week, everybody was talking about it. Nobody quite got it right. The girls knew that Terry was caught with somebody doing something, but they couldn't quite figure out who it was and what they were doing. Some thought it was a boy from the Jesuit school. One briefly held rumor conjectured that she was pregnant with Father Ray's child. A few came close, at least with regards to Terry—a group of girls believed she had been caught kissing the janitor's daughter in the furnace room.

The scandal meant little to me. Girls talked around me, they gossiped and lied and giggled, they passed notes and made up stories. I did not care. For weeks I lived in the world of the article, rereading it every night in bed, looking between the lines for some sort of clue, for another piece of information, imagining what Raymond Cino looked like. As I walked to school I looked into the faces of the people I passed, into the eyes of the middle-aged men, and I wondered, *Is that Raymond?*

I spent my evenings in the fort. After dinner, more often than not, I simply tossed the contents of my plate down the garbage disposal and wandered out onto the cold back lawn empty-handed, gazing up at the dark sky. But there were still some nights when I brought my uneaten dinner out with me in the greasy paper bag. When I showed up with the bag, Shadow wagged her tail and whined, her paws kneading the ground in anticipation. I took some pleasure in watching Shadow eat, in making the poor mutt happy. When she finished she would lick her chops and sniff my hands, looking for one last morsel. I pushed my face into her fur and breathed in the cool, wet smell of her.

One day, while we were in the bathroom outside history class, Susanna Spindale leaned close to the mirror with a tube of lipstick in her right hand. As she guided the tip of the bright red stick across her mouth, she glanced over at me. "What do you think of the rumors about your friend Terry?" she asked.

I closed my backpack and looked up at her.

"I know you know what I'm talking about."

"Don't you all have something better to do than talk about other girls' business?" I asked.

"It's your business, too, isn't it?" She raised one eyebrow. "The rest of them may be blind, but I'm not." She capped her lipstick and was gone.

Nobody else connected the Terry Situation (as it had come to be known) with me. We were both called to guidance. We had both disappeared the night of the Read-A-Thon. I could have walked through the school halls stark naked and nobody would have stopped me, not even for a uniform infraction. You could say I was lucky—carte blanche at seventeen to do anything I wanted—but I was also caught, encased in plastic like Mrs. Henderson's butterfly. I could not be anything other than the-girl-whose-brother-died. There was a barrier between me and the rest of the girls. It had been there since Roy died, but only now, as I took my first steps back into the world, did I sense it. My classmates were cautious, the nuns overprotective, and the teachers never entirely honest with me. I could have handled all of this, but that I was helpless to aid Terry, that I could not stand up for her, this I hated. I wondered if she was right, if anything I did to call attention to myself would only end up reflecting badly on her. And I wondered, too, if my mother was right, if we would burn in hell. I started showing up at school looking more distracted and bothered than usual.

The whole fiasco, from the debate inspired by Miss Beal to the lack of supervision at the Shakespeare Read-A-Thon, did not reflect well on the Sisters' ability to mold young Catholic minds. As much as they hated to discuss the situation, they had to do something. Mrs. Phillips had not gotten anywhere with me. So they found me another mentor, Mrs. Pinkerton. An English teacher, she had certainly proven that she was comfortable with the subjects of sex and romance.

"Girls," Mrs. Pinkerton said to us on the day we began studying *A Farewell to Arms*, "this is the most important book you will ever read. This is important because . . ." She paused, pulled at the waist of her sweater, and continued with increased bravado. "Through the self-sacrificing character of Catherine you can learn what it means to be . . ." She paused again, turned her back to us, and wrote on the blackboard: "A Woman in Love."

She smiled down at us, leaned against the blackboard, and looked out the long classroom windows to the school's soccer field. Her poker-straight bottle brown hair fell in a lank pageboy. Her durable plaid skirts and thick-soled brown oxfords lent her a rough, boyish air.

"Love means making compromises for your man," she said in her breathless southern drawl, a copy of *A Farewell to Arms* held loosely in her right palm. She closed her eyes. She dabbed at her bright red lips with the tiny white linen handkerchief that she stored in the sleeve of her sweater.

Mrs. Pinkerton loved Hemingway. But then she loved most things indiscriminately. She was in her sixties, resilient, terminally cheery, and completely out of her mind. She taught us the secret to analyzing literature: turn to the last page of the book, note how many pages are in the novel, divide that number in half, and that will give you the page at the middle of the novel. Turn to that page, and there you will find the message of the book. One day in midwinter, as we filed into class, Mrs. Pinkerton cried, "Oh, my beauties!"—this was her signature manner of addressing the class—"I forgot to put my girdle on this morning and I feel so *free*!" and she proceeded to skip around the room. Once, when Mary Elizabeth was called to the front of the classroom to pick up her term paper, Mrs. Pinkerton handed it to her and announced to the class, "Mary Elizabeth wrote a fine paper. And she has great breasts!"

Despite what some may have perceived as her shortcomings, Mrs. Pinkerton was well liked. She spent every afternoon in the basement offices under the convent helping girls lay out the yearbook or make selections from the vast number of submissions we received for the school literary magazine.

She loved reading Great Literature aloud. After *A Farewell to Arms* we read *The Great Gatsby*. In the midst of one of her long recitations from the text, just as Nick bends over to kiss Jordan for the first time, she clasped the tattered paperback to her chest and let out a breathy sigh. "Oh, my beauties," she cried. "I can't wait till you all get married so you can have sex!"

When the bell finally rang, she called me up to her desk. "There you are, my beauty!" she whispered in her southern drawl. "How are you?"

I told her I was fine.

"Did you like the discussion today?"

I nodded. After *Pride and Prejudice*, *The Great Gatsby* was my favorite novel.

"Come for a walk with me," she said and grabbed her L.L. Bean tote bag.

"I have to get to physics."

"I'll write you a pink slip." She leaned against the oak door and waved me over. "Come on."

She led me down the hall to the English teachers' office, a converted classroom. Tall bookshelves acted as dividers for makeshift offices. Mrs. Pinkerton had taught at the school for longer than anyone could remember, even Sister Daniel, and over the years had amassed quite a collection of odds and ends in her book-lined partition. There was an overstuffed Victorian love seat, a collection of porcelain teapots gathering dust on top of the bookshelves, and a portrait of Carson McCullers.

Her desk was piled high with secondhand copies of novels, a Shakespeare Folio edition, and several boxes of Dove soap. She smiled. "We are going to have a private heart-to-heart," she said, and she squeezed my hand.

"We are?" I asked.

"Take your shoes off, honey," she drawled and took off her own. She rubbed the bottoms of her feet, encased in a pair of knee-high hose, along the threadbare nap of a small Oriental throw. "Ahh. That's better," she said. She pointed down at the rug. "It's divine, isn't it? Just cozies up the whole place." She leaned forward. "Nine ninety-five at the Goodwill. You'd never know."

I stood with my book bag and my copy of *The Great Gatsby* and looked down at the worn Goodwill carpet beneath her feet.

"What's the trouble? Take a load off," she said. "Can I make you a cup of tea?" she asked.

"Mrs. Pinkerton?" I stepped onto her rug and eased into a corner of the Victorian love seat. "Is there a problem with my last essay? Because I can rewrite it."

"Oh, no!" she said as she pulled two teacups off the shelf. "It's just wonderful. All of you girls are so smart. I don't know how I got so lucky." She shook her head in amazement. Her pageboy swung from side to side. "Kick off those old penny loafers." She leaned back in her metal rolling chair.

As I pulled off my shoes, the springs of the love seat squeaked.

"It's hard, isn't it?" she asked, and she handed me a cup of tea. "Milk or sugar?" I shook my head.

"What's hard?" I asked.

"Oh, you don't have to hide from me. The nuns told me all about it."

I spilled tea on my knee. "They told you?"

"Yes. I hope you don't mind. They thought I could help, being a woman of the world."

"A woman of the world?"

"I may be an old married lady now, but in my day I was in the very same position you are in."

"You were?"

"Of course! When I was sixteen, why, I was so in love that my eyes just crossed with desire."

"Really?"

She nodded.

I scooted forward in my seat and said, "What was her name?"

"*Her* name?"

"The girl you were in love with."

"The girl?"

I sat back in my seat, set down the cup of tea, and asked, "What did the Sisters tell you?"

"That you were confused, that you had love trouble, that a boy broke your heart—at least that is what they implied. Isn't that what happened?"

"Yes," I said. "I mean, no. Not the way you think."

She leaned forward and patted my knee. "You poor baby. I know it's so hard to talk about these things. What was his name?"

"There is no boy!"

"It's too painful to say, isn't it?"

"No! That's not it."

"Shhh," she said, and she poured more tea. "It's okay. I understand. Poor thing!" She patted my knee again. "You just stay right here with your auntie Pinkerton and everything will be all right. The trick is to get this boy off your mind. Do you think you can do that?"

I nodded. "I think I can manage it."

She slapped her hand against the desk. "That's the spirit!" She beamed at me, grabbed a book of Milton off her desk, and ran her finger along the spine. She leaned toward me. "I have hatched a plan to help you along," she whispered and scooted forward on her seat. "I want you to come out with me on Friday night. Do you think you can get your parents' permission?"

I guessed I could.

"Good."

39

AND THAT IS HOW I found myself on Friday evening in the women's ward of the state hospital, a sewing needle in one hand and a Simplicity pattern in the other, surrounded by lobotomy patients.

Mrs. Pinkerton delivered me herself—a half hour late. When we arrived, twelve pairs of very docile eyes looked up from their sewing patterns and gazed at us. I stepped back toward the door and whispered, "Mrs. Pinkerton, what are we doing here?"

"You're going to love this," she said. "Just what you need to take your mind off your troubles."

Sister Daniel grabbed my arm and ushered me into the one empty seat at the end of the table. "This is Mrs. Gold," Sister said, indicating the woman on my left. "She's making a very pretty apron."

I looked down the row of women bent over their patterns, plastic scissors in hand, and realized that they were all making aprons. The same pattern, each one in a bright solid color. I grabbed Sister's arm and pulled her away from the table. "Sister, do you really think that I need to be put in here, with these women?"

Sister stared at me, blinked, and said, "What on earth are you talking about?"

"Why did Mrs. Pinkerton bring me here?"

"To teach them how to sew." She smiled at me.

By now Mrs. Pinkerton had lassoed one of the patients, pulled out a copy of *A Farewell to Arms*, and was pressing it into the bewildered woman's hands. "You are going to eat this with a spoon," she said to the woman I would soon learn was called Dotty. "The best thing about love ever written." Then she glanced over at me, grinned, and gave me a thumbs-up. I realized Mrs. Pinkerton had fallen back on the Sisters' old standby, their answer to every problem: Service.

"You were my prize student in home ec," Sister Daniel said. "The only girl who took three whole semesters with me."

I nodded. "Thanks to Sister Lawrence."

"What was that, dear?"

I shook my head. "Nothing."

Since nobody wanted to find out what would happen if we gave patients unrestricted access to needles and scissors, sewing classes were pretty much limited to lobotomy patients, who, as a rule, were very compliant. Since lobotomies had gone out of style in the fifties, most of the women were quite elderly. They shuffled in every Friday night, filed into their seats, and waited.

Progress was slow. They remembered little, approached everything with the same bland, unchanging wonder. The project that Sister Daniel had planned, to teach them to make aprons, was a rather silly undertaking; they were not allowed to cook for themselves. But they seemed to enjoy it, to find purpose in making these useless things. Every week, I taught them to thread the needle, to cut out their patterns, and every week they looked on with fresh amazement. They leaned over my hands and watched me lick the thread to a point and guide its tip through the oversized needle eye. They ran their hands over the soft gingham of their dresses, smoothing them down, and they stared.

I thought it an odd punishment for Unnatural Desires—to be forced to teach these women how to sew—but then Mrs. Pinkerton didn't know anything about the unnatural part of my desire. In the end, I found strange comfort in these Friday nights. The sewing room was on a high floor of the hospital, in a quiet corner of the old wing. From its windows you could make out the lights of the city twinkling below us.

Pale, pasty, and blank, like a linoleum floor that had been scrubbed too many times, these women had had the shine rubbed clean off them. But there was something in their soft obliviousness, their ability to escape the confines of a personality, of a past, that captured my attention. Sometimes, they seemed to have risen above the horrors of the locked ward. Even though they were quite old, they looked young, their faces free from worry lines—the childlike gestures, the girlish giggling. They huddled in corners and told each other secrets. They chased each other around the room.

After the first two Friday nights at the mental hospital, Mrs. Pinkerton stopped coming. She wasn't much of a seamstress, and the atmosphere dragged her down. It was so rare to see Mrs. Pinkerton really laid low by anything that I didn't hold it against her. I convinced Mary Elizabeth to accompany me to the sewing classes. It was not hard. She was eager to show off her prodigious talents as a seamstress.

I am sure Mary Elizabeth heard the rumors that spread through the school about Terry. She could easily have guessed what really happened. She and Susanna Spindale actually saw me sneak out of the Read-A-Thon with Terry. But Mary Elizabeth would not entertain a word of the rumors, and in her own quiet, blindered way, she remained loyal to me. Perhaps she stopped by my locker a few more times than usual in the coming weeks, perhaps she stared a bit longer when she asked me a question about my homework, but she said nothing. She never mentioned the newspaper article or Terry. Mary Elizabeth may have lain awake at night in her four-poster bed in her attic room at the top of the house across from ours and contemplated all that had happened to her friend, but if she did, I did not hear about it. Instead, I heard about Jimmy, whose title had changed from Jimmy-the-Lead-Guitar-Player to Jimmy-the-Boyfriend. While I was miserably unsuccessful in love, Mary Elizabeth had gone off and landed herself a boyfriend. As we threaded needles and stitched patterns for the patients, Mary Elizabeth told me the love story.

It started when Mr. Henderson was called upon to direct a student production of *Guys and Dolls* at the public school in Brighton, just outside Rochester. Jimmy-the-Lead-Guitar-Player was not Catholic. Although Mary Elizabeth was one of the few girls who would actually hold that against a boy, she spent an admirably small amount of time fretting over Jimmy's religious convictions. Instead, in her poised and cautious way, Mary Elizabeth fell in love.

Jimmy had a sizable part in the musical and was having trouble with his solos. Although Jimmy was convinced he had a perfectly good singing voice, Mr. Henderson thought he needed a little extra help. So Mr. Henderson sent Mary Elizabeth over to Jimmy's house to play the piano for him and regale the poor boy with the powers of her perfect pitch. Mary Elizabeth drove herself over to Jimmy's.

"I got there and I was wearing that red sweater, the one with the row of hearts around the front, you know the one?"

I nodded.

"And I brought my music with me, and my songbook and also my flute, just in case. Anyway, I get it all packed into my arms, and I'm rushing up the front steps, and before I even get to the front door, he's opened it and he's right there, his hair curling around his ears the way it does when he's been playing for a while in the basement."

I nodded again.

"And I step inside after him and look around. They have a huge house. It's like room after room after room. The parlor opens onto the dining room, which opens onto the living room. Then there are these cool French doors that go into the music room, and guess what they have? Can you guess?"

"No."

"A grand piano." She grinned at me and handed Mrs. Gold her restitched apron. "I start playing. And he stands really close. I'm showing him the trickier parts of the harmony, and after a moment he sits down next to me. I feel his arm pressing against mine, and I hear him breathing, and then he leans over and I say, 'Are your parents home?' 'No,' he whispers, and he kisses me."

"Was it nice?" I asked.

Mary Elizabeth closed her eyes, her head tilted back an inch, her bottle-cap nose tipped up toward the tin ceiling, and she sighed. "Oh, yes." Then she snapped back to attention. "But I kept thinking, *His parents aren't home. Where are his parents?* And the little dog, he said it was his sister's, kept barking and running around the piano like he was going to announce it to the whole world that I'm sitting there with this boy kissing in the music room and his parents aren't even home." Her brow knit together. "What do you think?" she asked. "Do you think he likes me?"

"It seems like it."

"No, really *likes* me."

I had my suspicions that Mary Elizabeth wanted the parents to come home, not because she did not like kissing Jimmy but because she did not know what to do next. When Mary Elizabeth described it, that he leaned over, that it happened while they sat at the piano, I could only think of the stillness in the room, the silence, that it was a gray spring day. I don't know why it sounded sad.

For the next two months, throughout the rehearsal period for the musical, the two of them kissed on the piano bench. And then there were countless afternoons spent languishing in the Hendersons' basement watching the band practice, watching Jimmy sing. (His singing voice did improve under Mary Elizabeth's tutelage.) Jimmy-the-Lead-Guitar-Player made Mary Elizabeth genuinely happy. He began to take up most of her free time. But at the mental hospital it was just Mary Elizabeth and me, the sewing on our laps, the patients flitting around us, their seams uneven, their needles coming unthreaded.

On one Friday night drive to the mental hospital, Mary Elizabeth told me she was in love with Jimmy. I told her I was very happy for her. And I was, although it felt like she was slipping away from me. Soon I ran out of things to say, and as Mary Elizabeth pulled the car into the hospital parking lot, we both fell silent. She cut off the engine, and we sat for a moment staring up at the tall building.

She turned to me. "Tell me again, whose idea was this?"

"What?"

"Teaching this class to these ladies who never remember anything. I mean, do you think they care? Do you think we're actually making a difference?"

I thought of telling her that we had to teach lobotomized women to sew because I fell in love with a girl instead of a boy. Instead I shrugged.

"It was some harebrained scheme of Mrs. Pinkerton's," I said.

"Oh, Mrs. P! That explains it."

40

EVEN THOUGH SHE no longer sought me out at every lunch, every free period, every study hall, no longer waited for me in the mornings at my locker, walked with me to the buses, and called me every night, Teresa Dinovelli could not completely disappear from my life. Over the next three weeks I saw her almost every day—turning the corner by the library door, outside the third-floor chapel, just beyond Our Lady of the Broken Toes. She would appear on the edges of my field of vision, haunting the periphery, always just out of reach, her dark hair falling close about her face, her paint-stained uniform disappearing around corner after corner. I began to think she existed only in these liminal spaces. The missed chances to talk to her, to look at her for a moment longer, were too much. I wondered if she ever cared for me. I doubted my own memory. I wondered if I had dreamed it all.

Then one day, almost a month later, we spoke. I had stayed late to help Mrs. Pinkerton organize the submissions for our literary magazine and found myself reading in the basement office under the convent well into the afternoon. By the time I looked up at the clock, it was almost five. I shoved my books in my bag, slid the piles of submissions into their folders, and headed back through the underground halls to my locker. As I walked through the basement tunnels, the heating pipes hissing and dripping above me, I thought of Terry. I climbed the stairs and crossed to the school's main floor. I heard a tiny squeaking behind me. It sounded like a mouse, but the rhythm of the little voice was too measured, too even. It grew closer. It was almost right behind me. I turned around and found myself faced with a pair of black utility shoes, poking out from under the hem of a long habit. I looked up, and my gaze passed over the shiny black leather of the shoes to the dark blue weave of a habit, past the knotted rope belt at the waist to the face of Sister Aquinas.

I nodded. "Good afternoon, Sister."

"You're here quite late, Miss Smith."

"I was just"—I pointed down the first-floor hall—"going to my locker."

"But your locker is on the second floor."

"Isn't this the second floor?"

Sister Aquinas shook her head. "No, Miss Smith. This is the first floor." She pointed toward the stairs. "Do you need an escort?"

"No!" I leapt toward the stairwell. "I'll be fine, thank you."

The wimple bobbed up and down once. She was off, squeaking down the hall, the ring of keys tapping against her thigh as she made her way toward the statue of the Virgin. As she passed the light switch, Sister cut off the overhead lights. The hall fell into darkness.

I peered down the corridor. I saw Terry. She was at her locker, kneeling in front of the open door, rolling up a sheaf of drawings. She thrust her hand inside her backpack, rummaged around until she pulled out a rubber band, and began to wrap it around the paper cylinder. I took my hand off the banister, walked over to the lockers, and made my way down the row till I was standing in front of her. She did not look up.

I leaned against the locker next to hers and slid down it until I was sitting next to her. She pulled her calculus book out of her locker, held it for a moment, balanced between her palms, thought better of it, and slipped it back onto a low shelf.

"You can't ignore me forever," I said.

For the first time in a month, Terry looked at me. She blinked, and her lashes brushed against her cheeks. "I thought that's what you wanted."

Her hair was a bit longer, her skin had paled, and she had lost some of the glow on her cheeks, but she was still Terry. I could not stop looking at her. Then I noticed it. At the opening of her blouse, just below the top button, where the bone dips down at the base of the throat—there was nothing there. Her gold crucifix had hung in that spot for as long as I'd known her. It was gone. My hand reached out, touched the indent at the base of her neck.

Terry set down her book bag, leaned in toward me.

"You're not wearing it."

She shook her head. It was such a small gesture I thought I imagined it.

"Did you lose it?"

"No." Her cheek brushed the back of my hand. I could smell her hair. She was that close.

When she leaned over to pick up a pencil, I kissed her. It happened very quickly, and before I could stop myself, her lips were trembling against mine. She dropped the pencil and reached for me. Her fingers pressed into the bone of my back. I started to shake against her. I did not know where to put my hands. I did not want to let go of her. At the same time I regretted approaching her. I pulled away. "I can't do this," I said. I huddled against the locker.

She grabbed the tail of my shirt, pulled me to her, and pressed her face into my collarbone. "I know," she whispered into my neck. Her hair fell across my cheek. A loose strand flew up and attached itself to my lower lip. I breathed in the scent of her—sweet grass and lemons, laundry soap and turpentine. I closed my eyes, ran my hands down her arms till I reached her fingers and pulled them off me.

"Terry," I whispered. "I can't." I pressed my feet into the floor and unbent my knees. I hoisted my backpack onto my shoulder, and walked away. I made it as far as the stairwell before I turned around. "Will you call me tonight?"

She nodded.

"At six-thirty, when my parents are watching the news."

"I'll call."

That was it. We fell into it again. But it was harder this time. It was dangerous. The nuns kept their eyes on us, my mother watched us, and all the while, we took risks. We met behind the grotto after fifth period. We lay on the cold ground under the rhododendrons, our hands stuttering and hungry, pulling at the collars of each other's uniforms, shivering, half naked in the grass. After school, we met in the literary magazine office, wedged a chair under the doorknob, and kept one eye on the door. We listened for the sound of footsteps in the hall, and when they came, we fell into a stunned stillness. I wrapped my hands around her head and pressed her to me. Her breath warmed my neck. We waited for the noise in the hall to fade. Her sweet face hovered next to mine all through that difficult spring.

We started to meet at night, in my backyard, while my parents slept. She rode her bike twenty miles from the northern outskirts of the city to my house. The wet grass at our feet, the warm smell of her body, heated from the ride—I liked these nighttime visits best of all. The darkness protected us, and we would talk for hours. We talked about old movies, *Casablanca* and *Notorious*. I taught her the names of all the trees in our neighborhood. She always brought a book with her. Usually it was an obscure feminist text. One night, she spent the evening convincing me that there were not just two genders but seven. She took hours outlining the different types.

"Imagine what the world would be like if we could see all seven," she whispered.

The next night, she asked me to imagine a world without men. "What if it were only women?" she asked me. "Wouldn't that be amazing?"

I smiled and looked down at the dark grass by our feet. I thought of Roy, and I knew on this I could not follow her. I could not imagine such a place. "Last night, you said there were seven genders," I said. "How did we get back to just two?"

We talked over each other, her hand on the book, holding it open, holding her place, her mind wrapping around each new idea. I watched the color rise on her cheeks as her mouth curled around every word. The hours progressed. We sat huddled by the picnic table on the back lawn.

This is how I like to remember Terry, as she was on those chilly April nights, the dew rising on the grass, the ground softening beneath our feet, when we wandered alone together through the wide squares of darkened yards, from tree to tree, from hedge to hedge. Terry in her bike pants and a white windbreaker, and me beside her, my down jacket sliding off my shoulders, we roamed the darkened landscape of the pristine suburb. In those nightlong conversations, between the half-understood theories, the grand imaginings, I realized that sometimes you have to step outside of goodness to discover who you are. And as we grew closer, as we reached over our own private sorrows to find each other on the grass, the nameless thing inside me, the thing that had been floating loose, unmoored for so long, found its home.

It seems to me that those spring nights went on forever. I am embarrassed to admit, it was less than a month. For a few short weeks, for a few hours on a handful of nights, I was no longer my parents' daughter. I was no longer the child left behind, the vessel for all of Mother's and Father's dashed hopes, the sister without a brother. I was simply in love.

A few hours before dawn, she would leave me. I walked her to the end of the driveway and held on to her hand as she mounted her bike. I ran beside her until we reached the base of the hill. There, she let go of my hand, wrapped her fingers around the ram's-head handlebars, leaned into the hill, and called back to me, "I'll see you tomorrow."

After she disappeared over the crest of the hill, I turned around and looked back at our house.

Between its two top windows, there was a small, octagonal porthole. It was the only ornamentation on the spare colonial façade. I stared up at the eight-sided window, and that one blind, unblinking eye stared back at me. My parents' bedroom lay on the other side of it. I imagined them up there, behind the white walls. Just above me, above the fresh, greening world, above this nighttime romance, they slept, turning beneath the cotton sheets.

As I gazed back at the house, I heard a humming in my brain. I closed my eyes. A tingling sensation tickled my limbs, and slowly, slowly, my insides floated out of me, slipped through some imperceptible hole in the top of my head, into the spring night, and ran after the girl on the bicycle. I felt the wind rushing against Terry's face, the soft hairs on her arms rising in the chill, her feet pressing into the pedals as the road rolled on beneath her and she moved further and further away from me. Then I opened my eyes, walked around the house, down the stone path by the back porch, and pushed open the back door.

When I woke after a meager hour of sleep, it was still dark. Early mornings, before Father woke, before the first light of the sun, I would shake and shiver under the covers in my flannel pajamas. I pushed the blankets back, got down on my knees next to my bed, the cold floorboards pressing against my kneecaps, and folded my hands in front of me. I gazed up at the picture of the Sacred Heart of Jesus that hung at the head of the bed.

"God?" I whispered. "Are you there?"

Instead of God, I saw Roy's face burning in the van. And Raymond Cino, the postal worker, struggling up the hill. The smoke, the flames surrounded me. I could not breathe. Then I heard Mother calling from the doorframe of the house, *Don't run away from me. Don't you dare run away!*

Into the silence, in the chill of the morning room, into the blank face of Jesus hanging on the wall, I said, "I'll stop. I'll never see Teresa again."

I promised never to touch her, never again to smell the sweat and salt on her skin after a long ride. I vowed to break it off the very next night, right away, as soon as she arrived, winded and panting, pulling out her water bottle, striding her sure and hopping gait toward me, across the back lawn. All through the day I prepared my speech—exactly how I would put it, how I would tell Terry it was over.

And then she arrived, her white jacket floating toward me. A smile lighted across her face as soon as she caught sight of me, and before I knew it she was next to me, one hand on the bike, one hand reaching for me. I pulled her to me and buried my face in her warm neck.

Terry knew there was something tugging at me. She knew it was more than the chilly night air that made me tremble on the bench as we sat across from each other every night and talked. I would ask, "Why can't we tell?"

"Are you crazy?"

"I just need to tell someone."

"Tell them what?"

"About us."

"Why?"

"I don't know. I just need to." What I could not say was that I hated the lying. The secrecy and the hiding made what we did seem worse.

She stood up and walked over to my side of the picnic table. She sat next to me. "Wait till you get out, till you're in college."

I looked up at her. I had not thought of that. Was I going to "get out"? I could not imagine a world beyond this yard. I was not sure I wanted to.

Terry put her hand on my arm. I pulled back and turned away from her. She reached for me. I don't know what we did or said after that. What comes back to me now, from those stilted, halting conversations, is her voice, the sweet cadence of it, as she leaned in. "Tell me," she whispered. "Tell me."

41

AROUND EVERY CORNER, at the end of every hall, at the foot of my bed, I found my mother. She stared down at me, her arms crossed, brow knitted, light from my reading lamp reflecting off her glasses. She felt the shift in me that spring after I read the article. And although she never spoke of it, she never forgot the call from Miss Beal. I sat distracted at dinner, resting my head in my hand and staring into the middle distance for hours. Every night, as I gazed out the kitchen window, the water running in the sink, the dishes piling up, my hands resting in the soapy water, I felt her eyes on me, appraising, searching, waiting.

Mother shook her head a lot that spring. She said, "There's something wrong with you. Something very, very wrong." Or, "Where did you come from? You're not my daughter. You could not be my daughter." And then, as quickly and silently as she appeared, she would walk her tight-hipped gait down the hall, out the door, around the corner.

As the ground warmed and the light began to linger in the sky well after the dinner hour, she played an elaborate and dangerous game of Kremlin. A series of young men appeared at our front door. When the first one arrived, a book tucked under his right elbow, I thought little of it.

"Hello," he said through the screen door. "I brought by that book you wanted to borrow." He held out a volume of French poetry.

"I didn't ask for a book," I said. But there it was, in his hand, its heavy weight, its rich blue cover. "I didn't ask for this."

Mother arrived. "Oh, Dan!" she said. "How nice of you to bring it by." She gave me a little nudge in his direction. "Why don't you ask him in?"

I unhooked the latch and held the door open for him. Mother stepped between us. "Alison," she said, placing a hand on my shoulder. "You remember Dan, don't you? He was at the last Christmas party."

"Hi, Dan," I said.

We stood in the foyer and glanced at each other. "Would you like something to eat, Dan?" Mother asked.

He opened his mouth to answer, but before he got the first word out, she was talking again. "Offer him something to eat, Alison."

"We have some brownies." I started for the kitchen. Mother put her hand on my shoulder and stopped me. "I'll get them. You go sit in the living room with Dan." As she passed, she whispered, "Tuck in your shirt."

I led Dan to the couch, tucking in my shirttails. He sat down. Mother arrived with a plate of brownies and two glasses of Pepsi. And before I knew what was happening, I was sitting beside this boy on the couch, sipping cola and holding an overlarge volume of French Symbolist poetry in my hand. Mother stood in the living room doorway and said, "I'll just leave you two young people alone." As she left the room, she dimmed the lights.

I set down my glass and glanced over at Dan. He had curly blond hair, thick eyebrows, and a fine, square jaw. "Whose idea was this?"

"I don't know." He bit into a brownie. "I think your mother talked to mine."

I nodded. He chewed. "You want to go out sometime?" he asked. "I have a van. Me and my friend take it to the Dead when they're in town. We sleep out on the grass. It's really cool."

"Are you asking me to go to a Grateful Dead concert?"

He nodded and picked up another brownie. "These would be better if they had some hash in them."

When I told Mother about the van and the all-night concert, she said, "It sounds very nice. Why don't you go?"

I pointed at the door through which Dan had just exited. "A boy wants to take me out all night in his van and you think that's 'nice'?"

She smiled at me, holding the book of poetry in her hands, and said nothing.

Later, when Terry arrived, I was so flummoxed that I could not say a word to her. "Tell me," she whispered. But I remained silent. So she made up a game for us to play. She called it Blind. She wrapped a bandanna around my eyes, took my hand, and led me around the yard, the neighborhood, the back streets, taking me to new places and then removing the blindfold. First, she took me to a yard three streets away. I had never been in it before. When she took off the bandanna and I looked around at the apple tree, the birdbath, the bank of lilacs along the back fence, I was completely disoriented.

"Are we still in my neighborhood?" I asked.

She leaned toward me, tipped her mouth to my ear, and whispered, "You tell me."

The next night she led me up the slope of the hill to the top of the street and to the edge of the main road. I heard the rev of an engine and the rush of air as a truck passed. I shook my head. "No," I said. I pulled off the bandanna.

"You're cheating," she said.

I curled the bandanna around my hand and ran down the hill. I passed our house and I kept running. I ran to the dead end at the bottom of the street.

Terry caught up with me at the mouth of the gully. "What's wrong?" she asked.

"Anywhere but the main road," I said, gasping for breath. "I don't like that road." I looked down at the bandanna. "Why don't you let me blind you?"

I wrapped the bandanna around her eyes and led her through the darkness into the gully. We sidestepped down the steep ravine, her hands out, reaching for me. When we got to the bottom and the ground leveled out, she tucked her fingers under my elbow, and I led her all the way to the other side of the gully.

"I hear water rushing," she said as we took the low, ragged path by the stream. And then a moment later, "Where are we?"

"You'll see."

It was slow going. The path was rugged and covered in tiny stones. I had to concentrate to keep her from falling. It took us an hour of stumbling, of her feeling her way, putting her hands in mine and saying, "Which way now, Al?" till finally we stood in front of it, in all its sinking glory. I had never shown anyone this place before. Not Mary Elizabeth. Not Susanna, not Mother, not Father. I untied the bandanna. It fell off her eyes.

It had lost a good deal of its splendor in the years since Roy and I first found it, but the shock of it, that striking feature—a house completely halved—was not lost on Terry. She stepped forward, shivered, stared up the height of it, walked around it once.

"Where's the other half?" she asked.

I took a step toward her. "The other half?"

It was a question Roy and I had never entertained. In all our discussions of this mystery house, in our musings about the lost family and the road trip they took, our examinations of the rooms, its hidden treasures, Roy and I had never asked where the other half of the house had gone. I shook my head, stuffed the bandanna in my back pocket, and put out my hand. She took it. "Come on," I said, and I showed her the house.

After that night Terry and I played three more games of Blind. I took her to the hidden trail behind the Wilsons' house and to the field at the end of the road where Roy and I had played frisbee. The fourth place I took her was closer than any of our other destinations. It was a short walk and the last game of Blind we ever played.

42

THE AIR SMELLED of woodsmoke. The moon was out. I shivered on the back lawn, waiting for Terry. I knew I would hear the gears on the bike chattering against the chain before I saw her. After a half hour, the *tisk tisk tisk* of the chain cut through the spring air. She coasted into the driveway, stood up on her bike, swung one leg over the center bar, and balanced both feet on the left footrest. With the street rolling out behind her, she floated out of the darkness. Once she reached the van, she hopped off, ducked past the lilac bush by the chimney, and pushed her bike through the ivy, onto the back lawn.

I ran over to her and grabbed the bike. "How was the ride?" I asked.

"Long." She gasped.

I pushed her bike across the lawn, past the garage, and down to the back fence, where the forsythia grew. She followed me, pulled a bottle of water out of her backpack, and let the water pour over her lips and down her throat. She took my hand.

"I want to show you something," I said, and I pulled out the bandanna.

She smiled. "What could it be?"

I wrapped the bandanna around her eyes, tied it twice at the base of her skull, took her hand, and guided her toward the garage. By now the route back to the fort was overgrown with brambles. Wild raspberry bushes and skunkweed had nudged their way onto the path. All that remained was a narrow footpath from the end of the garage down through the underbrush.

"Duck," I instructed. I pushed the branches aside. When we

were standing in front of the fort, I pulled the bandanna from her eyes.

I do not know what it must have looked like to her, that run-down, half-neglected, half-loved pile of wood, whether in that first glimpse she found it a treasure or an eyesore. The roof of the second story had collapsed. All that remained were two buckled walls and a framework, slouching across the shingles of the fort. Terry blinked, shook her head, and stepped away from me.

"You have a hideout!" She grabbed the door and pulled it open.

Once we were inside, I latched the door, and the darkness closed around us.

"It's absolutely pitch-black in here. No one could catch us," Terry said. She reached for my hand.

Her fingers brushed my arm as I made my way over to the table and felt around till I had the lantern by the handle. I located the box of matches and lit the wick. I handed her the lantern. "Look," I said.

First there were the books—all those incomprehensible physics texts and his favorite novels—*Where the Red Fern Grows* and *The Count of Monte Cristo*. Next there were the walls, plastered with the copied pages from his journal. I had laid out his baseball card collection and his Boston Red Sox cap on the overturned doghouse.

Terry held the lantern very still as she looked around. The wind moaned as it rushed through the crack under the door, the crickets screamed in the tall pines by the side fence, but Terry was silent. She had her back to me. I could not see her face, but I could tell that something was wrong. Her neck straightened and went stiff. Her fingers, gripping the wooden handle, bore down till the knuckles lost their color and went white.

In that moment I realized how little we knew about each other. I knew she was the best physics student Mercy had ever seen. I knew she had three sisters and her father worked as a mechanic in a body shop on Ridge Road. He hated Terry, his eldest daughter, but I did not know why. I knew that something bad had happened in the school she attended before Mercy, but she never told me what it was. And I hadn't told Terry anything about Roy. She didn't know about the rebuilt van, or Paul, the Encyclopedia Boy, or the Before-People. She didn't know about the secret visits to the fort and the hidden food.

I thought about her taking the fall for me when we were caught in the dean of discipline's bed, and about the day in the art room when I asked her to leave me alone. Through all that, she never cried. Now she was crying. She was looking at the walls, at the photos and pages copied from his journal, and her cheeks were wet with tears. I had brought the newspaper article out with me. I slipped my hand in my back pocket and ran my finger along the edge of the page. The lantern held out before her, her shadow flung up against the wall, she looked at me. I pulled out the article and held it up for her to see. She did not look at it. Even from that small distance, she seemed far away. There was something in her eyes I had never seen before, not in all that we had been through, not in the fights, or the separation, or the hours of talking. It was pity. She stepped toward me. The lantern began to swing in her hand. "Al," she whispered. "What is all this?"

I dropped my hand and slid the article back into my pocket. I shook my head. "I'm cold. Let's go inside."

Then Terry noticed the daisy-print plate and the photograph that I kept beside it. She lowered the lantern, held it close to the plate. The flame inside the dome jumped and shivered. She stared at the photo of the two of us. In the photo, I am three, Roy is six, and we are standing outside our aunt Jeanne's house on the front walk. Roy is grinning. I have a bit of a scowl on my face. His arm is wrapped around my shoulder, holding me in place. Terry looked back at the plate. The remnants of last night's meal remained. A bit of broccoli collected in the corner. The only trace of the meat was a few smears of grease in the center of the plate. There was no silverware. She raised her eyes and looked at me.

"Do you eat out here?" she asked.

I shook my head.

"Yes, you do. You eat out here with him." She pointed at the photo.

I looked away from her.

"How come I never see you eat?" Terry looked from the plate to the photo and back again. Then she looked up at me, at my skinny arms folded across my chest.

"I don't—"

"You give him your food."

I stepped toward the door.

She stood up and put her hand on my arm. "That's why you're so thin."

She started to pace. The space was so close that I had to stand pressed against the door while she walked back and forth in front of me. I slid my hand around my back, grabbed the latch. She slammed herself into the chair by the window and tapped her knuckles against the pane of glass that Roy had installed.

"Don't touch that window," I said. "You'll break it."

Terry looked at me, then looked back at the window and shook her head. She tapped the window harder, studied its depth, the sharp edge of her knuckle. Then, as quickly as she had sat down, she stood up. She grabbed my hand and pulled open the front door of the fort. She dragged me back down the path, through the brambles, out onto the lawn, and toward the house.

When we reached the back door, she opened it and pulled me into the kitchen. There, in front of the refrigerator, she let go of my hand. She rummaged around in the refrigerator till she pulled out two Tupperware containers, one of broccoli, one of leftover chicken. She opened the cupboard, removed a plate, and dumped the contents of the two containers onto it. She handed it to me. I would not take it from her hands. She slammed the plate down on the table, grabbed silverware from the drawer, and pulled out a chair. "Sit," she commanded.

"You'll wake my parents."

"I don't care." She pointed to the chair.

"I ate dinner already."

"No you didn't. You brought it out there and fed it to that dead boy."

I started for the door. She grabbed me and shoved me into the seat. She picked up the fork, put it in my hand, and sat across from me, waiting.

"Terry—"

"Don't talk." She pointed at the plate. "Eat."

I picked up the knife, cut off a piece of chicken breast, put it in my mouth, and chewed. There we sat for the better part of the night while I slowly made my way through the plate of food. Terry watched the food travel from the plate to the fork, to my mouth, making sure I swallowed every bite. It was not exactly how I had imagined the evening. I had hoped to show her Roy's journal, his physics notebooks, his coin collection. I had hoped to finally share the article with someone and that, together, Terry and I would travel the distance between the dead and the living. But I had Terry all wrong. She did not want to fade away. She wanted to live.

I finished the food. Terry looked down at the clean plate and smiled. I felt queasy. I started shaking. It felt like my lungs were filling with smoke.

"Are you okay?" she asked.

"I guess something didn't agree with me."

I grabbed my stomach, lunged for the sink, and threw up.

43

I WAS AN EXCELLENT switchboard operator: devoted, constant, reliable, and efficient. Until the night when I crossed the threshold of Sister Barbara's room, I had never broken a single rule, never showed up late for work, never once slacked in my duties to the nuns. I wish I could say the same for my new career as a library page. I was terrible. I read more books than I ever shelved, never helped a single patron find a book, and one evening, I misfiled over a hundred cards in the card-catalog system.

When I wasn't inflicting irreparable damage on the card catalog, I was curled up in a back corner reading. I would arrive, grab a shelving cart, disappear into the miles and miles of metal bookshelves, find a deserted spot, usually around human evolution—a particularly unpopular Dewey decimal number—and read all evening. I looked up books on fire, on hyperthermia. I found some information on burn victims. There were accounts of great fires in history such as the fire in Coconut Grove or the San Francisco fire. When I became overwhelmed by the images from these fires, I researched the dominance of right-handedness, the domestication of cats; I read biographies of the painters Egon Schiele and Paul Klee, books of early Norwegian history, and books on magicians who ate glass and rocks.

About the same time that Dan arrived on our front stoop with a volume of French Symbolist poetry, I became obsessed with the Lives of the Saints. I pored over ancient hagiographies that I found on my evening library shift. I wrote out my favorite lives in a journal. I kept charts of miracles. Each night, I uncovered stranger and stranger stories. Saint Lucy became a particular favorite. I found a prayer card for her—a hologram, where objects in the picture move when you move the image. In this one, Lucy held a plate with two eyeballs on it—not an uncommon image for the Patron Saint of Eyesight. When you moved the card, Lucy's eyes closed, and so did the eyes on the plate. Together, they blinked out at the viewer, open and shut, open and shut. I could stare at the hologram for hours, watching the plate eyes blink.

I started going to church on my own. Not for Mass but just to sit. The blond wood of the pews curving beneath me, the padded kneeler at my feet, I tried to think. The afternoons in the silent church, the evenings of research, the nights on the back lawn with Terry, and the lack of sleep precipitated a slow and quiet unraveling in my brain. Despite Terry's efforts, I still ate very little. Saving food for Roy had become more than a gesture of grief. By now, self-starvation had become a habit. It was perhaps the hunger, the malnutrition, that superseded all my other troubles. Without food, I could no longer think clearly.

One day, when Mother drove me to my shift at the library, she parked the car, turned off the engine, and reached behind her for her purse.

"What are you doing?" I asked.

She smiled into her purse, unzipped the side pocket, pulled out her lipstick, craned the rearview mirror toward her, and began applying it. "I thought I would go in and have a look around," she said. She blotted her lips.

I pointed at the low brick building. Above the glass-fronted doors stood a sign that read BRIGHTON MEMORIAL LIBRARY. "In there?"

"Don't look so shocked." She pushed the rearview mirror back into place and stuffed the used tissue in her purse. "I know how to read."

Once inside, I checked in, grabbed a shelving cart, and rolled it toward the nonfiction section. I kept my eyes on Mother. She walked around for a while and stared at the signs above the card catalogs. She picked up a pencil from the pencil box by the bin of scrap paper on the main table. She examined it and set it down again. Mother found her way to the reference desk. She smiled at Mrs. Krauss, my boss. She picked the cardboard "Can I Help You?" placard off the desk tripod and pointed to it. "Yes, you can!"

I slunk behind my shelving cart and disappeared into the recesses of the nonfiction section.

Mrs. Krauss must have shown her how to use the card catalog, for the next thing I knew Mother was marching up and down the nonfiction aisles, with a scrap of paper in her hand, ticking off items on her list. She chose five books, and cradling them in her arms, she tracked me down in the 800s, near poetry, and waved good-bye. "I'll be back at nine to pick you up, baby."

The next night, at dinner, she began to read aloud to Father and me.

"The first year is the hardest," she recited. "When the first round of anniversaries passes, the grief lessens."

I glanced at the cover of the book. It was a slim volume; in bold green letters, it read, *On Death and Dying*. I looked over at the pile of books to her right. They were all Christian self-help books about grief. I set down my fork, closed my hand over the paper bag in my lap, and waited.

Mother set down her book and passed Father the potatoes. "It's supposed to get easier." She opened the book again and read a little further. "Is it getting easier," she asked, raising her eyes from the page and staring at me, "for you?"

I gulped. "Me?"

She nodded. "Is it getting easier, not having Roy here?"

Father jumped when he heard his son's name. "Vonnie?" he asked. "What are you doing?"

"I'm asking my daughter a question." She placed her finger on the page to mark her place and leaned back in her chair. "I want to know if it's getting easier, now that Roy's been gone awhile."

"Mom!"

Father stared across his mound of potatoes into Saint Jude's face. "Why does she do it, Jude?"

"I am her mother. I have a right to know." She turned to me. "What are you feeling?" she asked.

I picked up my fork. "You're kidding, right?"

"No, I am not kidding. What are you feeling, right now?"

I shook my head and stared into the tines of my fork. "I don't know."

"Well, you had better figure it out." She glanced down at her book. "It says here talking is important." She pointed to the page. "We have to talk about our feelings."

Father pushed his chair back. He threw his napkin over his plate. "I can't take this, Vonnie," he said, and he walked out of the room.

A moment later, he was back, standing in the doorframe. Mother and I looked up, waiting for him to say something, to explode or apologize. Instead, he bent over the table, picked up Saint Jude, and walked out again.

Over the next few weeks she read sections of each of these books and then returned to the library and checked out five new books. She became very attached to Elisabeth Kübler-Ross's *On Death and Dying*. I still remember her face leaning over the book every night at dinner, her loading peas onto her fork and saying, "First comes denial, then anger, and then bargaining."

"Mom, please," I pleaded. "Stop."

"I thought you liked books."

"Not those books." I pointed at her pile.

She grabbed my finger. "Alison, you need to know this."

"Vonnie," Father yelled. "I am sick of this." He threw his fork. It skittered across the tabletop and clattered onto the floor.

For a moment we were all quiet. I held my breath. Then Mother leaned over and said, "This must be the anger stage."

After that night, Mother stopped reading at the dinner table. Instead, she took to showing up every night at the foot of my bed, a book in hand, and reciting from one of the chapters on stages of grief. This was an improvement over the nights when she would arrive, no book in hand, cross her arms, stare down at me, and say, "There's something wrong with you." After a week of reading at the end of my bed, she sat down, smoothed her hands across the bedspread, and asked, "What are you feeling?"

"Not this again."

"Alison, you have to answer me." She looked at her book. "Do you understand that Roy is gone?"

"Mom!"

"It's the first stage, baby. If you can't get that one, you'll never get on to the bargaining."

"I know, Mom. I get it. You've read them to me every night for the last two weeks."

"We need to talk about your feelings."

"Okay," I said. I set down my book and crossed my arms over my chest. "What do you want to know?"

"First, you have to get out of bed."

"Why?"

"Because you're wallowing. And wallowing stalls the grieving process."

"The 'grieving process'?"

"Get up."

"It's ten o'clock at night. Aren't I allowed to be in bed at night?"

"But you're always in bed. You're always tired. You never show any interest in anything around you—"

I stopped her short. "Just because I don't want to go out with some boy in his van does not mean I'm wallowing."

"Something's wrong with you."

"Mom," I whined. "Please." I picked at the edge of the sheet. "Okay, look, you're right. Something is wrong with me. Very wrong. And I can't help it."

She grabbed me by the arm.

"Ow, you're hurting me!"

She pulled me down the stairway, her hand clamped on my upper arm, and into the kitchen. She slammed her library book down on the countertop and pointed to a chair. I sat in it. She stood over me. "How do you feel?" she asked.

"Right now? Bad."

"Bad how?"

I did not reply.

"I bet you miss Roy."

"Yes, I do. Can I go back to my room now?" I looked out the window. Terry would arrive in less than two hours, and I would be waiting for her on the back lawn. Ever since she found out about the food in the fort, she brought a snack with her on her nightly visits. If I wouldn't eat it, she grew angry with me. "I miss him," I said. "All the time."

Mother sat next to me. "Baby," she whispered. "He isn't coming back. You know that, don't you?"

"Don't say that."

"You can see him in heaven someday, when you're an old lady. But he's not coming back here." She shook her head. She tried to look into my eyes, but I moved away from her.

"I wish I got into the van with him," I said.

"What did you say?"

"I wish I died with him."

"No," she said. She got up. She shook her head. She looked around her. She picked up the book and then set it down. "You are not feeling that. You can't be feeling that."

I stared at the gold flecks in the Formica tabletop and watched as they blurred and washed over.

"Royden!" she called out. "Royden, she wants to die." She rushed out of the kitchen, into the living room, where Father sat in his green chair reading the paper.

After that conversation, Mother stopped showing up at my door at night. She stopped asking about my feelings. For a week, she retreated and left me in peace. I went to bed early, slept for a few hours, and set my alarm for midnight. I sneaked out onto the back lawn to wait for Terry.

I brought the hagiographies to school, and after last period, I sat on the lawn, spread the books out across the grass, and read while I waited for the bus. Mary Elizabeth and Susanna Spindale often joined me. Mary Elizabeth was teaching herself to crochet. She was making a set of matching socks and sweater vests for her first year at college. As she sat with long strands of lavender yarn looped around her fingers, Susanna perched across from her, leaning back, sipping dreamily on the end of an overlong plastic cigarette holder. In April, Susanna Spindale had finally seen *Breakfast at Tiffany's*. Almost immediately, she procured an old-fashioned holder and crammed the end of her Virginia Slim in its tip.

Holding the cumbersome cigarette filter between her first two fingers, she waved it about in the crisp spring air. "She's changed my life," Susanna said. She placed the tip of the filter between her lips.

"Who?"

"Holly Golightly," Susanna said, holding the filter in place with her teeth.

"I'm surprised it took you this long to see it," I said.

Mary Elizabeth turned toward me. "What's she talking about?"

"It's somebody in an old movie," I said.

Terry walked to the edge of the parking lot, looked around to make sure none of the Sisters were watching, and called my name. When I looked up, she was spelling something out for me with her hands. We had developed a series of secret gestures so that we could communicate during the school day. She was asking me to meet her at the grotto. I shook my head. Susanna was on to something. She had been watching me very closely over the last month. Terry made the same gesture again. I shook my head and signaled that I would explain later. She signaled one last time, telling me that she would meet me behind my house that night.

Susanna leaned back, sucked on her cigarette filter, and watched this interaction. After Terry had walked away, she slid her sunglasses down her nose and said, "That was weird."

"What was weird?" Mary Elizabeth asked. She did not look up from her crocheting.

Susanna sat up, plucked the filter from her mouth, and waved it in the direction of the parking lot. "Don't you see what is going on?"

"What?" Mary Elizabeth asked. She glanced at me.

I shook my head. "Nothing's going on."

Susanna sighed. She leaned back on her elbows and took another drag off her filter. With her free hand she flipped the pages of one of my hagiographies. "What's all this about?"

"I don't know," I said. "But isn't it interesting?"

"That you can't stop reading about saints?" She pulled one of her opera gloves over her elbow and peered up at the sun. "In a sick sort of way."

"It's funny how the saints were such failures."

"What do you mean?" Mary Elizabeth asked.

"Take Saint Lydwina, the patron saint of ice skating. She was such a bad skater that she fell on the ice and died. What kind of example is that?" Mary Elizabeth set down her hook and yarn. Susanna lay back and rested her head in the grass. "Then there's Saint Blaise," I continued. "Patron of sore throats. Why? Because he had his throat cut. Why do we pray to them?"

"Because they tried," Mary Elizabeth said.

"But they failed!"

"What do you want from them?" Susanna asked, flicking ash into the grass. "They did the best they could."

I turned away from her. "What do you know about it, anyway?"

Susanna sat up and snatched the book away from me. "You better watch yourself. This one"—she nodded at Mary Elizabeth—"and Terry are going to graduate. Next year, I'm all you'll have."

"Give me the book," I said.

"Give her the book," Mary Elizabeth said.

Susanna held it away from me. She started flipping through it. "Maybe I should take a look at it. Maybe I'll learn something. Like why Terry Dinovelli can't keep her eyes off you."

I grabbed for the book. Susanna stood up and held it behind her back.

I put out my hand. "The book, please."

"The buses are here," Mary Elizabeth said. She packed up her crocheting supplies.

"Walk home," Susanna said to me.

"I can't. I have to work at the library."

"I don't know what you're up to," Susanna said. "But I bet it's big trouble."

I grabbed my bag and ran away from her, toward the buses.

That evening, Mother's bedroom visitations resumed. Instead of a book, she arrived with a slim envelope, pulled out the pink slip of paper, and laid it on the bedspread. It was an application for a learner's permit.

"Sign this," she said.

I grabbed the paper off the bed. "I'll get my learner's permit. But that's all."

She nodded. The next afternoon, I found myself in a long line at the DMV, holding my birth certificate and my Social Security card.

44

THE FOLLOWING MONDAY, as I squeezed through a crowd of girls rushing the chapel doors on the third floor, Jenny Silan squealed and put her arms out toward me.

"I knew we would both get it," she cried. "I voted for you!" Jenny had not spoken to me since the afternoon of the debate. Now she stood in front of me beaming. "Did you vote for me?" she asked.

I stepped away from her, clutching my books against my chest. "What are you talking about?"

"We both got in!"

"In what?"

"The May Court, silly."

Behind her the crowd grew. Girls in back stood on tiptoe, craning their heads to see a white sheet of paper that had been taped to the chapel door. I could not make out the words on the page, but I could see that it was a list of names.

Beth Mier pushed her way out of the throng of girls. Her face was red and blotchy. Tears streamed down her cheeks. Jenny nodded at her. "Beth didn't make it," she whispered. "You beat her out."

"*I* beat her out?"

"Well, somebody did. She made the semifinals, then got eliminated." Jenny eyed me for a moment. I had not combed my hair in several days, and it lay, matted and lank, in one long mass down my back. I glanced down at my sweater. It was inside out.

Susanna Spindale walked up, flipped her hair off her shoulder with one gloved hand, balanced her books against one hip, and sighed. "I suppose congratulations are in order. You got it. I didn't."

Jenny hoisted her backpack further up her shoulder. "I have a free fourth period. Do you want to hang out?"

Terry and I had agreed not to talk in the school halls, so when she walked up, pushing through the crowd, I pretended not to see her. She didn't even bother to look at the list. Her backpack bumped up against Jenny. Jenny stumbled forward.

"Will you watch it!" she called after Terry. Terry did not turn around. Jenny cut her eyes at me. "Do you still hang out with her?"

"Why?" I asked.

Jenny shrugged. A lock of curly red hair fell across her cheek. She unclasped her barrette and smoothed the strand back in place. "She's just weird, that's all." Jenny grinned. "It doesn't matter. You're in the May Court!" She spread her arms out as she spoke.

"There must have been a mistake," I said.

"Spare me the false modesty," Susanna said. She shifted her books off of her hip. She walked away, calling over her shoulder, "You're already in." Her sleek, black head disappeared into the crowd.

Jenny walked across the hall to congratulate the May Queen. I pushed my way through the crowd toward the chapel doors. There I was, third from the top, next to the words "Scroll Bearer." Mary Elizabeth was elected as well, as the Crown Bearer.

I walked through the day in a haze, accepting congratulations, nodding at my classmates, looking for a glimpse of Terry. When fifth period arrived, I skipped study hall and waited for her at our assigned spot behind the grotto. She didn't show. I found her at her locker after school.

"Where were you?"

She looked at me. "Oh. Hi."

"Why didn't you meet me during study hall?"

"I was studying for a calc test."

"You could have sent me a note or something. I was freezing out there."

"I figured you were busy."

"Busy?"

"Scroll Bearer, second in line for the throne. If anything should happen to the queen and she is unable to fulfill her duties . . ." She threw her textbooks in her book bag.

"You know I didn't want this."

"Like hell you didn't. Walking around the halls with those Saints' Lives." Terry slammed her locker shut and fiddled with the lock. "If you think that's going to make it okay, guess again." She shoved her calculus book in her bag, pulled her backpack onto her back, and walked toward the stairs.

I caught up with her by the stairwell and grabbed her arm. "I can't believe I have to apologize for being in the May Court."

Beth walked down the hall. Terry made a sign with her hand to keep quiet. Beth passed us and started down the stairs. Once she was out of sight, I leaned toward Terry. "You think I feel good about this?"

"Deep down, I think you feel just super," Terry said as she pulled on her wool cap. "You've fooled them all."

The news of my election to the May Court thrilled Mother. She hugged me when she found out. "I knew you could do it," she said, as if I had accomplished something. You did not run for the May Court. You were not supposed to campaign. You were nominated by your peers, in a silent ballot. This did not deter Mother.

"I'm so proud of you, baby," she said that night at dinner, her bright face beaming over the pork chops.

Members of the May Court were required to wear long white dresses to the May Day Mass. Mother made plans to find the perfect dress for me.

"How about a Gunne Sax?" she asked the next morning at breakfast. "Gunne Sax makes such pretty things."

"You're kidding, right?" I said.

She picked out a dotted swiss thing at the mall. White and virginal and two sizes too big. We took it to a tailor in the city to have it altered. They pinned me into it, took it in, in the waist, the bust, the hips—just about everywhere. They asked us to come back in two weeks for a final fitting.

Those were a difficult two weeks. Terry and I fought about the May Court. She would not let it go. At one point she stopped talking to me. Still, I waited for her during every free period, huddled behind the grotto, under the rhododendron. I waited for her after school, in the literary office under the convent, at night in the backyard, hoping that she would come and find me. She never did.

I could not figure out what Terry wanted from me. She was the one who wanted to keep our affair a secret. I had gone and stumbled upon the perfect cover—the May Court—and still she was angry with me. It began to seem to me as if she wanted it both ways. And it began to seem to her like I had it both ways. I was so filled with guilt and worry that I stopped eating altogether.

When we went back two weeks later to have the final fitting, the dress was still too large. The seamstress grabbed the extra fabric around the waist. "I know this was right. I pinned it myself," she said.

I looked down at the dress, hanging off me, and shrugged. "I think it looks all right."

The seamstress took Mother aside. "There's something wrong with your daughter."

Mother clutched at her purse. "What do you mean?"

"My measurements are never wrong." She glanced over at me. "She was already so thin."

Mother smiled. "There's nothing wrong with her." She relaxed her grip on her purse. "She's just thin. We're all thin. It's a thin family."

The seamstress wound her tape measure around her hand and shook her head. "She needs to see a doctor."

"There's nothing wrong with her," Mother repeated. She rummaged in her purse and pulled out her checkbook.

*　*　*

May Day dawned a week later. It turned out to be perfect weather, sunny and mild. Mary Elizabeth squeezed my hand as we crossed the parking lot in our long white dresses. "I'm glad you got in," she said, and she smiled at me. As soon as we reached the grass by the front walk, she started running. "I'll see you inside," she called over her shoulder as she rushed up the auditorium steps.

Susanna walked by, wearing a trim Jackie O knockoff. From her pillbox hat to her patent leather pumps, she was clad entirely in black. Susanna had grumbled for the first few days about her exclusion from the court, but she tried to make good. She even helped the Sisters weave the flowered wreaths for our hair.

"I'm not bitter," she told me as we stood outside the main steps to the auditorium. "Even though I have the most divine white muslin dress. It would be perfect."

"Nice outfit," I said.

She pinched the scratchy fabric of my dress between her thumb and forefinger. "Mmm," she said and wrinkled her nose. "Where did you find this?"

"Mother took me to the mall."

"At least it's sleeveless." She fluffed up the ruffle around the neck. "Maybe I should have carried around a copy of the Saints' Lives. It seems to have worked for you." She handed me the wreath of baby's breath. "Here's your crown of thorns."

"Give me a break, Susanna." I grabbed the wreath.

She squinted across the lawn. "Is that your dad over there?"

"It is. He must have taken time off from work to come to this." I waved to him.

"Well, I've got to scamper on, mourn with a few of the other virgins. Go in peace, my child," she whispered.

"Oh, shut up," I said, mashing the wreath down on my head.

As Susanna took off across the lawn, a dozen wreaths of baby's breath looped over her arms like enormous bracelets, Terry walked toward me. It was the first time she had come near me in a week. I was thrilled to see her, but my father was closing in. I took a step toward her, but when she saw Father approaching, she turned and started walking in the other direction. I did not see her for another three hours, till after the ceremony was over.

We processed down the main aisle of the auditorium, one at a time, while Sister Daniel played a Debussy prelude on the piano. I remember the flashes from the cameras popping all around us when the Queen placed the crown of flowers on the statue of the Virgin. I blinked into a bank of cameras, all those girls in summer dresses with their Olympus automatics held out to us. I was almost blinded by the brightness of the flashes. I remember being led off the stage and outside to the Virgin's Grotto, where we began the round of processing and posing and crowning and genuflecting all over again. And I remember, from the dizzy height of those grotto steps, staring down at my mother's smiling face.

45

FOLLOWING THE MASS and the crowning ceremony in the Virgin's Grotto, the Sisters of Mercy hosted a charity bazaar. The fund-raiser, a sort of indoor carnival, was held in the decrepit gymnasium. Under the efficient direction of Sister Rose, the aging gym was transformed into a sea of light and color. Sister Daniel baked the sweets. Sister Pat dressed as a clown and handed out balloons. Sister Robert played the banjo. And Sister Aquinas volunteered for the dunking pool. Those of us who had almost failed trigonometry lined up to exact our revenge. When she was dunked, in full habit with her glasses slipping down her nose, she always emerged from the cold tank water laughing.

Even Sister Barbara loosened up at the May Day bazaar. She snuck up behind her favorite pupils and hollered, "Drop and give me twenty!" When the girl turned around, a look of panic on her face, Sister Barbara pulled the girl's ponytail and chuckled. "I got you, didn't I?"

Sister Daniel flitted from booth to booth, handing out apple fritters and carrying a wicker basket for donations for next year's Valentine's Day party at the mental hospital.

"It's never too early to start donating!" she called over the din. I watched Sister Daniel slide her hand into Wendy Peterson's purse and pull out a pack of Virginia Slims. She clicked her tongue against her teeth and said, "Look what I found here, Miss Peterson." She plopped the box of cigarettes into her donation basket. "The patients will be so pleased with your contribution."

I was leaning against the far wall by the locker room, taking it all in, the streamers and the confetti, the girls in bright summer dresses, the nuns' laughter, Mrs. Pinkerton running from booth to booth, when Terry appeared at my side.

"Hi," she said.

I closed my eyes and took a breath. I smiled. "Hi." I turned to her. "It's finally over."

"Not quite." She tugged the ruffle on my shoulder. "You've still got to wear this fabulous dress."

I looked out across the gym. Sister Pat was handing a balloon to a girl in a white eyelet jumper. She couldn't have been more than five. As Sister leaned over, securing the bright red string in the girl's chubby hand, I heard her say, "I bet you want to be in the May Court someday."

I looked back at Terry. "How much longer do you have here?" I asked.

"What do you mean?"

"How much longer till you graduate?"

"Eighteen more days. And then I'm free."

"That's not so long," I said.

"It feels like forever."

I took one more look around the room, and then I grabbed Terry by the shoulders and pulled her to me. I kissed her, right there, in front of God, the Sisters of Mercy, my classmates, and everybody. She tried to pull away, but I held her steady, locked her into the embrace.

Over Terry's shoulder I could see the carnival spinning around us. Two freshmen girls stopped and stared at us. One of them grabbed the other's arm. Their mouths opened, forming two silent Os. The one on the left, the shorter one, asked, "Is that the May Queen?" Just beyond them stood Sister Barbara. Her head was nodding up and down, her jaw working, dimples pressing against the tight edge of her wimple. She started to turn around. She was just about to catch sight of us when I felt Terry's hands slip off my arms, and then they were on my collarbones and she pushed me away. I stumbled back and landed on the floor next to Sister Faith's penny-toss booth. Terry stood over me, wiping her mouth, furious. "What the hell are you doing?" she asked.

"I'm coming out of the closet," I said, and like the fool that I was, I smiled at her.

She grabbed me by the scruff of the neck and started steering me through the crowd, to the edge of the gym.

"Where are we going?"

"Out of here," she said. She kept pushing me.

"I don't want to go." I stopped, planted my feet on the ground, and dared her to move me. She was smaller than I, but I had lost so much weight that year that, within seconds, she overpowered me. She had both my arms pinned behind my back as she pushed me out of the gym and down the hall.

Where the gymnasium hall fed into the main building, there was a bathroom and, next to the bathroom, a janitor's closet. Terry dragged me to the door of the closet, opened it, shoved me inside, and turned the skeleton key that was in the lock. The closet was fitted with shelves, and I could not stand up. I crouched in my white dotted swiss dress, amid the pails and sponges. I pulled my feet out from under me, sat back, and kicked the door a few times, but with the May Day Carnival just down the hall, no one heard me. I got onto my knees and peered through the keyhole, but I could not tell if Terry was waiting on the other side of the door or if she had left me there and returned to the gym.

I don't know how long I spent in the dusty mop closet breathing in the chalky odor of ancient mop ends. Kneeling in the dark, in the closeness of the closet space, I felt as if I had found myself in a makeshift confessional.

If you'd asked me at the time what I had to confess, I would have told you that I had committed the sin of lying, of pretending I was good when really I was bad through and through. When I kissed Terry in front of the Sisters in the gym, I was trying, in my own muddled and troubled way, to make it right, to own up to all that I had become, to finally tell the whole terrible truth. I wanted to stop lying. But what I did not understand until years later was that the only sin I committed was kissing Terry in public, pushing her out into the world before she was ready. I betrayed her.

I must have known I had already lost her. After the kiss in the gym, she would never trust me again. But as I grabbed the door-knob and twisted it, as I rammed the heel of my hand against the door and called her name into the darkness, I wanted her to give me one more chance.

After a while, the sounds of the carnival died down and I heard a scuffle in the hall outside the door. Then I heard her voice. "Are you all right?"

I sat up on my knees, pressed my mouth to the keyhole. "Terry, I'm sorry."

"Don't, Al."

I slumped back deeper into the closet. A bucket jabbed me in the kidneys. I rubbed my back and pleaded, "Let me out."

The door rattled and thudded against its frame. Terry slid the key in the lock, turned it twice to the right, and the door creaked open. The hall was dark, except for the two security lights by the main office. They lit the side of her face. I slid off the step stool at the back of the closet. She knelt down, glanced at the white dress. It was covered in dust, dirt smudged, the ruffle torn off the right shoulder.

"I must look ridiculous," I said.

She tried not to, but she smiled. She shook her head. "No, you look . . ." She started laughing. "Yeah—you do."

I took her in my arms for a second time that day, but this time gently. I let my head fall onto the worn cotton of her shirt and closed my eyes.

46

TERESA DINOVELLI SLIPPED out of my life just as quickly and mysteriously as she had entered the day she arrived midsemester, a transfer student in a new uniform, the folds from the box still creasing her jumper. After Terry and Mary Elizabeth graduated and went off to college—Mary Elizabeth to a small school in Iowa and Terry to Berkeley—things quieted down. I did not hear from Terry for a month. Then, in late September, she called me in the middle of the afternoon from a pay phone on a street corner in San Francisco. She told me she hadn't slept in her dorm the night before. I asked if she was all right.

"I met someone," she said. The sound of the cars and the people in the teeming city pushed through the phone line and into my tiny dormered bedroom in Rochester. "It meant nothing, though," she said.

"What meant nothing?" I asked.

"We spent the night together."

Someone walked by with a radio, and for a moment, Simon and Garfunkel blared out through the phone line.

"What?" I said. "I can barely hear you."

"I feel dirty," she said.

I had not been many places in my life. I had fallen in love only once. But somehow I had an inkling of the slippery ground Terry was entering. "Did you have a good time?" I asked.

She was quiet for a while, and together we listened to the sound of the cars passing outside the phone booth. "Yes," she said. "Yes."

"Then there is no reason to feel dirty."

She told me the name of this girl: Amy. Her name was Amy.

In November, Terry's grandmother died. She came home for the funeral. I went to the church service. I rode with her to the cemetery. Her grandmother was buried in the same cemetery where Roy lay. We had had a frost but no real snow yet, and I wore a pair of thin cotton pants. As I shivered in the freezing wind, I kept staring over the shoulder of the priest, out past the line of trees, to the simple stone that marked Roy's grave. Afterwards we went back to Terry's family home.

Whenever I entered a room in the Dinovelli house, Terry, it seemed, was just leaving it. I could not catch up with her. So I sat with Thisbe for a while. I held her on the couch and fed her gingersnaps. She clutched the frayed edge of a baby blanket. Terry's mother tugged at it and said, "You're too old for that." Thisbe tucked the blanket further under the bend of her arm, and Mrs. Dinovelli touched the child's cheek, picked up a serving plate from the side table, and walked on.

Terry was standing in the doorway between the living room and the kitchen, the ends of her ink-dyed black peasant blouse hanging over the waist of her slacks, her dark hair falling across her eyes. She still had her homemade haircut, the edges ragged and choppy, the right side longer than the left. It gave her a permanently windblown air, as if she had just stepped off the beach. She was staring down at the pink sateen edge of Thisbe's blanket, just running her eyes along the shining line of fabric. Her brows quivered, riding some secret argument. She slouched against the doorframe. Then her gaze shifted. It slid off the blanket, across Thisbe's pouting face, and met mine.

For a moment—her hands poised, halfway in the front pockets of her slacks, the thumbs hooked through the belt loops—she froze. I thought of the day I first saw Terry, in the hall at Our Lady of Mercy, when she tipped her chin up toward me, paint staining her new blouse, her hair in disarray. I had looked into those eyes and noticed their brightness, mixed with the odd, golden color. Now, almost two years later, she stood in her parents' home, three months into her college freshman year, just back from her first taste of freedom. Her mouth opened slightly, as if she was going to speak.

She pushed her elbows into the wall behind her and walked into the kitchen.

We said good-bye in a parking lot on the edge of the inner loop, the lights of the outlet mall smearing across the sky behind us, the expressway roaring overhead. It was as far as she could take me in her mother's old jalopy. They needed her at the house, she said. Thisbe came with us. She sat on my lap, her warm body curled against my thighs, her head tucked under my chin. "When will I see you again?" Thisbe asked, her button brown eyes pleading. I smoothed back her bangs. "Soon, monkey," I whispered, and I kissed her on the cheek.

Someone, a neighbor or a friend, whom Terry had called and convinced to take me the rest of the way home, stood outside in the cold to greet us. As she walked with me across the pavement, Terry kept looking away from me, back at her mother's beat-up car. The wind picked up. It blew her dark hair off her face, and for a moment, I caught a glimpse of her ear and the skin on her neck. Finally she turned to me and said, "Look, you don't want this. It's not for you."

I stepped toward her, put my hand out to touch the sleeve of her jacket. "Terry, I—"

"Go kiss some boy."

She took a few steps back, nodded at the other driver, and started to walk toward her mother's car. After she popped open the driver's side door, she stopped for a minute, looked down, took a breath, and turned back. She said something to me, but the wind whipped the words from her mouth. I could not hear her. She opened the car door and stepped inside. The wind cut through my pants, and my legs trembled. The sky was darkening, and I could barely see her face behind the wheel. The engine turned over. She put it in gear. Light from the streetlamps flashed across the roof of the car. She turned a corner and was gone.

Part IV

The Drive

47

I ACCOMPLISHED ONE thing senior year: I learned to drive. At Mother's insistence, Father tried to teach me. He took me out in Mother's Chevy Chevette. He thought the best way for me to learn would be to watch him drive as he talked me through what he was doing. All through the chilly fall we traveled the streets and back roads, the highways and the interstate, my father at the wheel, while I sat beside him and took notes. He took great care with his descriptions of the mysteries of shifting, the uses of the turn signal, and how to change lanes. "Watch the yellow line in the middle of the road," he would say. "Never cross that." Once he stopped, pulled over to the curb, cut the motor, and turned to me. "Do you understand, baby? Never cross the dividing line." Ice frosted across the windshield. Cold crept in as the engine cooled. A pencil poised over my notebook, I stared at him.

"Baby," he said. "Answer me."

I looked into his red-rimmed eyes and repeated, "Never cross the dividing line."

He pointed at my notebook. "Write it down," he said.

"Don't you think it's better if I memorize it?"

He nodded and ran his hand through his hair, smoothing it down. He turned the key in the ignition and pulled back onto the road.

After the first month, he forgot about the driving lessons. He just drove around, pointing out sites of interest. He showed me the Cobb's Hill Reservoir, Kodak Park, and Nazareth College. He relaxed. He began to enjoy himself. He drove like he lived— quietly, with great care. And he loved cars. Years later, long after I had graduated from college, soon after he retired, he tried to get a job as a car salesman.

"Why?" I asked him.

"It would be fun," he said.

"To spend all day around cars?"

He broke into a grin. "Of course."

Inside the warm cab of the Chevette, Father's hands cradled the wheel. The heel of his palm pressed the gear shaft, his left knee rising when he engaged the clutch. He slid the car soundlessly into the next gear. The heat of the engine rose up, and he told me stories.

His first car was a 1950 Ford convertible with two-tone gray exterior and leather seats. He liked to drive it to the lake at Charlotte on the weekends. Whenever he could, he took his nephews with him. He bought them ice cream at the beach. He let the boys eat their ice cream cones in the backseat. He kept the top down and drove around the lakefront while the two boys, my cousins Tim and Greg (who later attended seminary and took orders), jumped on the leather seats, waving their free hands above their heads, catching the wind in their outstretched palms.

I looked at my father as he drove the darkened streets of Rochester. "You let them eat ice cream in the backseat? And no seat belts?"

"Baby, we were young."

I tried to picture him behind the wheel of a two-tone gray convertible, windswept, a wide, easy grin spread across his face. In the photos I had of him in his youth, he was combed and buttoned and Brylcreemed—an earnest, pale-skinned boy in sweater vests and long britches. I could not imagine this messy, carefree young man.

"How did you afford a car?" I asked.

"It was my one luxury. I was twenty-two. I had been working for four years already. I had saved." He took another turn, pulled onto the highway, upshifted, and smiled. The car sailed along the black pavement. "The police stopped me once."

"What?"

He chuckled. "Yes. An officer pulled me over and asked how I knew the boys and what I thought I was doing driving them around like that, them jumping on the backseat with the top down. He let me off with a warning. By the time I got home, Aunt Catherine had got wind of it, and oh, she was mad. She put her hand out and said, 'Give me the keys.'"

"What did you do?"

"I gave her the keys."

"What did she do with them?"

"She told me she'd give them back when I was old enough to drive."

A week later she handed them back. Father bought seat belts for the backseat.

The highway dropped away, and we moved onto a deserted country road. Outside my window the trees—dark heaps of gray against a dark sky—whizzed past.

Mother waited for us at the door each night. "How did it go?" she would ask.

"Good!" Father would say. "I think she's improving."

I would nod in agreement. "I'm getting the hang of it."

One night when we returned home from a driving lesson, Mother opened the door and held it with her foot. We rushed in, stamping the snow off our boots. As she stood back and watched us take off our hats and gloves she said, "Maybe you should let her practice backing down the driveway, Royden. She needs to learn how to do that, too."

I realized she did not know that he never let me drive. She assumed that, at some point, after we pulled out onto the street, Father turned the car over to me. I stood in the front hall looking into their impassive faces. My father stopped, his hand on the wool plaid of his scarf. Just his eyes moved as he glanced at me and waited.

I turned to Mother. "That's a good idea," I said.

Father smiled. He slid the scarf off his neck, took off his coat, one sleeve at a time, and tucked them away in the front hall closet.

As we walked through the dining room into the kitchen, he put a hand on my head. The cool skin of his palm cupped the back of my skull. He called to Mother. "So what's for dinner?"

It was on one of our drives that we saw the dog get hit. An old yellow Lab stepped off the curb in Brighton, about a mile from home, and loped across the street. Father braked. The wheels skidded against the pavement. We came within two feet of it. The dog passed us without looking up. It crossed the yellow line. Another car came toward it. We were sure they were going to brake. They had plenty of lead time. The sound of our squeaking brakes should have tipped them off. It was a bone white Volvo—old, a late-seventies model. It hit the dog square in the center of its body. The dog bounced off the grillwork and was thrown ten feet into the bushes at the side of the road. The Volvo didn't even slow down.

We pulled over. I leapt out of the car and ran toward the bank of bushes where I saw the dog disappear. Father rummaged in the back of the car, looking for a flashlight. By the time Father arrived, I had found the dog. I could tell by the gray around her muzzle and the matted fur on her back that she was an old girl, probably deaf and half blind. She was definitely dead, her eyes wide open and still. I tried to pull her onto my lap, but she was too big for me. Father trained the beam of light up and down the dog. He knelt down and felt the dog's throat, looking for a pulse.

"She's dead," I said.

He kept feeling for any sign of movement. After a minute he sat back on his haunches and ran his hand across the animal's body, caressing the fur. He nodded. Father held the flashlight over the collar. I read the address off the name tag. We looked up at the street sign. It was right there.

"You go for help. I'll stay with her," I said.

"No. You go. I'll stay."

I got up and sprinted down the street. I turned back once. He had pulled off his coat and was wrapping it around the dog.

When we drove home Father was agitated. His hands kept moving up to adjust the heat knob, to pull at the collar of his coat, and he shook his head. The lights from oncoming cars flashed across his stricken face. "He never even saw it coming," he said.

"She," I said.

"What?"

"It was a female dog. She."

He nodded, took the next turn, shifted twice, and shook his head. "He never saw it coming."

48

WHEN SUSANNA SPINDALE beat out ten women with years of acting experience to play the role of the blind girl Susy Hendrix in a community theater production of *Wait Until Dark*, no one was surprised. Susanna was destined to play Susy Hendrix. She was a dead ringer for Audrey Hepburn (who had made the role famous in the 1967 film), and she prepared more assiduously than any other girl had ever prepared for a role. Susanna knew the key to the role was becoming believably blind. For this, she enlisted my services. During the month of October, Wednesdays after school, I met Susanna in front of her house and walked with her while she practiced being blind. My job was to make sure she didn't bump into anything. She didn't need me. Susanna—sporting dark glasses, a Burberry trench coat, and a white cane—took to blindness like it was second nature.

As she navigated her way around a third postal box without any prompting from me, I glanced over and peered at the space between her sunglasses and her face, checking to see if she peeked. She didn't.

"What's the news from Iowa?" she asked.

"Mary Elizabeth has a new friend."

"What's his name?"

"Michael."

She nodded and tapped her cane some more. "And the news from Berkeley? How's the physicist?"

"She has a new friend too."

The tapping of the white cane stopped. A horn blared in the distance. A car rushed past, close to the sidewalk. The wind from it rustled through our hair. Susanna checked her wig, fluffed her bangs, and placed her hand on her hip. "You mean?" she asked.

"I think so."

"You don't know?"

I glanced at her. Her large-framed dark glasses engulfed the upper half of her face. "Are you sure you're not peeking?" I asked.

"Of course not. What would be the point of that?"

"It's just that you're so good at this."

"I've been practicing at home with a blindfold."

"And your mom doesn't mind?"

"Didn't even bat an eye."

She had filched a Hermès scarf from a secondhand store. Draped over the wig and wrapped twice around her neck, its floral detail emphasized the fine line of her cheekbones. With the wig and the dark glasses and the cane, the whole getup, I could not imagine Susanna ever going unnoticed.

"Your parents really didn't notice?"

She pinched my emaciated upper arm. "Do yours notice this?"

Susanna readjusted her grip on the cane and resumed tapping. We walked the rest of the way to her house in silence.

Susanna wore the most outrageous outfits and pulled absurd stunts, but except for a few detentions for uniform infractions, no one cared. Which was a pity, because Susanna was dying for attention. When *Wait Until Dark* closed, Susanna played Agnes (the novice nun who believes she is carrying God's child) in *Agnes of God*. She worked for months to develop stigmata like Agnes did. She tried everything from strange elixirs to satanic rituals in an effort to get her palms to bleed like the wounds of Christ. In the end, she resorted to chopping wood for hours at a stretch and then applying a nail file to the blisters till they bled. She came to school wearing a novice's white habit, with bandages around her hands, and practiced fainting in the halls. No one looked twice.

My skipped meals and attendance problems didn't make much of a mark at Mercy. I slept through most of my classes senior year, and by the time I graduated, I weighed eighty-five pounds. I lost my period. I grew a pelt of fine hair on my legs and arms. A smoky, sour spice rose off my skin. The nuns assumed my parents had it under control, and my parents thought the nuns were handling everything.

At lunch, I choked on the first bite of my sandwich. My throat closed, and the gag reflex kicked in. I tossed my sandwiches in the garbage bins by the cafeteria hall. The three of them—plastic with beveled sides—were cradled together on a metal trolley. The cafeteria cook wheeled them out at the start of lunch period. I stood over the bins every day and dropped my sandwich into the center one. Nestled in a plastic Baggie, it disappeared into the dark mouth of bin number two. I thought, *There's something wrong with throwing out the sandwich,* but I could not grasp what it was.

I walked out of the cafeteria, past the apple machine and the candy machine, and I disappeared. I walked through the halls under the convent. The heating pipes hissed and sputtered above me. Most afternoons, I went to the school literary office in the basement. During the school day, it was deserted. I opened the door. I pushed aside the piles of papers, climbed up on the big pine table, and fell asleep. While I slept, I dreamed. In this dream there were no cars. The guardrail that bore the imprint of the crash had disappeared. The road itself was gone. Only the bright, keenly lit forest remained. In the dream Roy ran toward me. That is how I saw him in those days. I would sleep in the afternoons during my classes, and while I slept, he ran. The sun full out, it fell in speckled patches on the trees around him. His legs were mud splattered. His feet barely touched the ground. The sugar maples and the pines, the sycamore and the old oaks rose around him, shuddering in the wind. The dark branches bent down, brushed his shoulder, his neck, the crook of an arm. In the dream, his face held no expression, just a hard, beautiful concentration as he ran out of the woods—a young man, a boy still, too skinny for his age. A boy with height he had yet to grow into.

Susanna showed up once in a while. "Come on. We've got chemistry," she'd say. Her brow would furrow. Her eyes would shift. "What's with you?" she'd ask.

* * *

I did attend Sister Rose's senior religion class. She never saw us for what we were—restless, disillusioned girls, itching to get out of high school—and this served her well. Sister Rose talked to us about God as if it were the first time anyone had thought to mention Him. She told us about how God appeared to her when she was sixteen: "I was a junior at this very school when Jesus came to me." He ordered her to become a nun. She told us stories of her early days as a novice with the Sisters of Mercy. We were so stunned by her faith that we sat silent, rapt, waiting to hear what she would say next.

In November, Sister Rose fell ill and Sister Daniel covered her classes. Sister Daniel preferred math and home economics to the vagaries of faith. She was not used to talking about God. For a while, she clung to the facts: the age of Christ when He died, the number of wounds He suffered, the names of the criminals crucified along with Him. We recited the Seven Joyful Mysteries, the Seven Sorrowful Mysteries, the Nicene Creed, and so on. When she ran out of facts for us to memorize, she did not know what to do.

"What did Sister Rose teach you?" she asked.

Jenny Silan raised her hand. "She talked about her faith."

Sister nodded, made a note in her blue ledger, and dismissed us twenty minutes early. The next day, she drew a cylinder on the chalkboard with a series of vertical lines coming out of the top of it—a birthday cake. She pointed to it with her chalk. "Faith," she said, "is like a German chocolate cake. Every layer is richer than the last."

After that, she resorted to moral riddles.

"There are three people in a boat," she read from a book on ethics for teenagers. "A mother, a child, and a man with one arm. If you do not throw one person overboard, the boat will sink and all three will drown. Who should you throw overboard?" She stared at the page and silently reread the riddle. She shook her head and closed the book. "Break into groups of four. You have fifteen minutes."

Susanna was in my group. She was chomping on a wad of gum, wearing a baseball cap and dark sunglasses. I don't know how she got away with the gum and the cap, but she had been granted permission to wear the sunglasses. She had convinced Sister Barbara that she needed to wear them for artistic purposes.

"It's part of my preparation for the play," she said as she slammed shut her locker earlier that day.

"They bought that?" I asked her.

She slid the glasses down her nose and winked at me.

The other two girls in our group were Jenny Silan and Beth Mier. Jenny pulled out a piece of paper and started drawing lines across it.

"What are you doing?" Susanna asked.

"I'm drawing a graph so that we can plot the pluses and minuses of throwing each person overboard."

Susanna put her hand over Jenny's paper. "Okay, Miss Perfect."

Jenny looked up. "Who should we start with? The one-armed man?"

"I think we need more information, don't you, Al?" Susanna asked.

I shrugged.

Susanna raised her hand. "Sister, we have a question."

Sister Daniel stepped out from behind her desk. "Yes, Susanna?"

"How did they get there?" she asked.

"What do you mean?"

"How did these three people wind up in a leaking boat in the first place?"

Sister nodded, adjusted her wimple, and turned to the book. "Well, let's see here." She flipped the pages. She reread the moral word problem aloud. She nodded some more and said, "It doesn't say."

"We don't even know if these guys were baptized," Susanna said. "We can't send someone overboard who isn't baptized. I'd feel terrible about that. How would they get into heaven?"

Sister cleared her throat. "It doesn't say anything about baptism."

"And who is this one-armed man?" Susanna asked. "Is he a priest? Because if he is, that changes everything."

Sister nodded. "It does. Doesn't it?"

I leaned over and whispered to Susanna, "How does it change everything?"

"Beats me."

49

WINTER ARRIVED. ON windless afternoons, as I waited for Father to arrive home from work and take me out for a driving lesson, the air turned to crystal. I watched the frozen world through the window in the dining room. Parting the lace curtains, I looked out on the lawn and the road. Occasionally a car would drive by, its engine working, breaking the stillness. As the frost crept up the windowpane, I leaned my cheek against it and let the ice sink into my forehead and cool my brain.

I wrote Terry. I never got an answer.

I wrote Mary Elizabeth long letters. I had won an award in history class, and I made much of this small victory. I told her about Susanna practicing to be blind and about Daniel and the German chocolate cake. In those letters I was someone else. I wrote of a lighthearted, hardworking girl, a girl who was on track. Mary Elizabeth answered with cheery missives in colorful, fine-point marker. She made drawings in the margins, and ended each letter with a heart. The letters came intermittently—three one month and then nothing till just before Thanksgiving. I cherished them—the orange hand-drawn heart, the Winnie-the-Pooh stamp on the envelope. I pressed them against my chest.

I sniffled through the whole chilly season, sneezed and coughed and rubbed my aching head. Having a simple cold—a known illness—was a relief. I found comfort in the decongestants, the expectorants, the antihistamines. The names tripped off my tongue as I pored over the labels, reading the instructions for use, the child's dosages and the warnings. I lined up bottles of Dimetapp and Robitussin and codeine-laced cough syrups along the windowsill and stared at the amber- and green-colored liquids.

When I was not sick, I spent most afternoons in the gully. I had sidestepped down the steep ravine first with Roy and once with Terry. Now, I went alone. I brought my backpack, filled with library books, and read in the cold woods. I continued to work as a clerk, shirking my duties, misfiling, and reading on the sly. I crouched in corners of the library and scanned the shelves for new material. I peopled my life with dusty tomes such as A Syllabus of Mortuary Jurisprudence, Elizabethan Puritanism, and Early Norse History. Some days I took the long walk to the outdoor skating rink and watched the skaters make their slow circles around the bumpy ice. My skates remained in the basement toy cupboard where I had placed them the summer Roy left.

Sometimes it occurred to me that my biggest problem might be loneliness. But I had stepped so far into the life of a dead boy that the path back to the living world seemed impassable. My classmates felt far away. I watched them apply lip gloss and whisper secrets to each other while we waited for the buses. I could not imagine reaching across the great chasm between us to say hello. My mind shimmered on the edges of sanity. I hovered above the living world—stunned, sullen, watching. When the words and thoughts blocked up inside me floated back down, they pointed in one direction: Roy. He haunted every quiet, voiceless moment of my life.

My parents still stared at me through the fogged glass of their minds, trying to clear it, trying to see me. And I stared back. Blinded by my own confusion, I had little compassion for how they struggled. We clashed often, over useless things. Movies I should not be allowed to see. Places I should not want to go. Colleges I should not consider applying to. Mother did most of the talking. Father hid behind his paper.

With the help of Sister Daniel and three semesters of home economics, I had picked up a few practical skills, and I found one useful way to pass the time now that Terry and Mary Elizabeth were gone: I sewed. I made pants and shirts, aprons and skirts—anything I could get my hands on, in any pattern and any fabric. Mother and

I set up the sewing machine and the ironing board in Roy's room. We worked side by side till long past midnight. Father watched television in the basement while we sat two flights up, the pale blue walls cocooning us.

One night, the subject of God came up. Mother was ironing her blue flowered skirt (she planned to wear it to church the next day) when she told me that I was not allowed to play in the gully anymore.

"Why can't I?" I asked.

"It's dangerous," she said. "I asked God about it. You ask Him. You'll see."

"I'm not going to ask God."

She stopped. "Of course you are. We ask God."

"I don't."

She was not wearing her glasses. Steam from the iron had fogged them, and she had taken them off and placed them on Roy's desk. She pursed her lips and resumed ironing. "Next you are going to tell me you don't believe in God."

"Mama."

She shook her head.

"I don't."

Mother pressed her skirt against the board and guided the nose of the hot iron across the fabric. Steam hissed. Water in the iron's central chamber sloshed against the sides.

"You don't what?" she asked.

"Believe in your God. He left me. Right after Roy died, He left."

She picked up the iron. Steam fogged off the brushed steel bottom. "My God," she said. "My God!"

She set down the iron, wound the temperature knob back to zero, pulled the plug from the wall socket, and walked out of the room. She left a pile of rumpled clothes in the hamper. The door to my parents' bedroom unlatched and squeaked open, and then just as swiftly, it shut and a silence fell back around the house.

Father came upstairs. He poked his head into Roy's room and

found me sitting in front of the sewing machine, a bobbin grasped in the palm of my hand. I stared out at the side yard.

"Where's your mother?"

I looked up. "She went to bed, I think."

He left. I tried to slide the bobbin into the cradle beneath the sewing arm of the Singer, but my hands were shaking and I kept dropping the end of the thread down past the spindle. I gave up, turned out the sewing light, and went to bed.

Father came to my room a half hour later, wearing his pajama bottoms and a T-shirt. His hair stood on end. He did not knock. His eyes were watery. His breath came in shallow gasps. "What did you say to her?"

I set down my book.

"What did you say"—he pointed at the door—"to your mother?"

I shook my head. "Nothing."

"Did you talk to her about God?"

"She asked."

He walked out of the room.

I leapt out of bed and followed him. "What did I do?" I asked.

He stopped outside their bedroom door. His eyes flicked up and caught the edge of my face. He looked down and stared at the matted carpet. "Why did you do it, baby?"

I rested my hand on the bathroom door to steady myself. I shook my head. I felt as if my mouth was filled with liquid. If I opened it something would spill out of me, something that would leave a mark.

"How could you do this to us?" he asked.

I stepped toward him. He slipped into the bedroom, closed the door behind him, and latched it. I stood in the hall and listened to the night sounds, the wind in the bare branches of the trees, the creak of the eaves as the winter cold settled deeper into the house. I waited. But I could hear nothing through the door. I went to my room. I pressed my ear to the far wall, the one that lay between our rooms. Again I heard nothing. I walked back to the door of their room, raised my hand to knock, and then thought better of it. I sat down. I laid my cheek against the painted wood. I ran my head along the door till I found the hard groove where the molding began. I pressed the bone of my cheek into the cut line of the painted wood, hoping it would leave a mark. I pulled my legs under my nightshirt. The night wore on. The silence continued. I fell asleep.

The next morning, when Father opened the door, I fell onto the pinewood floorboards of their bedroom. He pushed me out of the room, away from my mother's sight. I saw her for a moment—a slim, trembling lump under the eyelet bedspread. I felt Father's hands under my arms as he pulled me up. He pushed me into the hall.

"Daddy," I said.

He stepped past me and walked into the bathroom. I heard the toilet flush, and then he emerged. He took the stairs gently, quietly, and dashed into the dining room to the wall phone. He called the factory and requested that the switchboard operator tell his supervisor that he was not feeling well and would not be in today. "It's just a cold," he said. "Thank you. Yes, thank you, Edna. I'm sure I'll be fine." He hung up the phone and walked to the kitchen. He poured cereal into a bowl, brewed coffee, pulled a blue beveled glass from the cupboard, and located the carton of orange juice at the back of the refrigerator.

Twenty minutes later, he walked up the stairs with a breakfast tray in his hands. He knocked on the bedroom door, and when there was no answer, he balanced the tray against the wall, turned the knob with his free hand, and disappeared into the darkened room. This time I heard voices—Father's plaintive tones, Mother's curt responses. And then silence. After a few minutes Father would begin again and Mother would cut him off. It went on like this for the better part of the morning—Father's querulous voice pleading, Mother's refusals, and then the silence again. No one even thought to call the school and report my absence. At two in the afternoon, their voices pitched up higher than I had ever heard. Someone cried out—a wild wailing, so strange I could not tell which of them had made it. I heard a crash, the sound of glass shattering against a wall. I hovered in the hall, walking back and forth between the bathroom and Roy's room. Father emerged from the room with the tray minus a juice glass. He pushed past me and returned to the kitchen.

It went on for three days. In those days I heard something I had not heard before—not in the weeks after Roy died, not on the Cape when she realized that he was gone for good, not in the two and a half years we had lived together without him. Mother was crying. At first it did not even register as crying. I thought it was a bird outside the window, or a car horn in the distance, or the wind in the eaves.

When the crying started, Father began a sort of house arrest. He locked the doors, drew the curtains in the living room and dining room, and unplugged the phone. He sat on the stairs at their base near the front hall, a spot he had sequestered the day his son died. He did not move, except to bring Mother trays of food.

Once again, I wandered the rooms of the house, walking from living room to dining room to kitchen. Whenever I passed Father, his eyes grazed across my face and then he looked away, shaking his head. I walked around in the daze that deep silence induces. I touched the discarded toys in the toy cupboard, the silverware in the drawers, the plastic body of Saint Jude. When I had finished wandering the rooms of the house, I climbed the stairs, walked down the hall to Mother's room, leaned my cheek against the door, and listened to her cry.

I remembered the winter, long ago, when our goldfish, Swimmy and Fred, had died. Roy and I had attended the Saint Thomas More Church Carnival the previous summer and had won two fish in the Ping-Pong toss. We had the fish for five months before they committed double suicide, jumping to their deaths from the bowl on the mantel to the fire one night while Mother was making popcorn and Father and I were reading. Roy was the only one to see them go. He stared dumbstruck. Mother served popcorn. Father was all the way through the business section of the paper and on to the classifieds page, making his nightly count of "Thank You, Saint Jude" notices, when Roy finally said, "The fish are dead."

"What!" I cried and ran to their bowl. "Where'd they go?"

Roy explained what had happened. I peered into the flames. Nothing was left of them. I cried. Father cried.

"They were fish, for heaven's sake. Cheap carnival goldfish," Mother said as she piled more popcorn in my bowl. "We'll buy you another one."

"I'll talk to Saint Peter," Father whispered after Mother had left the room to make more popcorn. "I'll ask if he will let them into heaven."

"Do you think he will?"

"I don't see why not. They were very good fish, and they are the Lord's favorite meal."

I wrinkled my brow. I did not want the Lord to eat my fish. I wanted Him to offer them eternal salvation. "Will Jesus take care of them?" I asked.

"Ask and you shall receive," Father said.

"Royden, what are you promising her?" Mother yelled from the kitchen.

"Is that my bride calling?" Father asked.

"What are you telling that child?" Mother asked.

Father smiled. He began to sing. "Too-ra-loo-ra-loo-ral, Too-ra-loo-ra-li."

He pulled me off the couch, took the book from my hand, and danced me through the front hall and around the dining room table. Roy ran after us, trying to step on my heels. We laughed. Father's touch was so light on my back that I could barely follow him. I leaned into his hand, resting in his palm. Mother came into the room from the kitchen. She had a bowl of popcorn balanced against her hip. She flipped on the light. "Enough of this," she said. Father dropped my hand and turned to her. He pulled her into his arms, set the bowl on the dining room table, and guided her around the room as he sang.

"Royden," she said. "Stop." She let go of his arm. "Stop."

Even before Roy died, my mother was a mystery. Inside her— tucked under the smile and the crispness, the rowdy zest for life— there lurked a fugitive sadness. The hidden, unrealized pieces of my mother were part of her allure. When the four of us would wander into the backyard after supper to look for the Big Dipper, the sadness crested and rolled off her into the evening air. Like a scent, it mixed with the lilac blossoms and skunkweed, marigolds and cut grass. The mosquitoes always found her first, landing softly on her neck and shoulders. Every night in the yard, she would let my hand fall, hug her arms to her chest, and wander away from me on the cool lawn. I thought there was a reason she dropped my hand and that if I could figure out what that was, then I would never lose her.

Father made Mother a ham sandwich and a cup of tea. He placed the food on an orange metal tray, marched up the staircase, tapped twice on her door, and disappeared into the darkened bedroom. I waited. Once again, Father returned alone, the tray of food untouched. He walked down the stairs till he reached the third step. He sat down and set the tray on the fourth step. He picked up the tea and drank it. When he had finished, he returned to her room one more time, knocked, waited, and entered. I heard voices again. He talked, she cried. And then the door flew open and he stormed down the stairs. He found me in the kitchen, where I had taken the tray to wash the dishes.

"Take it back," he said. "Go up there and take it back."

He had not changed his clothes since the night he came into my room and asked what I had said to her. The skin under his eyes looked thin and bruised. His narrow arms trembled as he flexed his fists.

I shook my head. "I can't."

He ran his hands through his hair and stepped toward me. "Why won't you help me?"

I wish that I had told him how sorry I was that I did not believe anymore, but I was scared and stunned and too uncertain to risk such a move. I shook my head. I stared at the refrigerator door. There, pinned in place with a magnet, was a faded green card that read, "One-Free-Game." Roy and I had won it at the mini-golf course years ago. Nobody had bothered to put it away. "I can't lie," I said.

Father squinted and raised his hands to shield his eyes as if he were looking into a bright light. The veins on his wrists were watery blue and prominent. "Are you trying to kill her?" he asked. He shook his head, lowered his arms, and walked out of the room.

The next morning, when the door opened, I jumped off the sofa. Father and I sprinted up the stairs. She hobbled down the hall to the bathroom and disappeared behind the door. She was in there for a long time. We stood on the stairs, gazing up at the door. After a while, the door opened and she stepped into the hall. She glanced down at us where we stood on the stairs, and nodded.

She walked over to the hall window and looked out at the rope swing in the yard. It was the spot where, years before, she used to set down her laundry and watch us play. We were shy, awkward, earnest children, the world opened out for us from the pages of our books; she loved us, but our studious nature scared her. She feared what they might do to us—the strange ideas we might find in books. As Father and I watched her from the stairs, she raised her arms and held them in front of her, embracing her firstborn, the infant Roy.

I trudged through the snow and pushed aside the ice-covered bushes. In daylight, our secret hideout did not look quite so spectacular. I could see the torn cushions on the moldy easy chair, the ice rising up the sides of the doghouse-table, the pages on the walls—all those meticulously copied journal entries—rippled with water marks, the ink smudged and illegible. There were his books, and the photos and his journals—a room full of useless mementos hanging there like lonely party favors, waiting for a celebration that would never arrive.

I tried to read the journal pages that I had pored over for so many nights, but I could not make out a single sentence. I pulled a page off the wall. I just wanted to hold it up to the light. I wanted to get a better look at the words. I tore another page off the wall, and then another, and another. When I got to the back wall, I stopped at the bookcase. I ran the back of my hand across the shelf, and the books tumbled to the floor. Then I started into the pile of photos I kept in a Ziploc bag. I pulled them out and threw them on top of the mess of papers and books. When I had finished, I stood still and let the breath rush in and out of me. Something bright—a sharp corner, a glossy flash of color—poked out from the pile. A photo, a recent print, gleamed up at me. I bent down and picked it up.

It was one of the last pictures of the two of us together. Father took it in June, on the day Roy and I had taken out the camper-van, looking for summer work. He had just arrived home from the factory when we pulled in with the van. Father said, "Our young man," and a soft smile spread across his face. He touched his hand to his temple, smoothed back his hair. "Don't move," he said. He rushed inside to get his Minolta.

Father was a meticulous photographer. He would focus and refocus, stepping backward and forward, making slight adjustments. The dance went on for fifteen minutes. It took him so long to frame the perfect shot that, by the time he got around to taking the picture, we had forgotten about the photo. As we stood in front of the van waiting, Roy pulled out his science books. Father caught us in that moment, Roy rifling through the pages, his mouth open as he tried to explain the fourth dimension to me for the second time that day. In the photo, I lean over the book, my hand on the page, squinting up at Roy. Light filters through the Lovells' oak tree and falls in mottled patches across the drive, the two of us, and the van. And he says it once more, *Indissolubly, Al. Indissolubly.*

As I sat on the edge of my seat in the ruined fort, it wasn't the light, or Roy's hand splayed out across the page, or my pained, quizzical look that captured me. What caught my eye was the camper-van. *That's it*, I thought. I let go of the photo. It fell onto my lap. *The van.*

50

So MUCH HAPPENED in cars. We traveled across the country twice in a small white 1972 VW camper. The cross-country trips were long, inexpensive vacations. When work at the factory had slowed to a halt and Father was laid off for the summer, we took a road trip. Roy was eight and I was five when we headed out on our first excursion. The final destination was a small suburb outside L.A. where our grandmother lived. Mother made a sign that read CALIFORNIA OR BUST and fastened it to the back of the VW. The morning of our departure the Hendersons came by to wish us a bon voyage. They brought a bottle of champagne. Mr. Henderson popped the cork. It shot out across the lawn. Roy caught it, trapping it in his cupped palms. His hands stung for hours afterwards. We said three Hail Marys before leaving the driveway. Father led the prayer.

The VW had no air-conditioning, and on hot days, on the long drive through the Painted Desert, my brother's eyes would droop. He would slide his head into my lap, curl himself around me, and sleep. Periodically, we would stop and Father would pose us carefully in front of a monument. On those early trips I remember only harmony. The two of us were blessed with long attention spans and an undying enthusiasm for card games. In the back, the seat cushions pulled out into the camping bed, we curled on top of sleeping bags and ate apples and Butterfingers and played endless rounds of spit or war. I remember counting license plates and cows, waving at truckers, motioning for them to pull their horns; they always did. Later, as Roy approached puberty, on long trips, tensions boiled up. Our family never fought. We never talked through differences. Instead there were just silent, restless moments and, later, the sight of my brother leaving. Running down the road, zipping closed his tent flap, riding away on his bicycle—more and more often, he left me behind.

The summer after he turned fifteen, we went to Cape Cod as usual. But Roy was different that year. He did not want to walk the beach walk together. A few minutes into the walk, he started jogging ahead of me. "I'll catch you later, Al," he said and disappeared off the path into the trees.

At the beach, he was plagued by fits of restlessness. Suddenly he'd rise up off his towel and run down the beach by the water, leaving me in the hot sand with my books. At night in the tent, we did not play cards. Instead Roy spent every evening sitting at the communal fireplace in the center of the campground feeding sticks into the fire pit. It was clear he didn't want me around. So I squatted in the scrub pines by the bathhouse and watched him. He moved a lawn chair up close to the fire. Even from that distance, I could see the reflection of the bright orange flames playing across his face. Firelight cradled his fine, high cheekbones, the soft slant of his tall forehead.

One night, Mother joined me in the underbrush, and together we watched him as he sat in the faltering light of the flames. It was close to midnight.

"You should be in bed, Alroy," Mother whispered.

"What about him?" I jutted my chin in the direction of the fire.

"He's got growing pains," she said.

"What's that?"

"It's when your thoughts are too big for your head."

"Does it hurt?"

"I think it can."

"Will he die of it?" I asked.

Mother glanced down at me for a moment. Then she laughed and pulled a twig out of my hair. She stared at Roy. "No, he won't die of it."

It was clear that I had come to symbolize everything that was confining and babyish, everything that was beneath him. I watched him on the ten-hour drive home, holding his head, staring out the window longingly, answering Mother's questions with clipped, stilted phrases. I didn't dare ask him to play cards. He tried to hold his irritation in check, to keep from hurting me. I think this pained me even more. I did not want his pity.

When we returned from the Cape, Roy remained distant. He had acquired a small radio and began to carry it with him everywhere. We had built a glorious fort earlier that summer, but he did not want to spend time in it. Something on that trip, on the long drive back, confined in the camper-van with his family, had changed him.

In the northwest corner of the yard, under the jungle gym, Roy began to dig. He unearthed things: a defrocked doll with no eyes, a piece of antique willowware, a filthy, wheelless Tonka truck. The treasures grew by the day. I circled the hole, playing around the lip, begging him to give me a job.

"But what can I do?" I asked.

"Nothing."

"I want to help," I whined.

He kept digging. He said nothing.

When Shadow came by, she stopped dead in her tracks about five feet from the hole. After a few minutes she sidled up to it. She sniffed around its edge, stared into its dank bottom, and watched Roy dump shovel after shovel of dirt into the fern bed. She barked at the hole. She whined and howled. She caused such a commotion that I walked her out of the yard, gave her three dog biscuits, and sent her on her way. I think it was the smell, something in the uncovered earth that spooked Shadow. The clay-mottled dirt had a powerful raw odor.

Mother watched from the kitchen window as Roy descended into the earth. First his knees, then his thighs, then his waist. Soon even his shoulders disappeared into the hole. By the end of the second week all she could see was the hard edge of the shovel and the earth landing in damp, loamy mounds by the fern bed. I lined up his collection of unearthed objects along the back fence.

Then one day, he called to me. "Hey, Al."

I scrambled over to the edge. "What?"

"You want to get in here and dig for a minute?"

I jumped in before he even finished his sentence. The hole was so deep that my head was well below grass level. He handed me the shovel, and I began to dig.

"You're doing it all wrong," he said.

I rolled my eyes. "How can I be shoveling wrong, Alroy? You put the dirt on the shovel, you throw it over your shoulder, like this." I undershot. The dirt hit the wall of the hole and scattered back down on our heads.

"Don't call me that."

"Call you what?"

"Alroy."

"But it's what she always calls you . . . and me."

"I know. I don't like it."

"You don't—"

"Just don't call me that anymore." He took the shovel from my hands. "You need help getting back out."

I stared at my muddy sneakers.

He waved his hand in front of my face. "Are you in there? Do you need—"

"No," I said and scrambled toward the opening. But I was too short. I could not get a good hold on the lip of the hole.

Roy knelt down. "Here. Step on my knee."

I looked down at him. His face was smudged. His arms were still skinny, still not much bigger than mine, but they had grown taut with the work of shoveling, and his ropy muscles moved like small animals under his skin.

At eight feet the dirt was as dark as pitch and filled with odd-shaped stones. My heart leapt as the tip of his shovel pinged against the rocks. I thought Roy had reached the top of the city of hell, that he had come within an arm's length of the devil himself. I thought he was going to be pulled down into it. I begged him to get out of the hole, but he would not listen to me. In the end, I decided to save myself. I stepped back away from the hole and sprinted into the garage. The wind picked up and rustled the leaves. A storm threatened. Father returned from work and sang in the front hall as he removed his heavy work shoes. At six o'clock, Mother called, "Alroy, dinner!"

I ran toward the house, kicking up divots of grass. When I reached the back door I called back to Roy, "Mom said dinner!"

He climbed out and stood on the edge of the hole. He had pulled off his shirt hours before. His body was covered in dirt. His shorts and his work boots were indistinguishable from his skin. It started to rain. Mother called again. "Alroy!" This time he looked up and saw us: Mother silhouetted in the fuzzy half-light of the kitchen window and me by the back door, my hand on the latch, my face pressed into the coming evening.

In my memory he emerges from the hole, runs across the lawn, and steps into the dark mouth of the camper-van, driving down the road and disappearing forever. This is not how it happened. Three years passed between the summer he dug the hole and the morning he drove away for the last time, but in my mind the two events are linked.

A few days after I had found the photo of Roy and me in front of the van, Father took me for another driving lesson. He drove me down East Avenue to show me beautiful, ramshackle mansions. I looked out the window. A woman in a tweed coat with a fur collar walked her spaniel down the snowy sidewalk. Father stopped at a stop sign. I got up the courage to ask him if I could try driving.

"Are you sure you're ready?" he asked me.

I watched the clouds of breath around the woman's mouth dissolve into the icy air. I nodded. "Yes."

Father looked both ways, drove through the intersection, and circled the block once more. He found a deserted section of the street, pulled the car up to the curb, and cut off the engine. His shoulders slumped. He leaned against the cold pane of the car window. He pulled the key out of the ignition and stared at it. He curled it into his palm, heaved himself out of the car and onto the street, the hard-packed snow crunching under his boots. We walked around the car. When he got to the passenger side, he pulled the handle, slid the door open, and began to step inside.

"Dad."

He looked up. "What, baby?"

"The keys."

He raised his hand, picked out the key with the black handle, and passed it across the hood of the car. I reached out. It was still warm from his palm. I opened the driver's-side door.

I drove toward the dead end. I shifted into second, sped up a bit. I began to think that maybe you could learn to drive just by watching. But once we reached the bottom of the street, I could not get the car in reverse. The engine stalled. I restarted it and shoved the shifter into reverse. I took my foot off the clutch too quickly. The car began to tremble and buck. Father pressed his hands against his thighs and held his breath. I could see the blue vein on his temple flickering in and out. Finally, he burst out, "Ride the clutch!"

"I can do this."

"No." He turned toward me. His face was red. "Put your foot down on the clutch, press it to the floor, and keep it there."

I obeyed. He unbuckled his seat belt, reached across the dash, grabbing the wheel in one hand, the stick shift in the other. Leaning over me, shifting and steering, he said, "Now keep your foot on the clutch."

I nodded.

"Give it some gas."

I did.

We drove the rest of the way home like that, him leaning over me, his hands on the steering wheel, telling me when to brake, when to give it gas. He never took me out again.

* * *

My parents enrolled me in a driver's education class. Mr. Barber conducted driving lessons after school in the back parking lot at Mercy. He had lost a son. It happened in 1980. There was a rifle with no safety and two boys. His boy died.

Mr. Barber was a good driving instructor—calm, measured, with a wry sense of humor. I looked at him at every stoplight, at every corner, every pause in traffic, my hands on the wheel at ten o'clock and two o'clock, and heard my father's voice saying, "He lost his son too, baby." For my parents this death was significant. They could trust him. They could put me in his hands because he knew how careful he had to be.

Susanna Spindale was in the class with me. We were the only girls over sixteen in the group. She preferred riding her Schwinn three-speed to driving. But Susanna had finally fallen victim to the seductions of a boy. She wanted her license so that she could drive to Billy's house.

One day after last period, just before driver's ed, I waited for Susanna to finish touching up her makeup in the bathroom on the third floor.

"What you need is a boyfriend," she said, applying lipstick.

"What happened to the Ken doll?"

"What are you talking about?" She stared at her reflection in the mirror.

"'I'll be the only girl at the dance who, when she grows tired of her date, can shove him in her purse.' Don't you remember that?"

"That was a long time ago. We've grown up." She ran her pinkie along her upper lip. "Look, I'll find you a boyfriend and we can double-date. Billy knows somebody."

"Have you been talking to my mother?"

"No. Why?"

I shook my head. "Nothing."

"We'll go to the drive-in. I'll lend you my red poodle skirt and I'll wear the blue one. With a white poplin blouse, you'll be adorable."

"Susanna, life is not one long costume party."

She snapped her compact shut. "Isn't it?" she asked. "You could have fooled me."

When driver's education came to a close, Mother signed me up for a driving test. She took Thursday afternoon off work, picked me up at school, and drove me downtown to the testing site. We sat in the car awaiting our turn for the test that would qualify me for a license. Mother found the wait unbearable. After about ten minutes she handed me the keys, told me to stay put, and stepped out of the car. "I'll be back when you're done," she said through the car window. She walked around the corner looking for a diner where she could purchase a cup of coffee. Shortly after Mother left, the tester arrived. Miss Lynn threw open the passenger-side door, plopped into the seat next to me, and pulled out her clipboard.

"Learner's permit," she said, holding out her hand.

I handed her the form.

She made some marks on the test sheet and peered down at the form. "Now, Miss Smith," she said. "Let's see what you can do."

I turned the key in the ignition. The Chevette rumbled to life. I sat there, the car idling away under us.

Miss Lynn was a large, pretty woman, with a pouf of blond hair teased up off her head. She looked over at me, raised her eyebrows. She folded her hands on top of her clipboard and began tapping her foot against the floor mat. "Are you waiting for something, Miss Smith?" she asked.

I cleared my throat. "I'm warming it up."

"Right." Miss Lynn leaned forward, felt around under her seat for the hand lever, pulled it up, and pushed the car seat back. She stretched out her legs. She crossed her arms over her chest, shifted her weight so that she was staring right at me, and asked, "How warm does it have to be?"

"I guess I could start now," I said.

"I guess you could."

I nodded at her. I paused.

"Now, Miss Smith."

I leaned over the steering wheel and stared into the side-view mirror at the traffic. The light behind us changed. The road flooded with cars. "Kind of busy today," I said.

"Not really."

I leaned out even further, craned my neck around, and looked back at the street. I turned back toward Miss Lynn. I smiled at her. I adjusted the rearview mirror.

"You've had half a dozen huge openings," Miss Lynn said. "Do you plan to pull out onto the road or not?"

I leaned over the steering wheel and looked out again.

"Go, Miss Smith, or I'm failing you."

I remained still. I could not put my foot on the gas and roll forward.

Miss Lynn pulled out her clipboard, marked a big red F across the driver's test sheet, and handed it to me. "Bring that into the office." She unbuckled her seat belt, popped open the Chevette's side door, and hoisted herself out of the car.

Mother returned from the diner on the corner and saw me waiting alone in the parked car. She stood on the curb squinting into the side window of the car. She waved. She smiled. She opened the door and leaned in. "That was fast." She sat down in the passenger seat, reached under her for the hand lever, and pulled the seat up. "How did you do?"

I held up the test paper. The K-turn, stopping, parallel parking, changing lanes—every section had a red F written across it. She shook her head. "How could you have failed all of this?"

I glanced out the side-view mirror. Miss Lynn walked to the next car in the row. A perky girl with a brown ponytail rolled down her window. Miss Lynn clamped her clipboard under her elbow and shook the girl's outstretched hand.

Mother handed back the test paper. "Next time," she said.

* * *

I took the test again a week later. Miss Lynn stepped into the car. "Hello, again," she said. She pulled out her clipboard, buckled her safety belt, adjusted the seat, clicked open her pen, and waited.

I turned over the engine, put the car in first, held on to the wheel, and stared.

"Is anything wrong?" she asked.

I shook my head.

We were in the middle of a parking lot this time. It would have been an easy start. I could just pull out of the parking space, point the car toward the exit.

Miss Lynn leaned her head back against the car seat and sighed. "I really don't have time for this." She held up her clipboard, wrote another big *F* across it. Just before she heaved herself out of the car, she said, "I don't think you really want to drive."

But I did. I wanted to drive.

51

SUSANNA SPINDALE delivered on her threat to find me a boy. It happened at a birthday party for a girl I barely knew, someone from the popular set at school, an actress, a friend of Susanna's. Susanna met me at the door in a floor-length watered silk tea gown with off-the-shoulder straps and a pair of nineteen-forties open-toed sandals. She held the neck of a peach wine cooler between two fingers of her gloved right hand, and with her left, she brought the tip of her black cigarette filter to her mouth.

"Darling," she cried, "where have you been?" She opened the door a little further and held it with her elbow. She looked at my outfit. I wore an oversized white oxford and a pair of jeans with holes in the knees. She took the cigarette away from her mouth, exhaled, and asked, "Is that the best you could do?" Her nose wrinkled.

"I didn't realize it was a formal."

"It's not, but this"—she pinched the worn fabric of my shirt-sleeve and shook her head—"this is just sad."

She stepped to one side, pressed her back into the door, and waved me in. I saw that Susanna was the only one in a watered silk tea gown. In fact, she was the only one in a dress at all. She flitted around the room, swigging her peach wine cooler and taking long drags on her cigarette filter.

It was a crowd I was not familiar with, and I was immediately ill at ease. I roamed around the deserted kitchen for a few minutes; then I retired to the living room where, sipping a 7UP, I curled into an armchair in the corner, found a magazine in the seat pocket, and began to read. Susanna came over and sat on the arm of the chair. "Don't tell me you're going to play wallflower again."

I turned a page of the magazine. "There are so many people here," I said.

"I know," she whispered. "It's divine."

I nodded, looked down at the magazine. "Divine."

She waved at someone across the room. A lanky, dark-haired boy in an REO Speedwagon T-shirt stepped away from a crowd of beer drinkers and headed in our direction. Susanna sat up on the seat arm, smoothed her dress, grabbed the magazine, and tossed it over the back of the chair. She whispered to me, through a smile, "I want you to be nice to him, Al. He's definitely available—just broke up with some girl from the public school." She winked at me.

Susanna stood up and introduced the boy. We shook hands. His palm was warm and damp.

I leaned forward. "What's your name again?"

He wiped his palm against his pant leg and repeated his name. I forgot it almost immediately.

Susanna waved her hand in the direction of the arm of the chair. "Have a seat," she said.

I looked up to catch her eye. She was gone.

The boy sat next to me, hunched, awkward. Tapping his fingers against his thigh, picking out a rhythm, he jogged his foot up and down a few times.

"You play the piano?" I asked.

He gave me a quizzical look. I pointed at his fingers tapping his thigh. "The piano," I repeated.

"Oh," he said. He shook his head. "No." He leaned over and said something to me. I could not make it out over the noise of the crowd.

"What?" I asked.

"Do you want a beer?"

I shook my head. Susanna caught my eye. She stood, poised in an arched doorframe, one gloved hand resting on the smooth oak of a side table. She set down her wine cooler, pushed her fingers into the corners of her mouth, and nodded at me. "Smile," she mouthed.

I smiled.

She pointed at the boy. "At him."

I smiled at the boy.

He pursed his lips, nodded. His mouth was pink, and he had a bit of a flush on his wide cheekbones. From the beer, I thought. I scooted to the end of the chair and said, "Let's get out of here."

He stood up. "Okay," he said, and he followed me across the living room, through the kitchen, and out the back door.

Fifteen minutes later, after some preliminary small talk about college, as we walked under a line of weeping willows at the edge of the apartment complex, the noise of the expressway whining in the distance, I put my hand on his arm, above the elbow. He looked down at my hand. I stepped toward him and placed my mouth on his. He smelled of watered-down beer. His hands hovered for a while around my back. He didn't seem to know where to put them. I kept thinking about his hands floating there above the pleated shirt back, and I started laughing. I pulled away, turned toward the parking lot, and tried to compose myself.

He ducked his head down toward me. "What?" he asked. He touched the tips of his fingers to my cheek, turned my head back toward him. "What's so funny?"

I shook my head. "Nothing."

He tipped my chin up toward him and placed his mouth on mine again. I felt his tongue brush against my teeth. His hands started floating in the small space between us. Then he pulled me to him, pressing his body against me. I could feel his hands tremble through my shirt, and I thought, *He's scared.* And then, *What did he say his name was?* And I waited. I listened for the click, the hum of desire to propel me toward him. But inside, everything remained still.

His hands moved off the small of my back and floated up around my shirtfront, closing in on my breasts. I felt his fingers brush against me, the soft nubbly fabric, and then, the warmth of his damp palm. I pulled away from him.

I took a few steps out toward the center of the parking lot. I tugged at the collar of my shirt.

He followed me. "Are you all right?" he asked.

I nodded. He stepped toward me. Under the buzzing electric lights, his skin was so white it was almost blue. His hair was dark and long. It hung in thin, inky curls, scrolling down the back of his neck. It was the darkest hair I had ever seen, especially on a boy so pale.

"Don't you want to?"

"You're so . . ."

"I'm what?"

"You're so." I shook my head. "I don't even know you."

He wiped his mouth, looked away from me. He sighed. "It's all right," he said. "We can just talk, if you want."

I looked at him one more time, at the hair that hung close around his ears and neck. I could not bring myself to look into his eyes. "Let's go back to the party," I said. A car engine revved to life. He pressed his palms together and nodded. We walked back in silence.

An hour later, as I stood in front of the apartment complex waiting for my ride, Susanna walked up holding two wine coolers, one in each gloved hand. She held one out to me. "So I hear you blew it."

I took the bottle from her outstretched hand and sipped. It tasted sticky and sweet. I swallowed. "I guess I did."

"I don't understand you." She sighed and ran her free hand down the length of her hair.

"It's okay," I said. "You don't have to."

She laughed, a high, hard sound. She was just about to say something when Billy appeared, a dark silhouette at her side. He wrapped an arm around her waist. She leaned into him. A car drove up. I handed the bottle back to her and walked toward the parking lot.

A week later, Mother and I drove to the DMV once again, stood in line, and filled out forms. This time, I was required to take a written test as well. Then I headed out to the testing lot and waited for Miss Lynn. Finally, after countless hours of practice and two failed tests, I pulled out into the traffic. I K-turned, I stopped, I looked both ways, I signaled, I changed lanes, I parallel-parked. When we returned to the testing lot, Miss Lynn sat in the passenger seat, adding up my score with her red ballpoint. She tore the test sheet off her pad and handed it to me. "By the skin of your teeth," she said, and for the last time, she stepped out of the car.

Mother let me drive home. Father met us at the door, as he had the last two times, his hands pressed against the bowed screen, waiting. Mother stepped out of the passenger side. I saw her give a little sign, a quick furtive nod to Father, and he rushed out onto the lawn. "Baby," he said. "You did it."

52

IT STARTED WHEN I got lost. I had taken the car over to a grocery store in Pittsford to pick up something for Mother, and on the way home I took a wrong turn, found myself in a strange neighborhood, and I kept driving. The sun set. Cars all around me snapped on their lights. They lit up like Christmas trees, streaking across the darkening road. My parents had gone to dinner at a friend's house. There was no way they could know how long I took coming back from the store. Mesmerized by the lights of the oncoming cars, I drove for hours.

At two A.M., the next night, I found myself up, the bottom of my nightshirt tucked into my jeans, standing in my parents' bedroom. I slipped a set of keys off Father's bureau. I drove around the dark suburb for an hour or so, coasted the Chevette back into the driveway, and slipped the keys back onto Father's bureau.

I did it again the next night, and again and again. After an hour of dividing my dinner in half, pushing it around the plate, I would watch Mother and Father leave the kitchen and finally flush the whole thing down the garbage disposal. I would visit Father in the living room, where every night he read the paper, and ask if I could borrow the Chevette for the evening. I said I wanted to visit Susanna or go to the movies, and Father fished the keys out of his pocket and handed them over. I did not visit Susanna and I did not go to the movies. I drove farther and farther out, away from home, watching the lights of the oncoming cars, feeling the engine vibrate beneath me, waiting.

I always told myself that I was going to go just around the block, just to the end of the street, just to the edge of town, but I could not stop. I would try to turn back toward home, but I could not do it. I could not make the car turn around. I would continue down the smooth, darkened road to Avon or Honeoye Falls and beyond. The straight country roads bannered out before me, the highway calling to me with its bright signs, its northern promises of Canada, the noisy pop music station fading as the vestiges of civilization dropped away on the roadside behind me.

When I did manage to get the Chevette pointed in a homeward direction, it usually took a few tries before I could bring myself to pull into our driveway. As the driveway moved closer on the right, I realized that I could not face the darkened house, the ringing silence of an engine just cut off, the ticks and pings of the cooling transmission. So after a short tour through the neighborhood, I would pass our house and keep going. Soon, I was back on the main road.

Grief can blind you; it pulls loose the seam of memory. It weakens your senses. The only time my heart woke up and noticed the world around me that year was at night, inside the metal box of Mother's car, driving through the outskirts of Rochester, the light from the oncoming headlights smearing across my wind-shield.

Summer arrived, fresh and bright and lovely. I drove more, rolled down the windows and waited for July, for the third anniversary of his death. In those weeks leading up to the anniversary, I saw only my brother's final minutes. No other memory seemed to exist. As if it were an accusation, a penance, an equation I could not solve, I would return to the image of the burning boy.

I remember the sky those nights, clouded and moonless or speckled with constellations, the engine overheating on the uphill climbs. I drove holding the steering wheel close, the radio voices calling to me, my eyes on the yellow dividing line. Sometimes, on the country roads, a truck would come barreling up behind me and ride my tailpipe, flashing its brights. I never knew how to manage the situation. The road was too dark for me to pull over and let him pass. The only sound was the revving engine of the impatient truck. How could he know that I could never speed up, that this nightly drive was a measured experiment? I waited and watched, counting the hours, counting how long it would take before that one errant car, an old blue Dodge with bald tires, crossed the dividing line into my lane.

53

ON THE THIRD anniversary of his death, I woke at 5:00 A.M. I padded across the hall into Roy's room, slid open the third drawer of his dresser, and found a cross-country T-shirt and a pair of his jeans. I dressed in his room in the dark. When I had secured the jeans with a belt, the waist bunching up around my midriff, I slipped into my parents' room and watched them sleep.

The sun was not up yet. Just the faintest hint of color seeped around the edges of the Henderson home across the street. Gray light streamed through the porthole window and washed across the bedspread. Father held his hands curled around each other as if in the midst of prayer. It seemed to me, as I sat in the wicker rocker and gazed at them, that the sky was dissolving. It washed over their sleeping bodies and held them there, suspended in time, motionless, weightless, staining dark circles around their mouths and eyes. I could hardly make out their faces.

For three years we had lived under the same roof without Roy. We traveled the distance between each other's bedrooms. In between the secret haunt of my room and the sweet quiet of theirs, in the middle of the hall, stood Roy's room—silent, waiting, its door hanging open, because no one had the heart to close it for good. It called to us, called us back, again and again, to a past we could never reach.

As I sat in front of them that morning, the night slowly loosening its hold on the sky, their passive bodies turning in the sheets, I felt again the warm rush of love that welled up in me every time I saw them sleep. Watching them rest was almost the same as resting myself. I remembered Roy and I huddled in his twin bed, his knobby spine pressing into me, after Father's morning blessing, after he had leaned over my bed and whispered, "Anything you want, baby, God will give it to you. Just name it." I asked Roy, "Can you name it?" He shook his head. "No, you name it." We knew, even then, that in our family, there were some things you did not dare name.

I wanted to change that. I wanted to rush over to the bed and shake them awake. I wanted to stop playing Kremlin, to stop hiding and waiting and biting my tongue. I wanted to tell them everything. *Someday*, I thought, *we will tell each other all our secrets.* Someday we will return to the beginning, to the Garden of Eden, where Adam first named every living thing, every plant and animal God gave him. And there, with Father and his relics, with Mother and her backpack of encyclopedias, I wanted us to say it all, to name every thought, every word, every kind of animal we had dreamed up in those three long years. I leaned forward in the rocker and thought, *Perhaps after this morning, after I am gone.*

The sun was rising now and the clock on the night table ticked out the minutes and I knew I could not stay any longer. I stood up, tugged at the ends of the T-shirt. The soft cotton caressed my bony shoulders. I slid Father's keys off the worn cherrywood bureau. But this time I did not take the keys to the Chevette. I took the keys to the camper-van.

54

I PASSED THE LINE of white clapboard houses, glowing pink in the rising sun. The stillness of the early morning rested on the wet lawns. The trees—the oaks and the sugar maples, the beeches and the sycamores—leaned over the dark lawns, dropping their leaves by ones and twos, onto the summer grass. I headed toward the top of the road. When I reached it, I signaled, and took a right. I pointed the camper-van east, toward the hill.

As the sun rose, the clouds broke apart and the air grew moist, releasing the nighttime dew. The cicadas screamed into the deepening blue of the morning sky. I could tell the day was going to rise hot and bright. No slick-wet road, no rainwater collecting in runnels. Just the dry pavement warming under the first rays of the sun. I wondered how it was going to work without the rain, but I figured it did not matter. It was the other car I needed. I needed that 1972 Dodge with bald tires to drive back, out of time, and find me in the van.

I passed Wilkins Dairy, where as children Roy and I ran the length of the muddy parking lot with empty milk bottles, racing for the door. I passed the old brick house where, once when we were children, Mother had stopped and introduced us to a tall woman in a pink smock; together, the four of us picked strawberries in her field. I was closing in on the farm stand at the top of the hill when I decided to check my watch.

Five-fifty-one A.M. I was a little early. I pulled into the dirt lot by the farm stand. I rolled down the window and smelled the wind off the sweet corn in the fields. A girl pulled crates of tomatoes, beans, and summer squash off the truck and lined them up at the base of the wooden overhang. She was hoisting the canvas tarp off the display tables when I popped open the driver's-side door and hopped out onto the dusty gravel. I squinted into the white sunlight and stumbled back, resting my hands against the side of the van.

"We're not open yet," she called. "Fifteen minutes." She yanked a canvas tarp. The muscles on her arms bunched up under her tan skin, flicking like a heartbeat. I did not recall her name, but I knew she attended the public school on the other side of the hill.

"That's okay," I called. I waved. As my hand floated back and forth in the cool morning air, I thought, *Will that be the last thing I ever say?*

The sun rose higher in the sky. The girl pulled at her canvas tarps. I climbed back into the van and turned the key in the ignition. I looked at my watch. Five-fifty-three A.M. I had two minutes.

The trees on the hill grew tall and close to the road. If I took my eyes off the road for a moment and looked up into the broad, bright leaves, I could imagine that I was driving into a wall of green. As the van and I dropped down the steep hill, I kept an eye out for the place where the guardrail broke away. When it came into view, I slowed down. I looked across the double yellow line. I heard Father say, "Never cross the dividing line, baby."

And then I saw Roy. In those last moments, adjusting the radio knob, shifting his weight, his hands palming the wheel. The radio whining out into the wet morning air. The rain rivering down the road. The car appears—a woman in an old Dodge struggling up the hill, her wipers soaked with rain, her pinched face peering out as the car begins to shake. She grips the wheel. She feels the tires spin beneath her. The rainwater is rushing hard now, floating them, and then in a breath, a split second, the car spins out and crosses the dividing line.

I looked at my watch again. Five-fifty-five A.M. I was closing in on that mangled railing, and still there was no car in sight, no one struggling up the hill in a 1972 Dodge with bald tires, a full tank of gas. No Raymond Cino pulling up the rear, driving the long hill in his steel gray uniform, guiding the postal truck through the wall of green. The road was deserted. I closed my eyes and gunned the engine.

55

MOMENTS LATER, I found myself in the deserted parking lot at the bottom of the hill, staring into the Panorama Plaza neon sign. I looked around me. I was surrounded by the remnants of my childhood. The ice cream stand where Roy and I bought soft-serve and marveled over its smooth coldness on our tongues. The pool where we learned to dive and I learned to hold my breath for half a length. The grocery store where Mother went every Wednesday with her red coupon book, a handkerchief tied around her hair. The Key Drugstore, where once when I was five, I lost my father in the stationery aisle. For a few terrible minutes, I had thought he was gone forever. The Fanny Farmer Candy Shop, where Father bought bouquets of suckers and saved the lemon ones for me. *Perhaps I was too early,* I thought. I turned the van around and headed back up the hill.

When I reached the crest of the hill, I pulled up to the farm stand. The girl stood behind her rows of vegetable bins, a cashbox at her side. She waved, pulled a strand of hair off her face, and tucked it behind her ear. "I'm open," she called. I parked the van and walked over. I ran my hand over the bright skin of an apple.

"It's early for apples."

"I know." She smiled. "These are the first." She picked one out, a Cortland. "These are the best, crisp and tart." She held it out to me.

I took it from her. "How much?" I asked.

"Twenty-five cents."

I dug into my pocket for change. Then I remembered I was not wearing my jeans. I was wearing Roy's. "I'm sorry," I said, holding the apple out to her. "I don't have it right now."

She pushed the apple back. "Take it," she said. She smiled. Her front teeth were crooked, one tipped over the other. She shifted her weight to one side and crossed her arms. "You're the Smith girl, aren't you?"

I nodded.

"I know you're good for it," she said.

I walked back to the van. Leaning against the bumper, I bit into the apple. Its white flesh broke off under my teeth. I wiped the juice from my chin and took another bite. When I reached the halfway point, I shoved the apple in the front pocket of Roy's jeans and climbed back into the van.

This time, there was an oncoming car. Right at the break in the guardrail. I braced myself, but nothing happened. The sedan passed by, keeping to its own lane. For a second time that morning, I found myself staring up into the Panorama Plaza neon sign, my hands white-knuckling the steering wheel, holding my breath.

I looked around the plaza. The Hess gas station boys, white bandannas hanging out the back pockets of their white jumpsuits, rested their backs against the glass-sided service room. A few cars arrived, made their way across the parking lot. A woman in purple spandex tights held two-pound weights in her hands and struggled across the empty lot. The sun hovered low in the sky, just above the plaza sign. The van was spread across three parking spaces at the west end of the plaza, close to the foot of the hill.

I let go of the wheel. I slumped back. Warm vinyl pressed into the back of the T-shirt. My foot hovered over the brake. I looked down. My legs were shaking, the knees jogging up and down against the van seat. I pressed my hands into them, but the shaking got worse. The heat at my back was rising. The trembling rose the length of my body. My torso started to shake, and the world dimmed. For months I had planned this moment. I had let the world fall away as I waited for the day when I would follow Roy, the day I could not live past. If I lived past the summer of my eighteenth year, the days would line up inside me, and for every one, every moment beyond that morning in late July, I would have to face that Roy died and that I—the little sister, the tagalong, the second-place girl—would surpass him. I rested my cheek on the rim of the steering wheel. I looked out the passenger-side window.

The first thing you come to at the northwest corner of the plaza just at the foot of the hill is a miniature golf course. Every summer of my childhood I played a round with Roy while Mother did her weekly grocery shopping. At the end of the eighteen holes there was one last shot, a long ramp ending with a maze, not unlike a pinball board. If you could get your ball in the center hole, you won a free game. Roy was a better shot than I was, and I always let him take both tries, first with his ball, then with mine. He came close a few times. He set it up, worked out the physics behind it. But still, we never won.

I remember nights when we would lie on the back lawn talking. After a while he would fall silent, and I would look at him and watch his face cloud over with concern.

I sat up on my elbows. "What's wrong?"

He stared up into the night sky, his brow furrowed. "Maybe if I bank it off the right top corner, it would ricochet in."

I flopped back onto the grass. "Are you still worrying about that free game shot?" I rolled away from him. "Face it. We're never going to get it. It's impossible."

He nodded. "You're right."

But the next week he was right there, lining up the shot with pinpoint precision, measuring the distances, banking the ball off the top right corner. I think he played that whole round every week just so he could try for the free game.

Then, one day, when we got to the end, after he took his free shot and missed, he stepped back. "Your turn," he said.

"But you always do it," I faltered. "You always take the shot for me."

He held the club behind his back. "It's your turn, Alroy."

I stared down at my well-worn golf ball. It maintained little of its toothpaste white golf-ball shine. It had been hit and tapped and dinged and slammed so many times by so many Putt-Putt clubs that it was just a collection of scuffs and stains. I didn't even like golf. I didn't even care. I squinted. I sighed. I set the ball down on its designated tee spot, pressed my hands into the handle of the club, positioned my feet shoulder width apart.

Roy crossed his arms and watched me. "Don't lean too far into it," he said.

I stepped back, shaded my eyes with my hand. "Are you going to let me take this shot or not?"

I resumed my position and squinted down the AstroTurf ramp into the tiny hole. I had a feeling that, even if I got the ball near the hole, there was no way it would fit in. I stepped up to the tee, closed my eyes, and swung.

The next thing I knew Roy was grabbing me around the middle, jumping up and down and yelping. "You did it! I don't know how, but you did it. Hole in one!" He beamed at me, put his hands out, palms up. I set down the club and slapped them. "Hole in one!" he kept repeating. "Hole in one!"

We picked up our free game voucher at the mini-golf booth and turned in our clubs.

"Let's go find Mom in the store and show her," he said, and he handed me the green card that read, "One Free Game."

"You hold on to it," I said.

"Why? You won it."

But I insisted. I wanted him to keep it in his pocket. "It will be safer there," I said.

He slid it in his back jeans' pocket.

"In the front pocket," I said. "In case somebody tries to pick-pocket you."

"It will get wrinkled."

"I don't care."

He nodded, slid it out of his back pocket, folded it once, and tucked it into the front pocket.

We ran the length of the plaza in two minutes flat.

The green One Free Game card hung on the refrigerator for years. Roy pointed to it every time he opened the door. He would slap his finger on it and say, "Look! It's One Free Game!" Every week, Mother would pull it off the refrigerator door and say, "Let's use this." Together, we would cry, "No!" Then we would pull out our weekly allowance and insist on paying for the week's game from our savings. We liked having our free voucher, knowing that, at any point, we could ride down to Panorama Plaza without a penny between us, and sign up for a game of golf.

I sat up, stepped out of the van, and crossed the parking lot. The booth where we waited in line to rent the clubs, where we held out our shirts and let the booth lady pour in a golf ball, a scorecard, and two pencils each, was boarded up. The 18 + 1 MINI-GOLF sign was covered in burlap sacks. I walked over to the fenced-in mini-green and hooked my fingers through the chain link. I tried to identify under which lump of burlap the nineteenth hole was located. The lights on the stores began to tick on behind me, and the birds in the tall oaks at the base of the hill chirped and twittered. I gazed out over the heaps of burlap and thought, *One Free Game*. I slid my hand into the front pocket of Roy's jeans.

I felt the juice from the apple seeping into the soft cotton of the pocket lining, the smooth arc of skin where it nestled against my palm. I pulled out the apple. The bite marks around the edges delineated the halfway point. Dark seeds at the core bulged through the meat of the apple. I brought it to my mouth and took a bite.

The second half was sharper than the first. Its crunchy tartness exploded in my mouth; the juice dribbled down my hand. My saliva came fast, burning the edges of my mouth. My jaw tightened, and the hunger rose up in me like a rash, searing my throat. I ate the whole thing. When I was done, I listened to my stomach rumble and come to life. I looked up at the hill that led into the Penfield valley, at the line of trees that banked the north face of the mini-golf green and, beyond that, out onto the road. I heard his voice. Morning light bounced off the van behind me, an apple core cradled in the palm of my hand. Roy leaned in, and he whispered, "It's your turn, Al."

Epilogue

THERE IS ONLY one burial plot left in the grass next to my brother's grave in Holy Sepulchre Cemetery. In the summer of 1997, Father started to worry about this. On my visit home, he spreads a cemetery map across the kitchen counter.

"We could have Great-Uncle Charlie moved. That will make room for two of us," Father says. "I don't know how we are all going to fit. Mother and I could go here and here"—he points to Uncle Charlie's grave and the empty space next to Roy. "Even if we move Uncle Charlie, that still leaves us one plot short. There's no space for you."

"How do you think Charlie's going to feel about the move?" I ask.

"Don't worry about Charlie. He's a shirttail relation."

On the other side of Uncle Charlie is an unmarked grave. According to state law, unidentified remains cannot be exhumed for any purpose but identifying them. "And that would cost a pretty penny," Father says.

Father looked into purchasing a family plot that would fit all four of us. When he found out how expensive it would be to exhume Roy's body, purchase a new, larger plot, and rebury him, Father decided to try a new approach.

He calls me the following autumn. "This is a good idea, baby," he says. "I haven't fixed it with the guys at Holy Sepulcher yet. But I think the lady in the front office is sympathetic."

"Dad, tell me your idea."

"How do you feel about cremation?"

"I haven't thought about it. Why?"

"If you agree to this we could all be together."

"What is it?"

"Would you mind having your body cremated?" he asks. "That way we could bury you on top of your brother."

In October 1997, Roy's best friend, Tim, got married in a church at Genesee Country Museum outside Rochester. The bride and groom rented cabins and spent their wedding night around a bonfire in Letchworth State Park with thirty friends—a collection of Air Force personnel, backpackers, bankers, former Jesuit school boys, and me. Tim arranged for me to bunk with Roy's friends, and so I found myself in a state park cabin with five men, drunk on home brew and playing euchre. At midnight John decided to turn the oven into a space heater. We opened the metal door and watched the coils glow in the darkened room.

After everyone else had fallen asleep, John and I huddled over the oven door trying to keep warm as we whispered and laughed. Roy and John met in eleventh grade, in chemistry. He lives in L.A. now, where he tries to find work as a stand-up comedian.

He told me a story about Roy, one I'd never heard: It was December of their senior year. Roy and Tim went running. A light snow fell. They found themselves outside Store 24, where John worked. Instead of going in to say hello, they jimmied the lock on John's Rabbit, hid in the backseat, and waited for his shift to end. After closing, John opened his car door, slid into the driver's seat, and started the engine. He reached behind him for the snow brush, and something grabbed his hand. He screamed. Roy and Tim popped up, holding the snow brush and laughing.

Four A.M. in a littered, freezing cabin, the only light in the room bleeding off the red coils in the oven, and I see my brother clearly once again. I see the ragged ends of his soft brown hair, I hear his laugh and the cadence of his voice, the angle of light as it fell across him on winter afternoons as he ran down the driveway.

John goes to bed. Tim sleeps in the far cabin with his new bride. Roy would have liked her. He would have liked all of it. Soon John and Peter and Greg and Chips and Bob sleep around me. I listen to them snore. From my spot at the stove near the center of the room, I can see all five of them. Together we have drunk seven six-packs, eaten twelve bags of Doritos and countless Little Debbie chocolate cream cakes. I watch the boys closely, looking for some clue, some sign, as if they have the secret decoder ring—the key to living. They have grown different from each other with age—one an account executive at a D.C. bank, another a backwoods guide in Alaska. But they are in constant touch. I wonder if they would have remained this close if Roy hadn't died, these men I insist on calling boys, as if they, too, were caught in time. As if, like Roy, they will be forever eighteen.

I wrap a sleeping bag around myself and step outside. A soft rain starts to fall. It patters over the autumn leaves. I lean against a picnic table and watch the embers in the fire pit. A figure comes weaving toward me. I can just make out the beam from a weak flashlight and a military cap. It is a boy I don't know. I saw him earlier at the ceremony. Tim must have met him in the Air Force. He stops and trains the light on me. "Who goes there?" he asks.

I hold up my hands, shielding my eyes.

"Sorry." He turns the flashlight off. He puts out his hand. "Billy Williams."

We shake. "Alison Smith," I say. "Have a seat."

I offer him the last Little Debbie cake. He declines. The wind picks up and rustles the trees. Leaves fall in heavy, wet bunches around the dying fire. Billy looks at the sky. He pulls out a rain poncho and offers me half. I take it.

"Thanks," I say.

"Friend of the bride or the groom?" he asks.

When I drive up to my parents' new house the day after the wedding, they are standing on the front porch adjusting their lawn chairs, looking past me at the horizon. Everything has been landscaped since my last visit. Mother folds her arms across her chest and holds her elbows. She points her chin toward a rose of Sharon.

"I just planted that in July."

They sold the house we grew up in, painted over the faded pencil markings that recorded our growing size on the kitchen doorframe, felled the rotting fort, and moved to a prefab housing development. In their new house there is an automatic fireplace. A light switch in the exposed brick interior turns it on and off. Mother flicks the switch, and two gas-fed flames flare to life, burning over the fake logs. My parents show me the treasures in their new house: the track lighting, the wall-to-wall carpeting, the security system that beeps every time you open a door, the ice machine.

"Do you want to see the Florida Room?" Mother asks.

"Excuse me?"

She leads me to a room walled with screened windows.

"It's lovely," I say.

"It's what my people call a porch," says Father.

Father has taken well to retirement. For a while he studied piano. He would call me up, set the phone on top of the upright, and plunk out a tune. But the piano did not hold his interest. He joined a golf club. At seventy he is the youngest in the group. The other men call him the Kid.

After supper, Father and I sit in the Florida Room. He looks out at the new backyard. He has been thinking. I can see it in the working of his jaw. It clenches and releases.

"All these years I've been asking God about Roy's guardian angel. I still don't get it." He shakes his head. "Where was he?"

I have not noticed my father aging. Perhaps he is a little grayer, perhaps his shoulders stoop a bit more this year. But this fresh wonder keeps him young. And it keeps him stuck in time. Unable to find the proper ending, he cannot step away from the story of his lost boy.

I lean forward. "Maybe he was there," I say. "Maybe he was the first one to see him die."

"Then why didn't he save him?"

"I don't know."

He nods once more, presses his fingertips together, and then leans over and picks up the paper.

I leave my father in the Florida Room and find Mother in her bathroom. She does not wear Roy's clothes anymore, except for the boots. She has been unable to part with them. She resoles them every couple of years. Even though they are heavy work boots, she wears them on hikes in the Adirondacks. Her hair has barely grayed. The glare from the mirror reflects off her glasses, and I cannot see her eyes, but it does not matter. I have memorized them—the intricate threads of green and gold and brown.

"You used to watch me like that when you were a little girl," she says.

"Did I?"

Later that night, at the foot of the stairs, she calls, "Alroy?"

I run to the stairs. In the silence that follows, the name hovers in the air between us. She looks away.

After they have gone to bed, I wander the halls of the strange new house. It smells of plastic and wood chips. I sit in the breakfast nook, in front of the glass doors to the deck. Light from the neighbor's emergency lamp snaps on: a stray dog, a raccoon, some feral thing has tripped the sensor. I listen as it digs through the garbage. The breeze picks up, the trees begin to whisper, and I can just make out the backs of the leaves as they shudder in the wind.

The next day Father and I go for a drive. We eat breakfast at Perkins. He leans over his scrambled eggs and whispers, "Mother and I are going on a cruise."

"That's great!"

"Shhhh!"

The waitress comes by and freshens his coffee.

"When are you going?" I whisper.

"The tenth of March," he whispers back. "It's for five days."

"Why are we whispering?" I ask.

"We haven't told anyone but you. We told our friends that we're going on a religious retreat."

"Why?"

"A new house, a cruise. What will people think of us?"

On the way home he explains what the ship looks like: the number of decks and their names. The number and types of swimming pools. He drives for half an hour. Suddenly, he looks at the street sign. "Where are we?" he asks.

In his enthusiasm about the cruise, he has forgotten himself. He drove to the old house. Since we are already there, we decide to take a look. We drive by slowly. The new owners have painted the shutters blue and planted a Japanese maple by the mailbox. A dog sits on the front step. Outside of these small changes, it looks the same. And then I notice it—from the flag post that Father hammered into the sugar maple in the front yard thirty years ago, shockingly bright, rippling in the early autumn breeze—hangs an enormous rainbow flag.

"Stop the car!" I yell. The dog barks. A woman comes to the front door.

"We better go," Father says. He speeds down the street.

I turn to him. "Who did you sell the house to?"

"A woman. She works at the hospital. She's some kind of therapist."

"Does she live there alone?"

"Well, she's got the dog."

"Do any *people* live with her?"

"There's this other woman. Mr. Lovell says she lives there too. They live there . . . together."

"Dad," I say, trying not to smile too broadly.

"What? What did I do now?"

"You sold the house to lesbians."

Father drives around for a while. We look at the old neighborhood. We drive past the dead-end sign by the opening in the woods that led Roy and me down to the abandoned house. "Remember the abandoned house?" I say.

"What abandoned house?"

I look over at him. His eyes are on the road. His hands rest loosely on the steering wheel. I remember he never knew about the dilapidated house in the gully. It had been Roy's and my secret.

"Let's go back," I say.

"Home?"

"To the old house."

"What if that lady's still there?"

"Then we won't stop. There's no harm in driving by."

He turns the car around.

This time, when we pull up to the house, the dog is gone. The front door is closed. There's no sign of the woman behind the door. The street is deserted. I open the car door.

"What are you doing?" Father asks.

"I just want to look."

I stand on the lawn and stare up at the house. After a while I hear the engine cut off behind me and then Father's loafers rustle across the lawn.

"They painted the shutters," he says.

I nod. "Yes, they did."

"I got a call yesterday," he says, "from the cemetery. It's official. We can cremate you and bury you on top of Roy. I had a bit of a fight with them, over the cremation, because it's not allowed in Catholic cemeteries, but I won. It will cost four hundred dollars to reserve the spot." He squints across the lawn, staring at the rainbow flag. "Ali, now are you sure want to be cremated and have your ashes buried on top of Roy?"

I follow his gaze and look at the flag. "You realize this is an odd question."

"I know, but the cemetery has to know and if you don't go there then we lose the four hundred dollars."

"Why do you want this so badly?"

"I want us to be together again, baby."

"Dad?"

"Yes?"

"Do you think about what it will be like when we die?"

"Oh, sure."

"What will it be like?"

"We'll be in heaven with Roy."

"You don't have any more details?"

"What do you mean?"

"What is heaven like? Is it warm all year? Is it pleasant? Do you get the newspaper there?"

"Baby, it doesn't matter. We'll be together."

I try to picture this heaven that my father persists in seeing. "Hey, Dad." I turn to him. "Remember Ghost Baseball?"

"Ghost what?"

"We used to play it on the front lawn." I point at the grass. "Right here."

Ghost Baseball was the first game Roy and I invented. Each of us was a team of nine: ourselves and eight "ghost men." These imaginary players peopled the outfield and the bases. We designed sets of intricate rules that became more elaborate with every game. The maple tree was first base. The Douglas fir grandfather planted in the front corner of the lot was third. If you hit the ball and it landed in Mrs. Brown's yard that was a two-run play. If you hit the ball and it flew by the maple, the Douglas fir, or the vaguely specified patch of ground that served as second, you were out. If, however, you knocked the ball clear out of the yard and it landed on Mrs. Brown's roof, you scored a home run, and all the ghost men ran home.

Ghost baseball required a lot more talking and negotiation than most sports, and the speculations on whose ghost man was where or how to account for fielding and fly balls were my favorite parts of the game. From the beginning I confused the Holy Ghost of the Trinity with my shortstop. I imagined the Holy Ghost, a shadowy, agile figure, an aureole of light surrounding his head, hustling between second and third. Then I imagined our outfielders were Jesus' apostles. In Catechism we learned that we were put on earth to love and serve Our Lord in this world to be happy with

Him in the next. But I was happy then. I had no thought of the next world.

As I swung and swung for that home run that never came no matter how slowly Roy pitched, I imagined them on the bases: Jesus and the apostles—my men, my team—crouched, expectant, waiting. They were ready to run for home if I could just catch a piece of the ball. I rarely did. When Roy was up to bat he always hit the ball.

"Ghost man on second and third!" Roy yelled as he dropped the bat and ran.

I beaned the ball at the Douglas fir and hollered, "No, ghost third isn't fast enough."

"You can't out a ghost man!" he called, his reedy voice pitching up into the sky.

I can still see his skinny legs pumping, his mud-splattered Boston Red Sox jersey pressing into the wind as he rounds first and slaps the bark of the sugar maple. I see his hands fly up. He tries to catch his baseball cap as it floats off his head. He rounds third and calls, "Ghost man running home."

Acknowledgments

I would like to thank the following people:

Kim Wiley for reading every single draft and, at key moments, housing and feeding me—this book would not exist without her; Katie Baldwin for believing in it long before I did; Valija Evalds for working by my side; Judy Fuller and Pearl Ratunil for more kindnesses than I can count; Charles Bock for Vermont and everything that followed; Carol Edelstein, Robin Barber, and Dori Ostermiller for letting me write in their living rooms; Paula Vogel, David Savran, and Jann Matlock for early encouragement; Sean Wilsey for making the connection; David McCormick for his integrity and his vision; Leslie Falk and Nina Collins for expert advice; Sarah McGrath for her keen editorial eye and extraordinary faith in this book; Nan Graham, Susan Moldow, and the staff of Scribner for incredible support.

And also: Joe Weisberg, Wyatt Mason, Rachel Sheinkin, Amy Kantrowitz, James Lowenthal, Mary Beth Brooker (and little Melle), Maria Healey, Fred Leebron, Rick Moody, Susanna Kaysen, Daphne Beal, Chaia Heller, Shulamith Oppenheim, Susan Stinson, Maddy Cahill, Quang Bao, Dawn Clifton Tripp, Charles Tsarnas, Christine Schutt, Julie Callahan, Heidi Thomson, the Virginia Center for the Arts, and The Corporation of Yaddo and the MacDowell Colony.

My deepest appreciation goes to my father, Royden Smith Sr., and my mother, Lavon Hansen Smith (born June 15, 1938, died April 8, 2003)—without whom naught.

What made you start writing about your family?

AS: In 1996 I had been writing short stories for a few years and was ready to take on a book-length project. I took a summer writing workshop at a college in Vermont.

At the beginning of the workshop we had each handed in stories. Mine were part of a series I was working on—rewritings of Greek myths from a female perspective. It was pretty dry stuff. My teacher took me aside one day and told me that my stories were well done. "But," he said, "I don't care. They're distant and cold. Why don't you write about your own life?"

"Why would I do that?" I asked. "Nothing ever happened to me."

He nodded. "Go home tonight and write a completely autobiographical, sentimental story."

I thought this was the worst advice anyone had ever given me. But I did it anyway. I wrote a short story about going to summer camp when I was twelve.

He read it the next night and said, "Now this is interesting."

Still, his advice threw me. I stopped writing for a while after that workshop. I reread my journals instead. (There were a lot of them—I had been keeping a diary since high school.) What I discovered was that when I was writing for myself, when I was not thinking about creating "literature," I wrote about my family, about my brother, Roy, about everything we had and everything we lost when he died.

Did the writing go smoothly once you figured out what you wanted to write about?

AS: It took six years and eighteen drafts to write *Name All the Animals*. It is the hardest thing I have ever willingly signed up for in my life. When I started it in 1996, I was quite naïve. I had no idea what writing a memoir would entail. And I made every mistake in the book. My first draft was eight hundred pages long and

I rarely appeared in it! Leaving yourself out of your own life story is quite an oversight. The most surprising thing that I faced was how hard it was to make myself the main character.

Why do you think it was such a challenge to put yourself in the story?

AS: Sibling grief is overlooked in our culture. When a child dies, we look to the parents. They are center stage in the tragedy. If siblings are noticed at all, it is only as an extension of the parents. They are told that they must make up for the lost child, they must look after their parents. I really bought into this line of thinking. When I started to write the book, I thought that I would write the story of my parents' lives, of everything they lost when Roy died. I thought that was the authentic family experience. It took me quite some time to realize that the sister's story was a very important story as well.

The book is filled with such vivid detail. How do you remember so much?

AS: At first what I discovered was how much I had forgotten. But as I looked closer I realized that I had not so much forgotten as locked away certain memories. Much of writing this book was about the act of remembering. When the memories started to come back, they were so vivid and visceral that I could not manage them easily. I cried quite often. I spent a lot of time just slogging through the intense images that were coming to me. Creating a narrative structure out of all these disparate and powerful images was my biggest challenge. Most of the time I was pretty sure that I would never figure it out.

What kept you going?

AS: I had made a promise to Roy that I would finish this book. And so I kept writing and revising. I became obsessed. As the years rolled by and it seemed I was getting more and more mired in the past, I just got more determined. By year five, I was completely consumed with the project. I had lost my waitressing job and

been evicted from my apartment, but I just could not stop working on this book. I put all my belongings in storage and was living in my car, driving up and down the east coast house-sitting
and staying with friends who offered to put me up while I wrote.
I finally finished the book in the spring of 2002 while house-sitting in Ithaca, New York.

**One of the things that strikes me about *Name All the Animals* is
how unjudgmental it is. We see your parents' failings, but you're so
understanding and humane.**

AS: I felt it was my job to portray them as complexly and as compas-
sionately as I could. Writing the book helped me understand
them. I think all of us have things we wish we could talk to our
parents about, but sometimes they're the hardest people to talk
to. By making them as real and as human as possible, I was able
to have a dialogue with them on the page.

Was writing the book like talking to them?

AS: Yes, it was. I was one of those kids who was born nostalgic. I was
always trying to get more stories out of my parents, more about
their past, more about the complexity or subtlety of their feelings. They found this personality trait of mine perplexing. "Why
do you have to ask so many questions?" they'd say. So I talked to
them on the page.

**Do you think that your life would've followed the same path had
Roy lived?**

AS: I think of the book as a family portrait. I would have written it
whether he lived or died. I still would have become a writer. I still
would have fallen in love with a woman. I try not to think too
hard about what life would be like if he had lived. It's too painful.
Instead, I try to think about what value I can take away from this
kind of devastating loss. When this sort of thing happens to you
in your adolescence, it is traumatizing; it is isolating. It makes
growing up so much harder. But it also makes you ask com-

pelling questions at a young age. What does it mean to have faith or lose your faith? Why do people die? Perhaps some of my peers had it easier. Perhaps they just memorized Madonna's song lyrics and tried on clothes, but I doubt it. That is a fantasy. Adolescence is hard for everyone.

You had a strange relationship to food in high school—saving food for Roy—and, at points, it seemed that you came close to starving yourself. Do you think you had an eating disorder?

AS: Yes. I did not have the same body-image distortion that accompanies classic anorexia, but I certainly had a complicated relationship to food. What started as a desperate act of grief turned into an addiction. I could not stop starving myself. When I went away to college and I got out of that house, that back yard where there were so many ghosts, the situation improved. Under the guidance of a therapist, I worked through a lot of it. There are still times when I catch myself dividing my food in half. But now I just eat both halves.

The book is very revealing. Did you have any qualms about opening up so much to the reader?

AS: Readers can detect dishonesty really quickly. I know I can, and if I sense any disingenuousness in a writer, I put the book down. It's important to think about what you have to offer readers when you're writing such a personal story. At a certain point I had to stop thinking about myself and start thinking: How do I take the reader by the hand and walk him/her through this story? And I think what you need to give the reader is a complete experience of a devastating loss and of an exciting first love. But you have to offer redemption as well, you have to open it up to a larger meaning.

What do you think would have happened if someone had shown you the newspaper article at the time it happened?

AS: I get asked that question a lot and I'm not sure what I think of it. I'd like to reframe it: What would have happened if someone, some editor or reporter, had chosen not to run that article? Was it news or was it the sensationalization of a tragedy? Who did it serve? I live with the image of him burning. We all do. And I ask myself, is that necessary? The article takes this beautiful, vibrant, clever, extraordinary, and completely ordinary boy and tears him out of his context. He is reduced to the victim of a freak accident. I think it's important that readers not see the article until they are well into the story. One of the reasons I wrote the book was as a counterbalance to that article. I wanted to create a written record that placed Roy back in context.

Do you think of this as a sad book?

AS: You know, I don't. I think of the book as a love letter to all of the compassionate, complicated, brilliant, eccentric people who helped me grow up. Of course, writing about losing Roy was very sad. But writing about growing up with Roy, writing about the Sisters of Mercy, writing about my school chums, about the passion, the heat of first love—that brought me a lot of joy.

How did the book affect your parents?

AS: I was the first person in my family to go to college. When I came home in the middle of my freshman year and announced that I was going to be an English major, my father shook his head. "We work in factories," he said. "What are you going to do, work in an English factory?" Years later when I decided to try to write a book, he thought that was just about the worst idea I'd ever come up with, worse even than being an English major! So I was really nervous about showing him the book. Would he like it? Would he be upset that I told our family's personal story? Would it break his heart all over again to read about Roy dying? Finally, the summer before publication, I got up the courage to send him a copy of the manuscript. I told him that he never had to read the book, or perhaps I would point out the funny bits and he could just read those parts. Well, he read the entire book in two days. He called me and said, "You're a good writer, baby. You did a good job!" It was the best review I will ever get.

My mother never got a chance to read the book. She died on April 8, 2003. She had breast cancer and was quite ill for the last years of her life. It is a great sadness in my life that my mother will never read the book. But something interesting has been happening. I get letters from mothers who tell me how much the book meant to them. More often than not, they found out about the book through their daughters. Much of *Name All the Animals* is about how we love in families—the insoluble familial bond. Mothers, especially, seem to connect with that. My mother never got to read the book, but it is a comfort to me that so many mothers will read *Name All the Animals*.

Do you have any special writing rituals? For example, what do you have on your desk when you're writing?

AS: I don't have any writing rituals. I don't have a set schedule. I believe in deadlines. Deadlines can be very inspiring. I try to meet them. Sometimes I succeed.

My desk is, more often than not, covered in papers—old drafts, notes-to-self, journals opened and folded back to a certain page, and several dog-eared novels. When it gets too crowded, I move the drafts to the floor. I spread them out around my chair. They usually end up covered with dust and footprints. Sooner or later I wind up crouching on the floor in the middle off this mess, reading and editing. I don't like to throw out old drafts. I'm superstitious about them. If I cut a passage, I always save it. You never know when you might need it again. Of course, the trouble arrives when I try to file all these drafts. I am constantly embarking on self-improvement plans. They usually involve tricking myself into getting organized. I buy Post-its and file folders. I am drawn to items with names like "vertical literature organizer." And still my desk is littered with paper.

What happened to Teresa Dinovelli?

AS: She walked away from me in that parking lot in Rochester in 1986 and I never laid eyes on her again. She really disappeared. And it broke my heart because she really was the great love of my life. For a while, I was always looking for her—at every gay pride march, at every coming-out event—but I never saw her. I always wondered what happened to her. When I placed *Name All the Animals* with a publisher, I knew I had to find her and tell her about the book. I thought it would be best if she heard about it from me instead of stumbling upon it one day in a bookstore. With the help of some other Mercy friends, I tracked her down. I sent her a letter informing her of the upcoming publication of the book. I was so nervous, I must have written about twenty different drafts of that three-paragraph letter! I sent if off and I did not hear anything for months. And then I got a phone call. "This is Terry," she said. I didn't recognize her voice. It had been so long since I had heard her. I said, "I don't know anyone by that name." She said, "Yes, you do. It's Terry." And then it all came back. We talked for two hours. It was quite wonderful.

Did your faith in God or Jesus ever return?

AS: When He walked away in the bathroom the day after Roy died, that was the last I saw or heard from Him. While I was in high school, I had to keep this loss of faith a secret. I was too ashamed to admit that God had left me. When I went away to college, it was a very different world. There, it was almost shameful if you did believe in God. So I was suddenly and quite unwittingly a "cool atheist." I didn't want to be an atheist. I wanted to feel God's presence, I just didn't know how anymore. Now I see that moment in the bathroom when Jesus walked away from me as a crisis of confidence. I did not know how to continue to believe in the face of such a devastating loss. I still struggle with that question.

These days I see faith as a more organic, fleeting thing. For me it dissolves and is rebuilt several times a day. I often think of writing as stepping into a void. You've just got to walk off the cliff over and over again to see where the words take you—that takes a degree of faith.

To download a free online Simon & Schuster reading group guide to *Name All the Animals*, go to www.bookclubreader.com